LET
ME
IN™

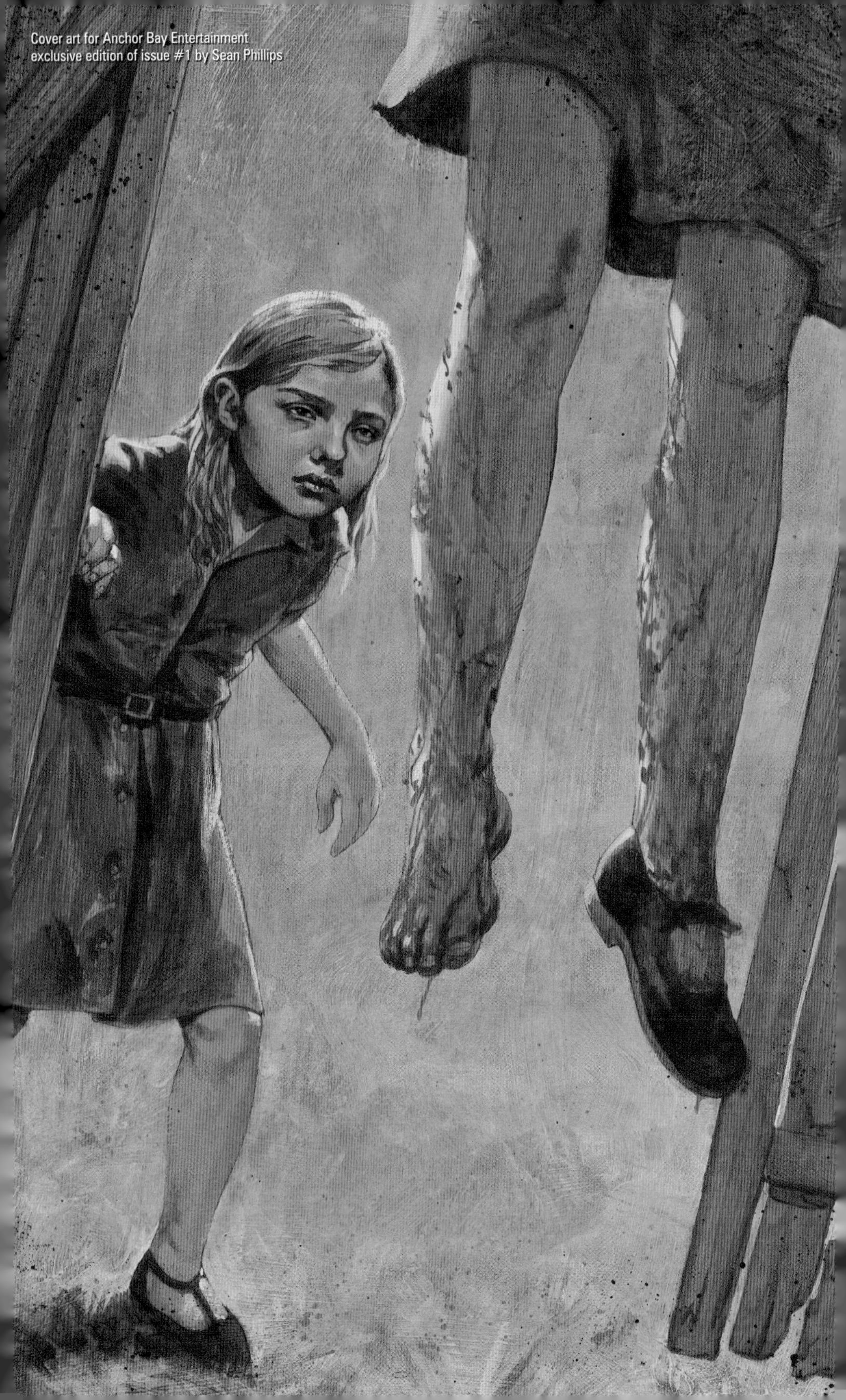

Cover art for Anchor Bay Entertainment exclusive edition of issue #1 by Sean Phillips

LET ME IN

CROSSROADS

script
MARC ANDREYKO

art
PATRIC REYNOLDS

colors
DAVE STEWART

letters
CLEM ROBINS

cover art
SEAN PHILLIPS

DARK HORSE BOOKS®

publisher
MIKE RICHARDSON

editor
SAMANTHA ROBERTSON

assistant editor
DANIEL CHABON

digital production
RYAN HILL

designer
KAT LARSON

chapter title page art
SEAN PHILLIPS

photos provided by
OVERTURE FILMS

special thanks to Simon Oakes, Alex Brunner, Ben Holden,
Adam Lewin, and Shira Rockowitz at Exclusive Media Group,
Adam Keen at Overture Films, Scott Allie at Dark Horse Comics,
and Matt Reeves.

This story takes place directly before the events depicted
in the 2010 Hammer film *Let Me In*, which was inspired by
John Ajvide Lindqvist's novel *Låt den rätte komma in*.

LET ME IN™: CROSSROADS © 2011 Hammer Let Me In Productions, LLC. Dark Horse
Comics® is a trademark of Dark Horse Comics, Inc., registered in various categories
and countries. All rights reserved. No portion of this publication may be reproduced or
transmitted, in any form or by any means, without the express written permission of Dark
Horse Comics, Inc. Names, characters, places, and incidents featured in this publication
either are the product of the author's imagination or are used fictitiously. Any resemblance
to actual persons (living or dead), events, institutions, or locales, without satiric intent,
is coincidental.

This volume collects issues #1–#4 of the
Dark Horse comic-book series *Let Me In: Crossroads*.

Dark Horse Books
A division of Dark Horse Comics, Inc.
10956 SE Main Street
Milwaukie, OR 97222

DarkHorse.com

HammerFilms.com

To find a comics shop in your area, call the
Comic Shop Locator Service toll-free at 1-888-266-4226

First edition: September 2011
ISBN 978-1-59582-796-8

10 9 8 7 6 5 4 3 2 1

Printed by Midas Printing International, Ltd., Huizhou, China.

CHAPTER ONE

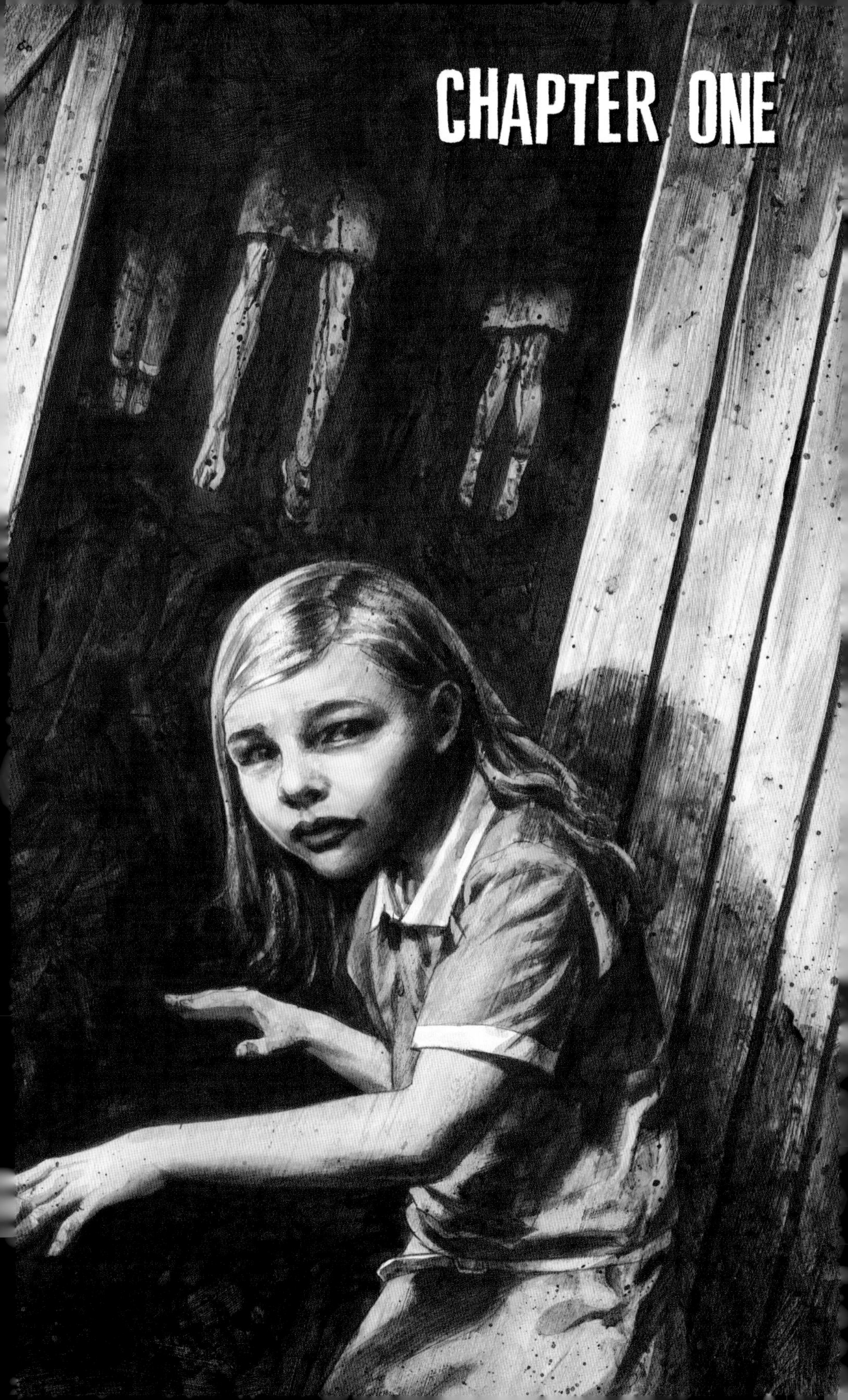

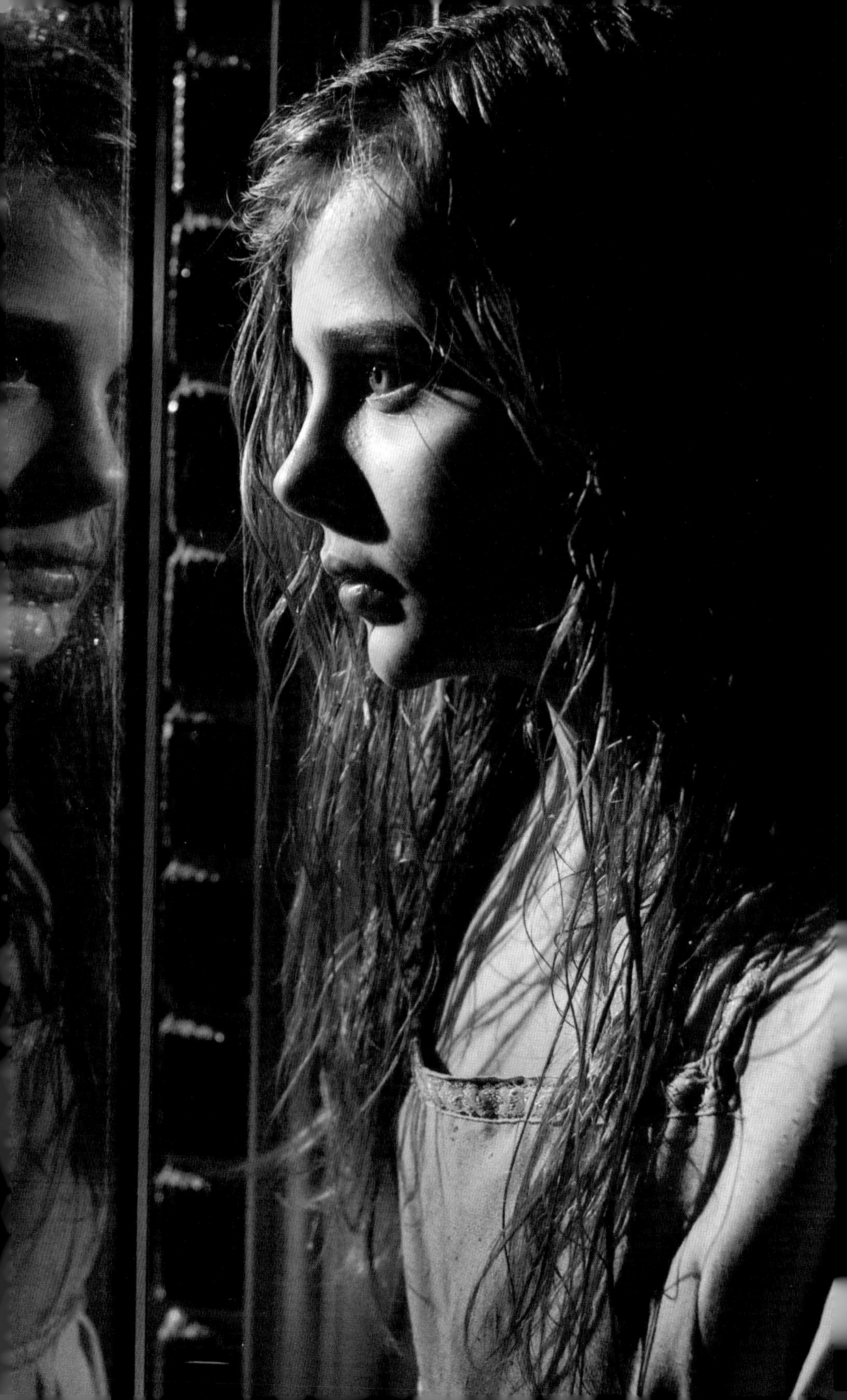

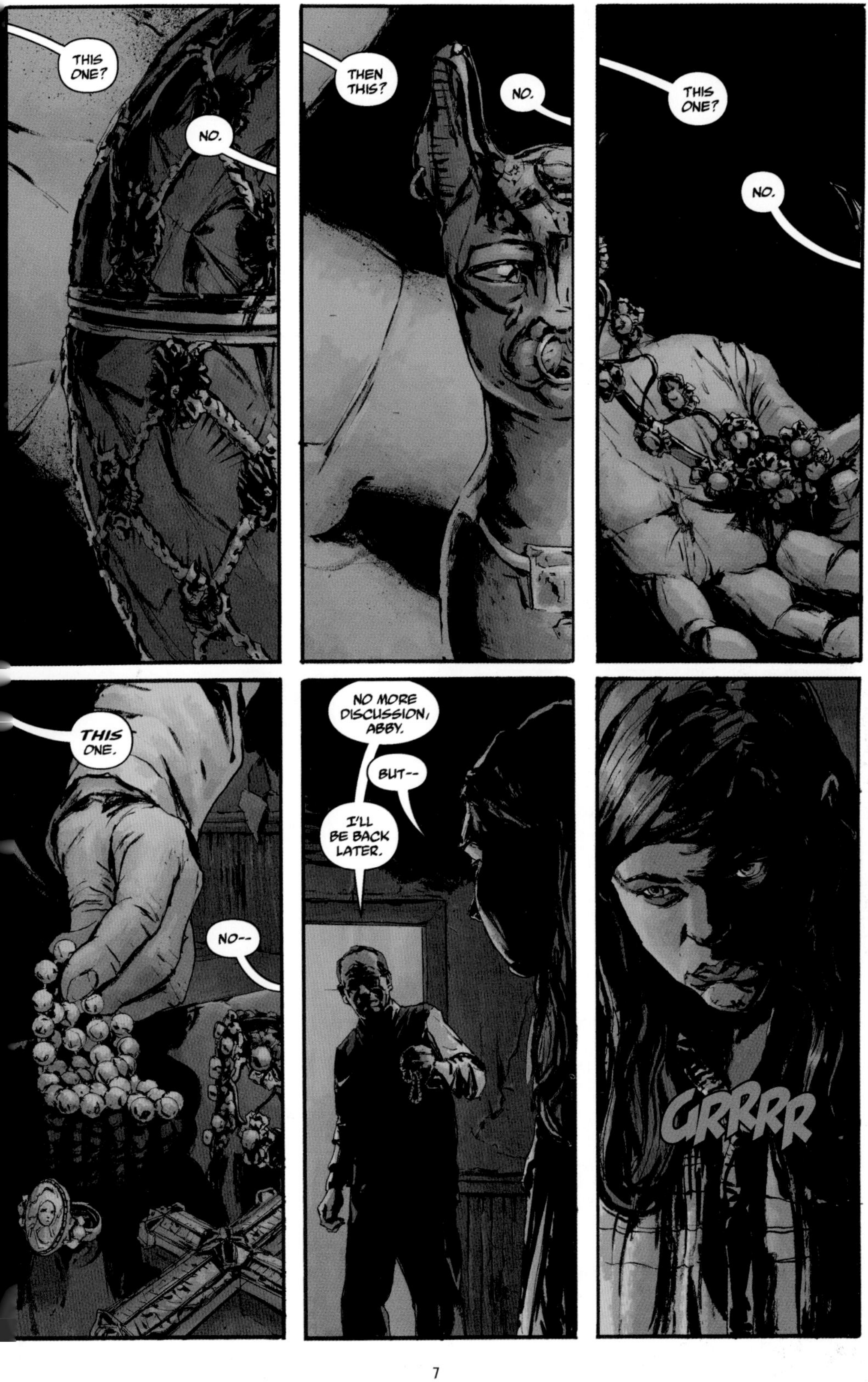
THIS ONE?
NO.
THEN THIS?
NO.
THIS ONE?
NO.
THIS ONE.
NO--
NO MORE DISCUSSION, ABBY.
BUT--
I'LL BE BACK LATER.
GRRRR

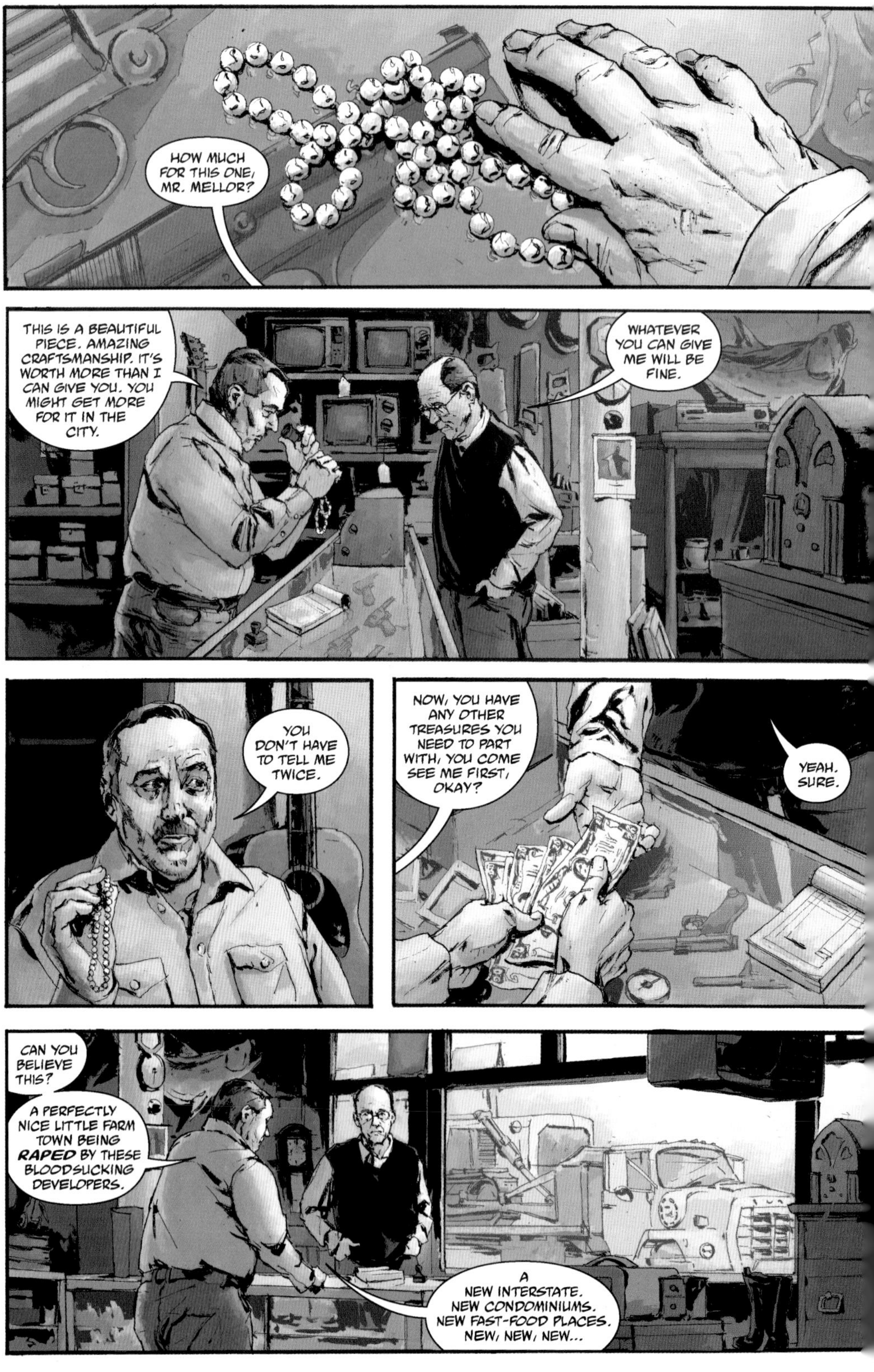
HOW MUCH FOR THIS ONE, MR. MELLOR?
THIS IS A BEAUTIFUL PIECE. AMAZING CRAFTSMANSHIP. IT'S WORTH MORE THAN I CAN GIVE YOU. YOU MIGHT GET MORE FOR IT IN THE CITY.
WHATEVER YOU CAN GIVE ME WILL BE FINE.
YOU DON'T HAVE TO TELL ME TWICE.
NOW, YOU HAVE ANY OTHER TREASURES YOU NEED TO PART WITH, YOU COME SEE ME FIRST, OKAY?
YEAH. SURE.
CAN YOU BELIEVE THIS?
A PERFECTLY NICE LITTLE FARM TOWN BEING **RAPED** BY THESE BLOODSUCKING DEVELOPERS.
A NEW INTERSTATE. NEW CONDOMINIUMS. NEW FAST-FOOD PLACES. NEW, NEW, NEW...

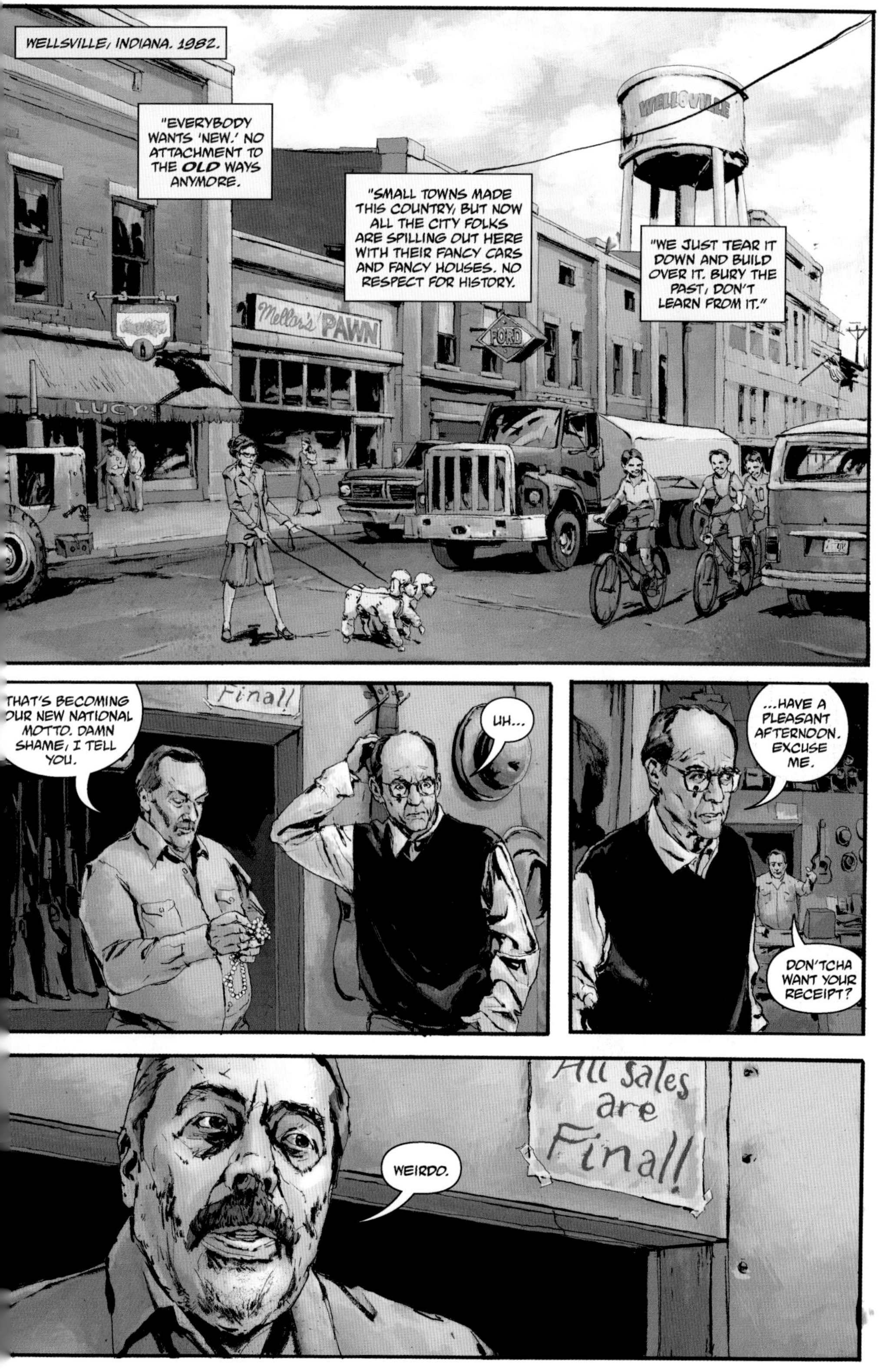
WELLSVILLE, INDIANA. 1982.
"EVERYBODY WANTS 'NEW.' NO ATTACHMENT TO THE OLD WAYS ANYMORE.
"SMALL TOWNS MADE THIS COUNTRY, BUT NOW ALL THE CITY FOLKS ARE SPILLING OUT HERE WITH THEIR FANCY CARS AND FANCY HOUSES. NO RESPECT FOR HISTORY.
"WE JUST TEAR IT DOWN AND BUILD OVER IT. BURY THE PAST, DON'T LEARN FROM IT."
WELLSVILLE
Mellor's PAWN
FORD
THAT'S BECOMING OUR NEW NATIONAL MOTTO. DAMN SHAME, I TELL YOU.
UH...
...HAVE A PLEASANT AFTERNOON. EXCUSE ME.
DON'TCHA WANT YOUR RECEIPT?
All sales are Final!
WEIRDO.

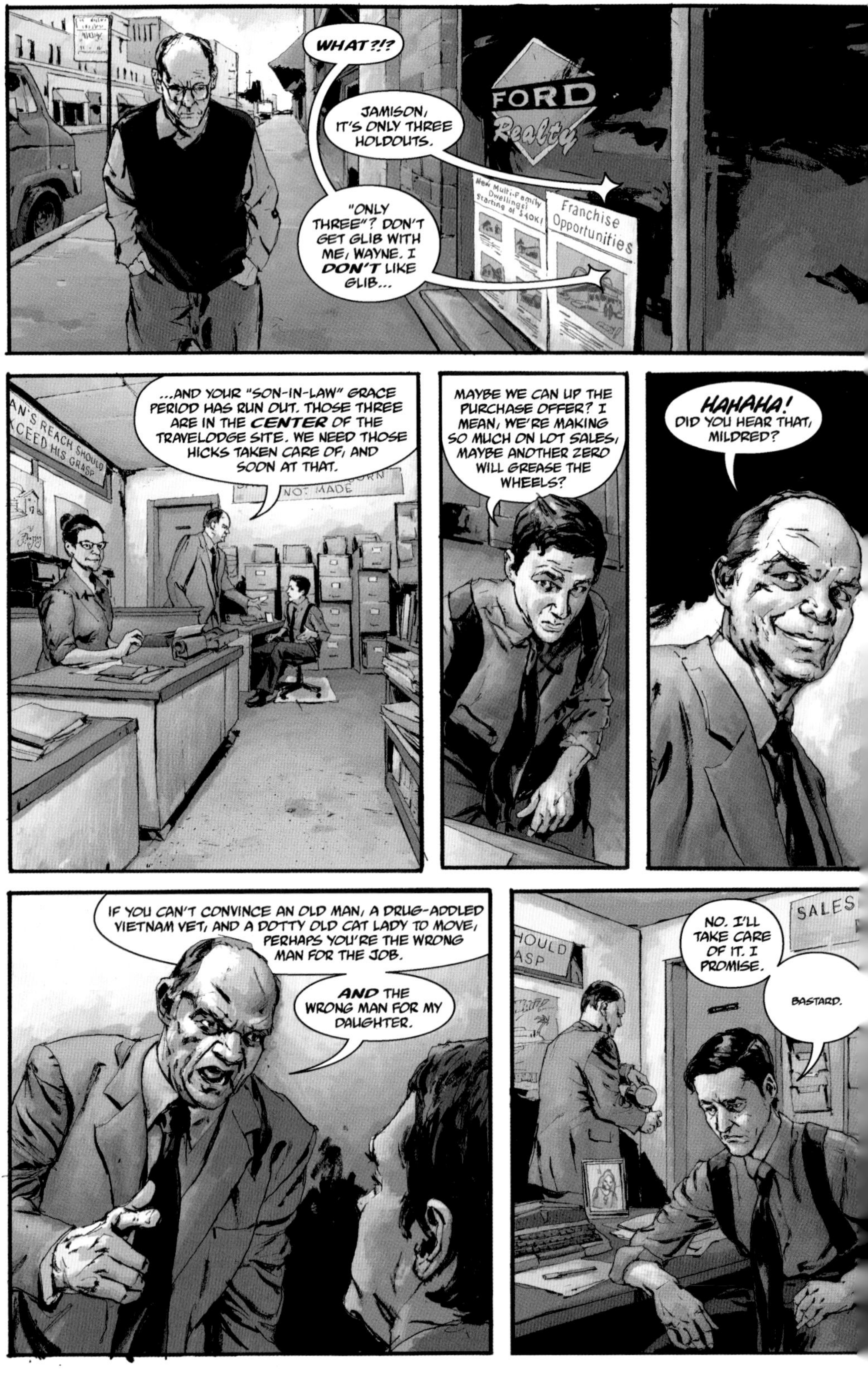
WHAT?!?
JAMISON, IT'S ONLY THREE HOLDOUTS.
"ONLY THREE"? DON'T GET GLIB WITH ME, WAYNE. I DON'T LIKE GLIB...
FORD
Realty
Franchise Opportunities
...AND YOUR "SON-IN-LAW" GRACE PERIOD HAS RUN OUT. THOSE THREE ARE IN THE CENTER OF THE TRAVELODGE SITE. WE NEED THOSE HICKS TAKEN CARE OF, AND SOON AT THAT.
MAYBE WE CAN UP THE PURCHASE OFFER? I MEAN, WE'RE MAKING SO MUCH ON LOT SALES, MAYBE ANOTHER ZERO WILL GREASE THE WHEELS?
HAHAHA! DID YOU HEAR THAT, MILDRED?
IF YOU CAN'T CONVINCE AN OLD MAN, A DRUG-ADDLED VIETNAM VET, AND A DOTTY OLD CAT LADY TO MOVE, PERHAPS YOU'RE THE WRONG MAN FOR THE JOB.
AND THE WRONG MAN FOR MY DAUGHTER.
SALES
NO. I'LL TAKE CARE OF IT. I PROMISE.
BASTARD.

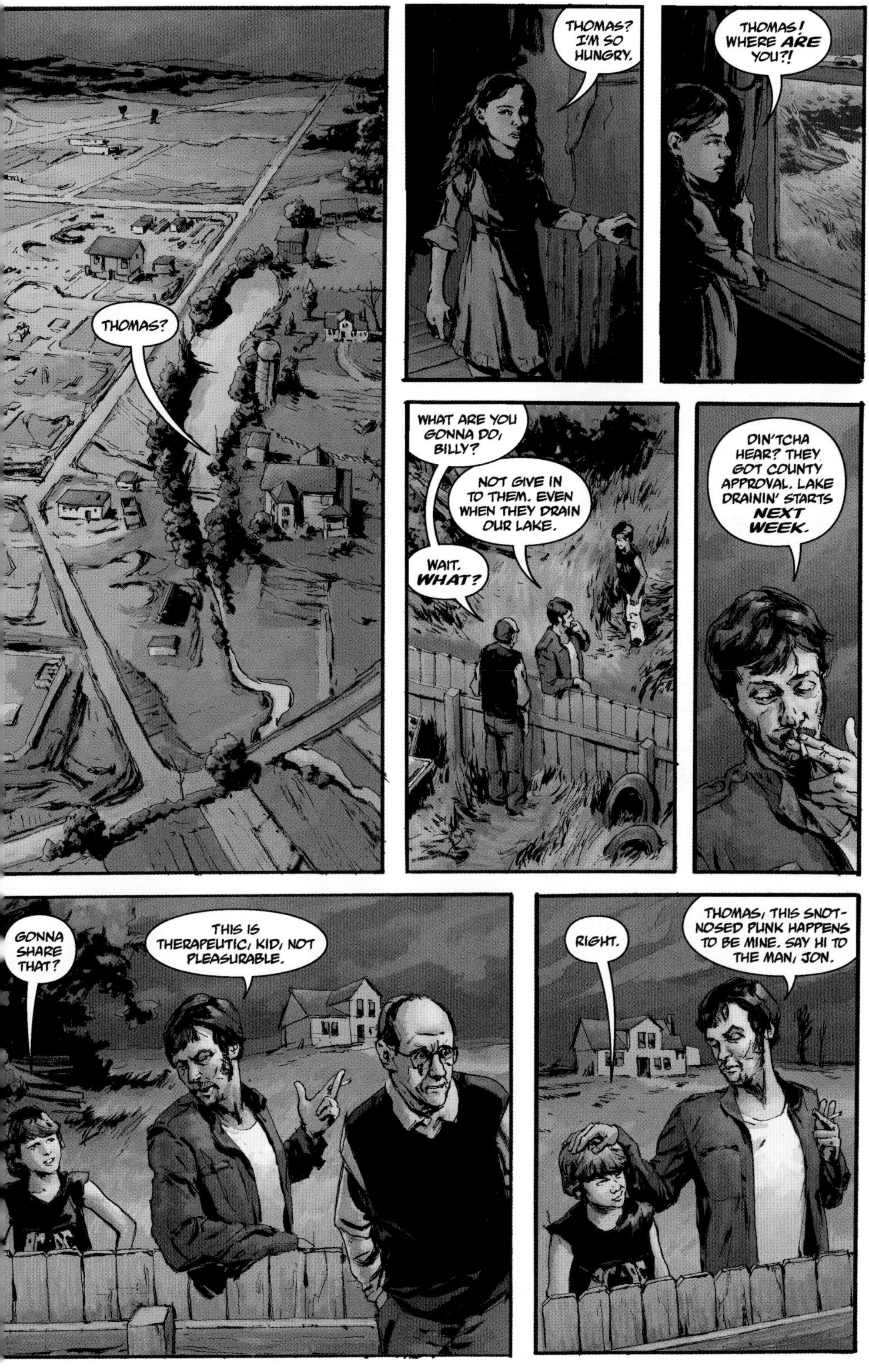
THOMAS?
THOMAS? I'M SO HUNGRY.
THOMAS! WHERE ARE YOU?!
WHAT ARE YOU GONNA DO, BILLY?
NOT GIVE IN TO THEM. EVEN WHEN THEY DRAIN OUR LAKE.
WAIT. WHAT?
DIN'TCHA HEAR? THEY GOT COUNTY APPROVAL. LAKE DRAININ' STARTS NEXT WEEK.
GONNA SHARE THAT?
THIS IS THERAPEUTIC, KID, NOT PLEASURABLE.
RIGHT.
THOMAS, THIS SNOT-NOSED PUNK HAPPENS TO BE MINE. SAY HI TO THE MAN, JON.

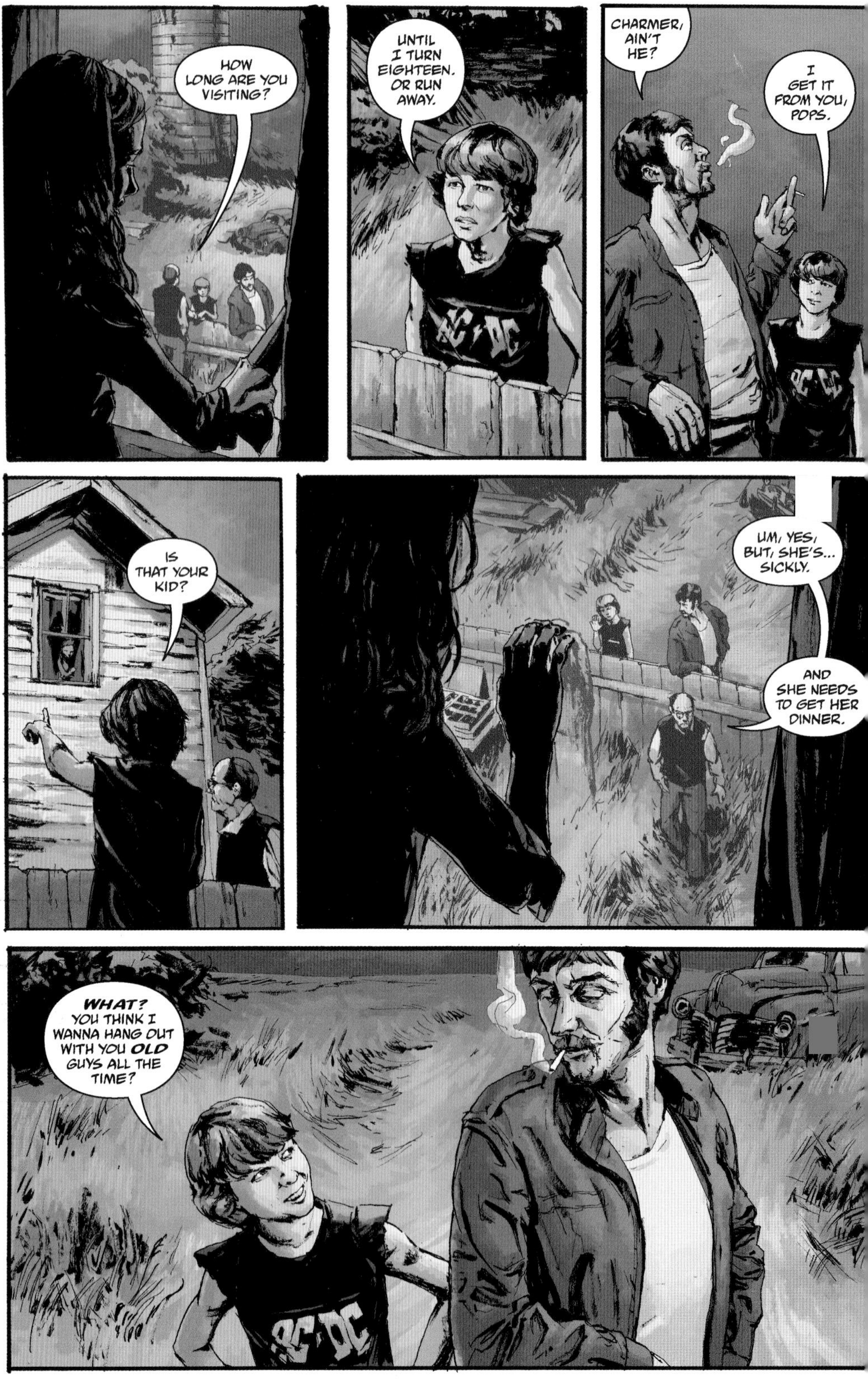
HOW LONG ARE YOU VISITING?
UNTIL I TURN EIGHTEEN. OR RUN AWAY.
CHARMER, AIN'T HE?
I GET IT FROM YOU, POPS.
AC/DC
IS THAT YOUR KID?
UM, YES, BUT, SHE'S... SICKLY.
AND SHE NEEDS TO GET HER DINNER.
WHAT? YOU THINK I WANNA HANG OUT WITH YOU **OLD** GUYS ALL THE TIME?
AC/DC

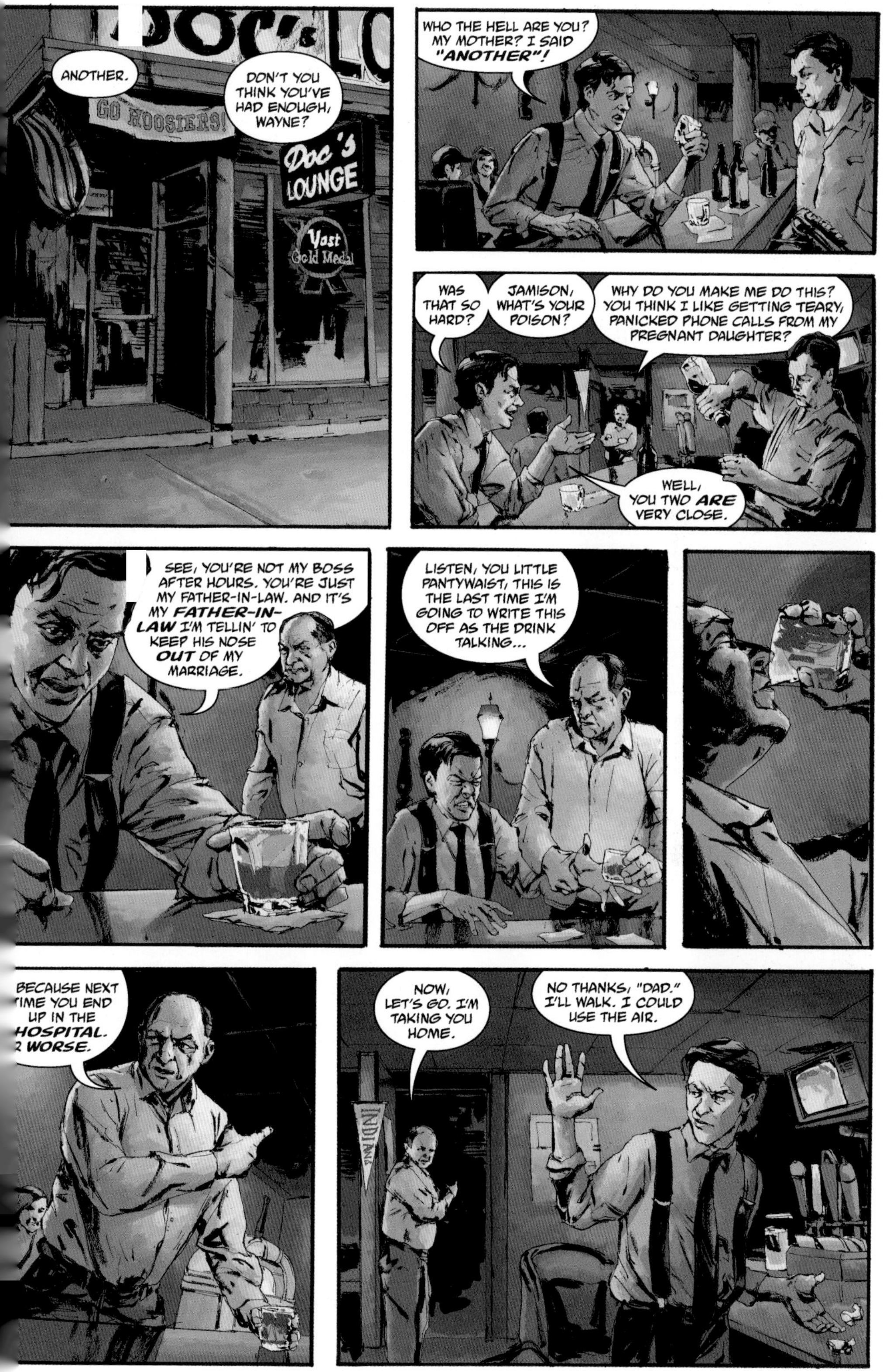
DOC'S LO
ANOTHER.
DON'T YOU THINK YOU'VE HAD ENOUGH, WAYNE?
GO HOOSIERS!
Doc's LOUNGE
Yost Gold Medal
WHO THE HELL ARE YOU? MY MOTHER? I SAID "ANOTHER"!
WAS THAT SO HARD?
JAMISON, WHAT'S YOUR POISON?
WHY DO YOU MAKE ME DO THIS? YOU THINK I LIKE GETTING TEARY, PANICKED PHONE CALLS FROM MY PREGNANT DAUGHTER?
WELL, YOU TWO ARE VERY CLOSE.
SEE, YOU'RE NOT MY BOSS AFTER HOURS. YOU'RE JUST MY FATHER-IN-LAW. AND IT'S MY FATHER-IN-LAW I'M TELLIN' TO KEEP HIS NOSE OUT OF MY MARRIAGE.
LISTEN, YOU LITTLE PANTYWAIST, THIS IS THE LAST TIME I'M GOING TO WRITE THIS OFF AS THE DRINK TALKING...
BECAUSE NEXT TIME YOU END UP IN THE HOSPITAL. R WORSE.
NOW, LET'S GO. I'M TAKING YOU HOME.
NO THANKS, "DAD." I'LL WALK. I COULD USE THE AIR.
INDIANS

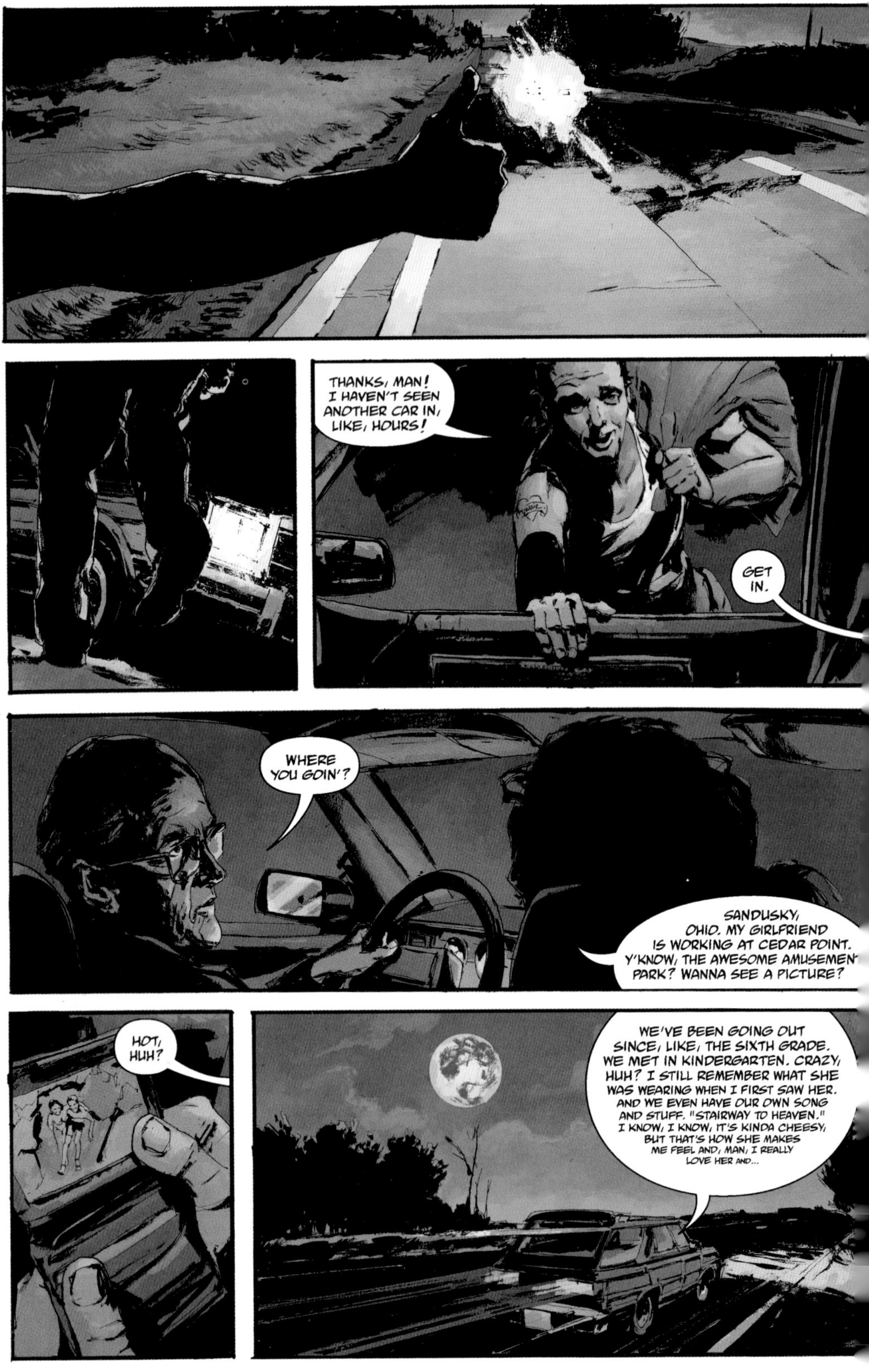

THANKS, MAN! I HAVEN'T SEEN ANOTHER CAR IN, LIKE, HOURS!
GET IN.
WHERE YOU GOIN'?
SANDUSKY, OHIO. MY GIRLFRIEND IS WORKING AT CEDAR POINT. Y'KNOW, THE AWESOME AMUSEMENT PARK? WANNA SEE A PICTURE?
HOT, HUH?
WE'VE BEEN GOING OUT SINCE, LIKE, THE SIXTH GRADE. WE MET IN KINDERGARTEN. CRAZY, HUH? I STILL REMEMBER WHAT SHE WAS WEARING WHEN I FIRST SAW HER. AND WE EVEN HAVE OUR OWN SONG AND STUFF. "STAIRWAY TO HEAVEN." I KNOW, I KNOW, IT'S KINDA CHEESY, BUT THAT'S HOW SHE MAKES ME FEEL AND, MAN, I REALLY LOVE HER AND...

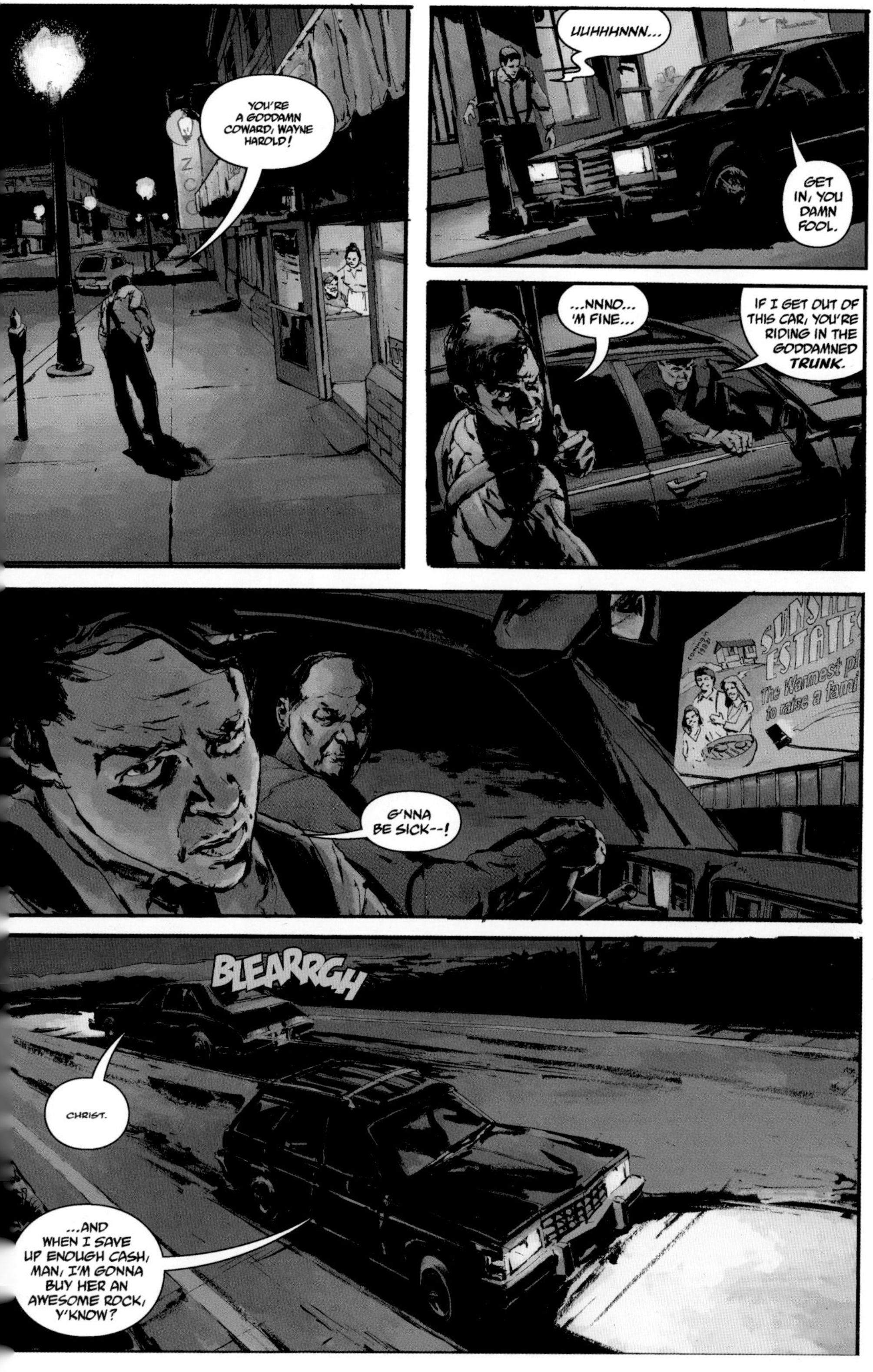
YOU'RE A GODDAMN COWARD, WAYNE HAROLD!
UUHHHNNN...
GET IN, YOU DAMN FOOL.
...NNNO... 'M FINE...
IF I GET OUT OF THIS CAR, YOU'RE RIDING IN THE GODDAMNED TRUNK.
SUNSHINE ESTATES
The Warmest pl
to raise a fami
G'NNA BE SICK--!
BLEARRGH
CHRIST.
...AND WHEN I SAVE UP ENOUGH CASH, MAN, I'M GONNA BUY HER AN AWESOME ROCK, Y'KNOW?

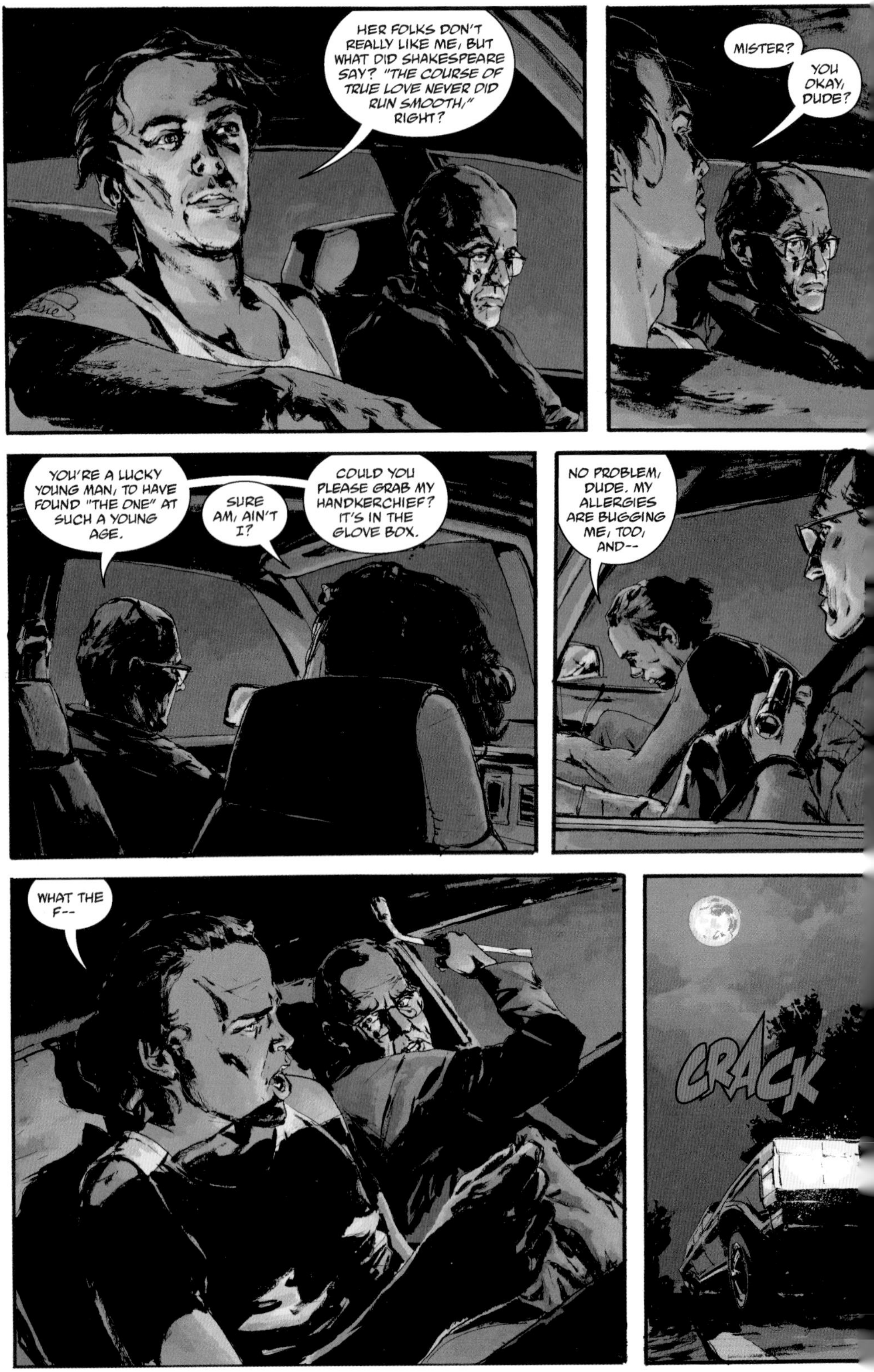
HER FOLKS DON'T REALLY LIKE ME, BUT WHAT DID SHAKESPEARE SAY? "THE COURSE OF TRUE LOVE NEVER DID RUN SMOOTH," RIGHT?
MISTER?
YOU OKAY, DUDE?
YOU'RE A LUCKY YOUNG MAN, TO HAVE FOUND "THE ONE" AT SUCH A YOUNG AGE.
SURE AM, AIN'T I?
COULD YOU PLEASE GRAB MY HANDKERCHIEF? IT'S IN THE GLOVE BOX.
NO PROBLEM, DUDE. MY ALLERGIES ARE BUGGING ME, TOO, AND--
WHAT THE F--
CRACK

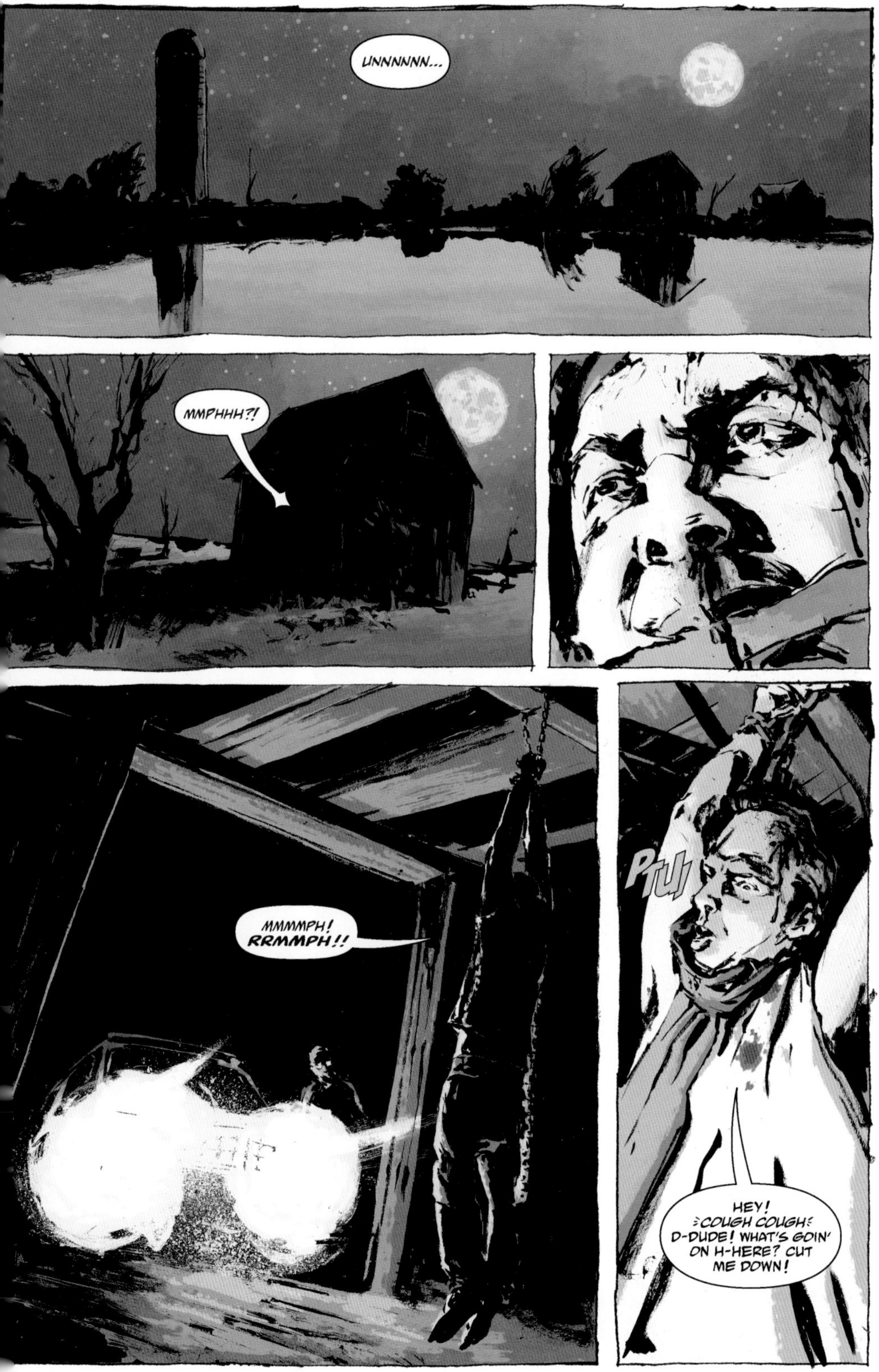
UNNNNNN...
MMPHHH?!
MMMMPH! RRMMPH!!
PTUI
HEY! ≷COUGH COUGH≶ D-DUDE! WHAT'S GOIN' ON H-HERE? CUT ME DOWN!

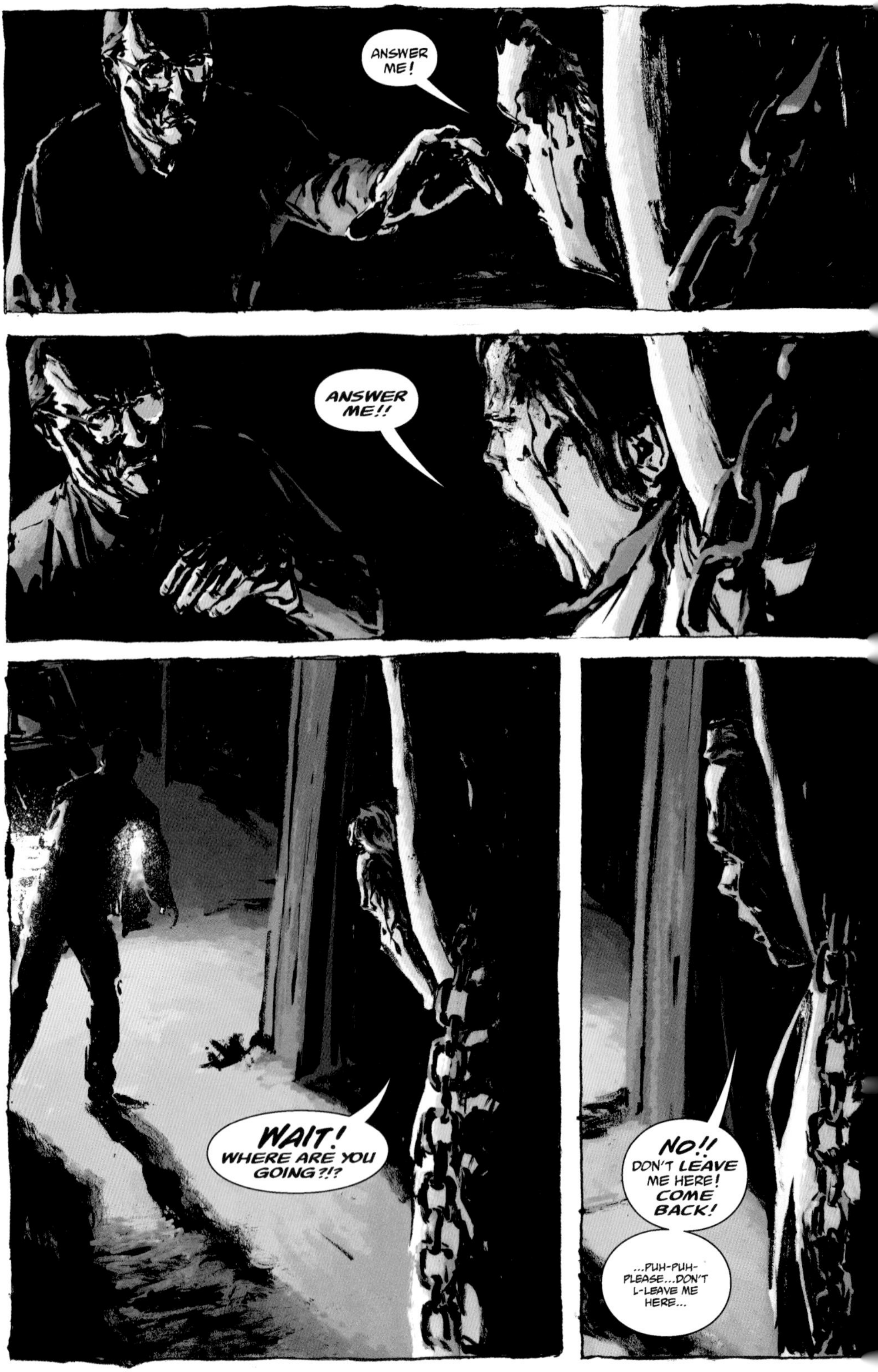
ANSWER ME!
ANSWER ME!!
WAIT! WHERE ARE YOU GOING?!?
NO!! DON'T LEAVE ME HERE! COME BACK!
...PUH-PUH-PLEASE...DON'T L-LEAVE ME HERE...

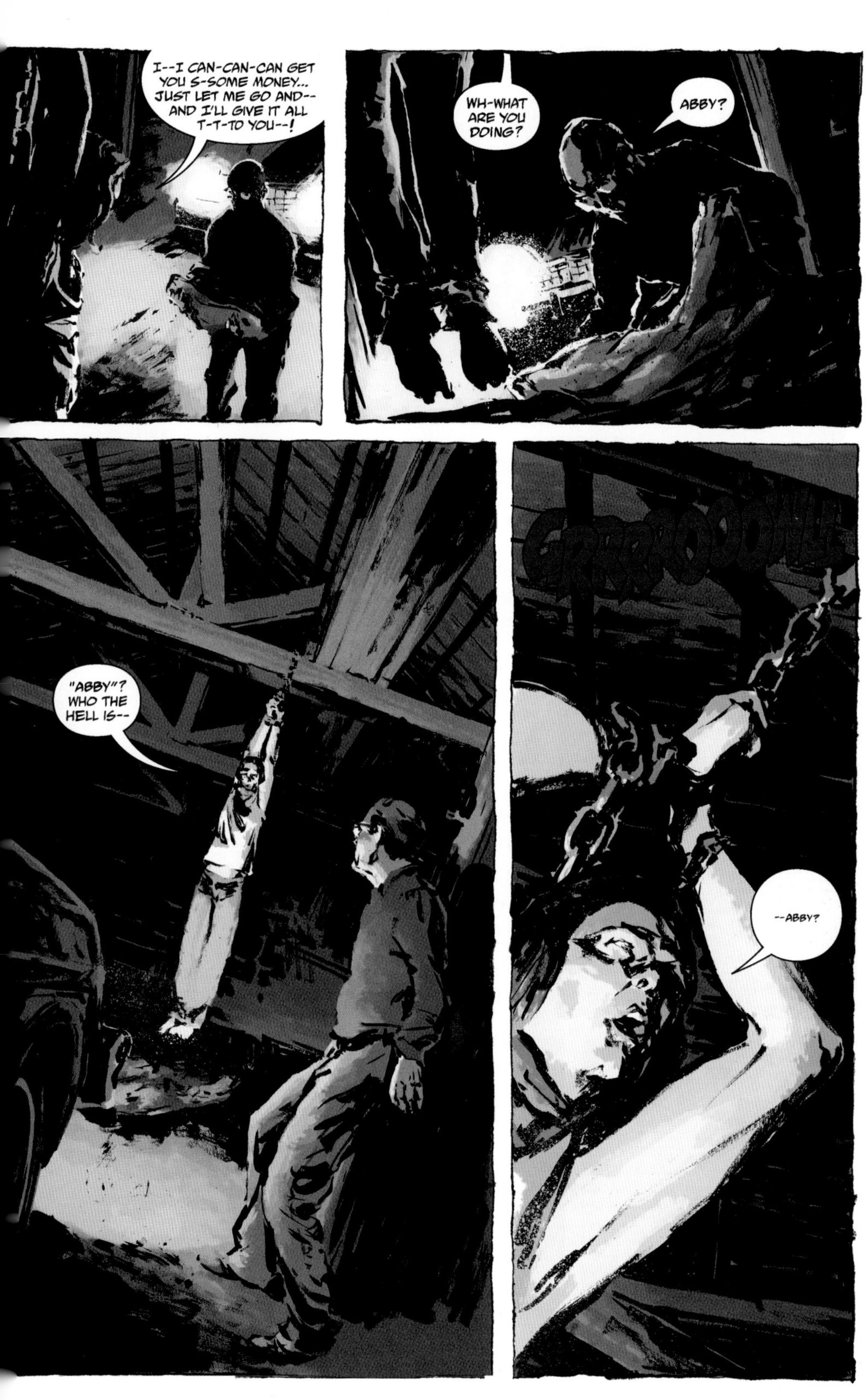
I--I CAN-CAN-CAN GET YOU S-SOME MONEY... JUST LET ME GO AND-- AND I'LL GIVE IT ALL T-T-TO YOU--!
WH-WHAT ARE YOU DOING?
ABBY?
"ABBY"? WHO THE HELL IS--
--ABBY?

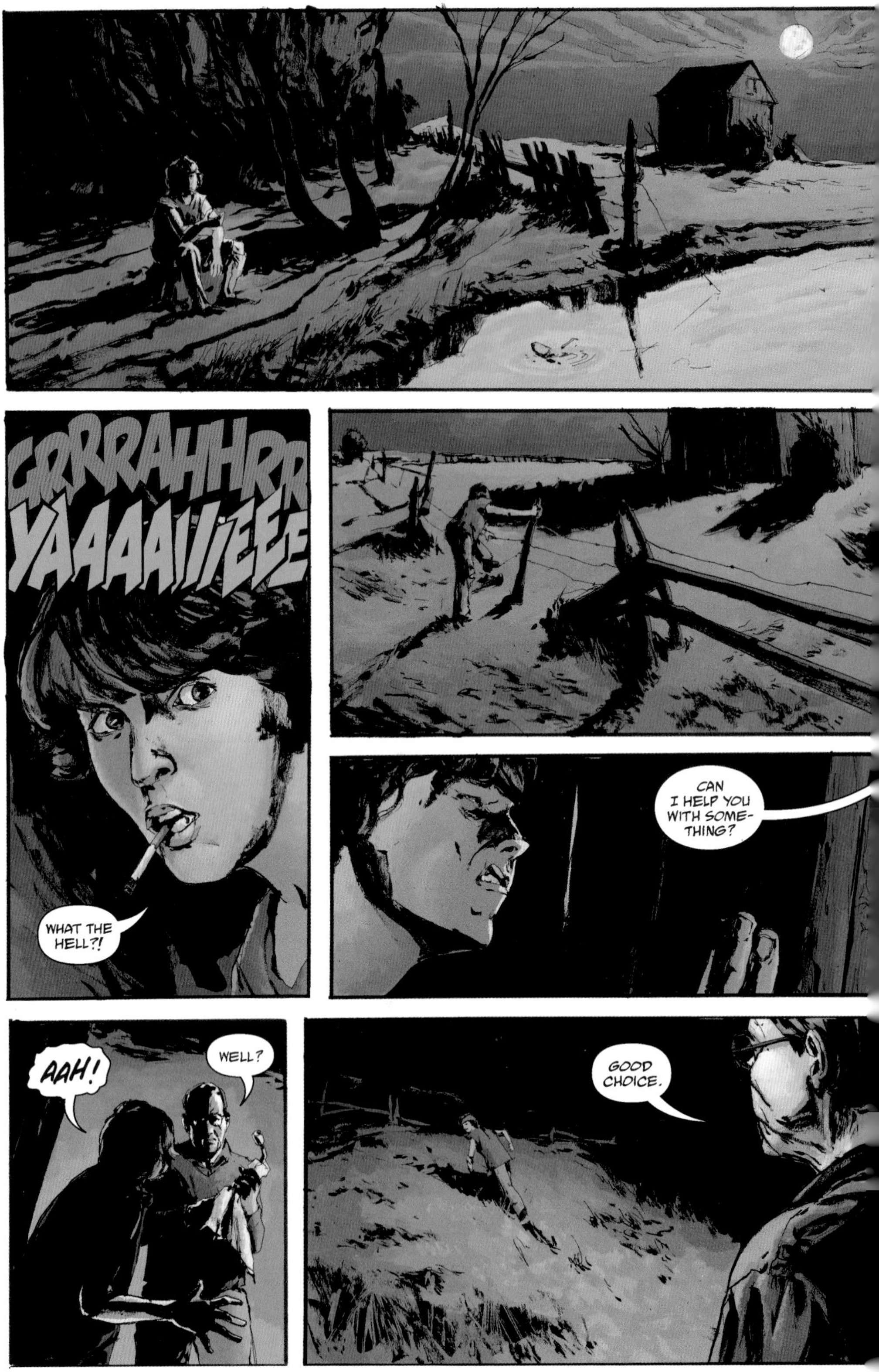
GRRRAHHRR
YAAAAIIIEEE
WHAT THE HELL?!
CAN I HELP YOU WITH SOME- THING?
AAH!
WELL?
GOOD CHOICE.

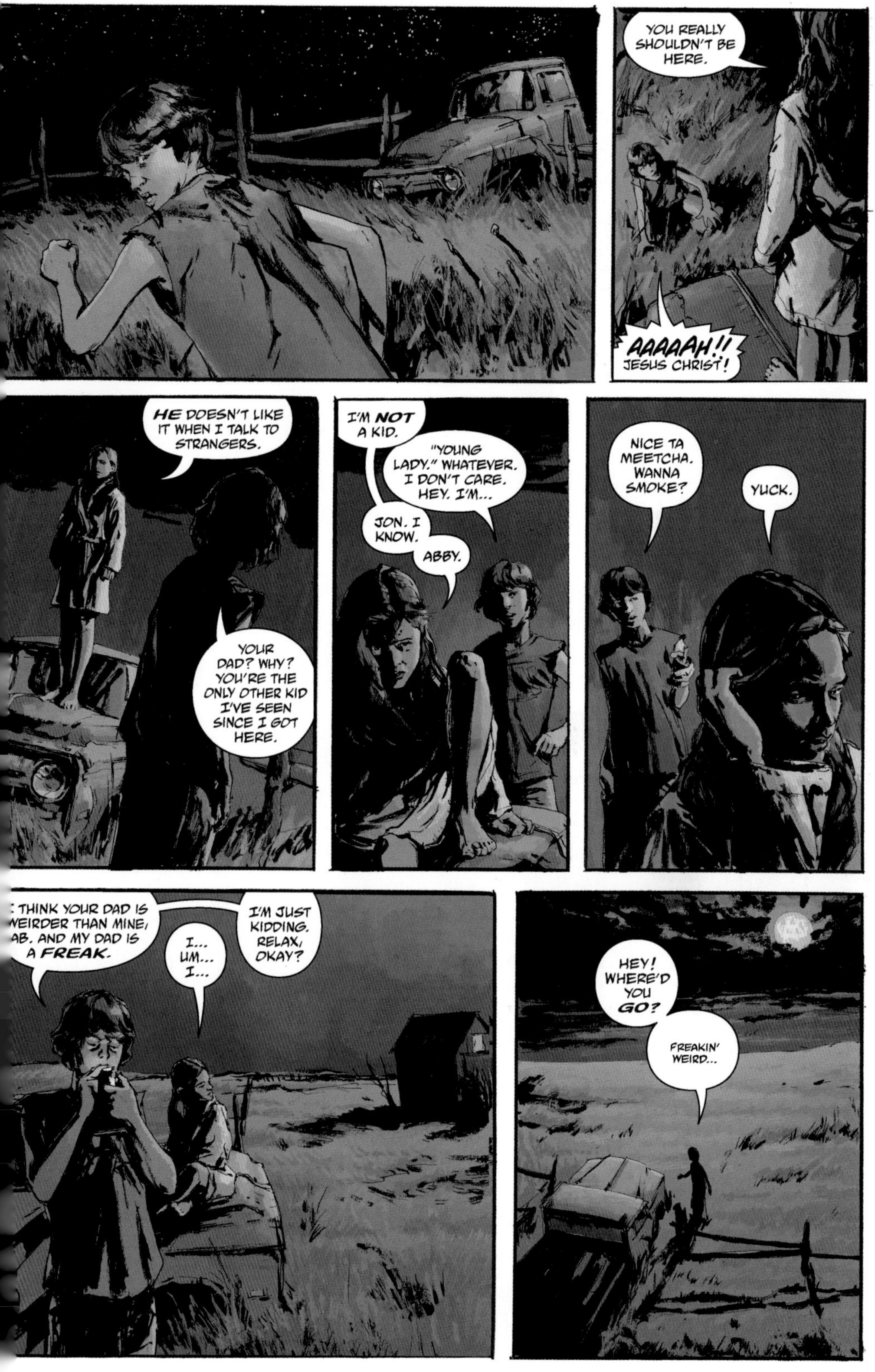
YOU REALLY SHOULDN'T BE HERE.
AAAAAH!! JESUS CHRIST!
HE DOESN'T LIKE IT WHEN I TALK TO STRANGERS.
YOUR DAD? WHY? YOU'RE THE ONLY OTHER KID I'VE SEEN SINCE I GOT HERE.
I'M NOT A KID.
"YOUNG LADY." WHATEVER. I DON'T CARE. HEY. I'M...
JON. I KNOW.
ABBY.
NICE TA MEETCHA. WANNA SMOKE?
YUCK.
I THINK YOUR DAD IS WEIRDER THAN MINE, AB. AND MY DAD IS A FREAK.
I... UM... I...
I'M JUST KIDDING. RELAX, OKAY?
HEY! WHERE'D YOU GO?
FREAKIN' WEIRD...

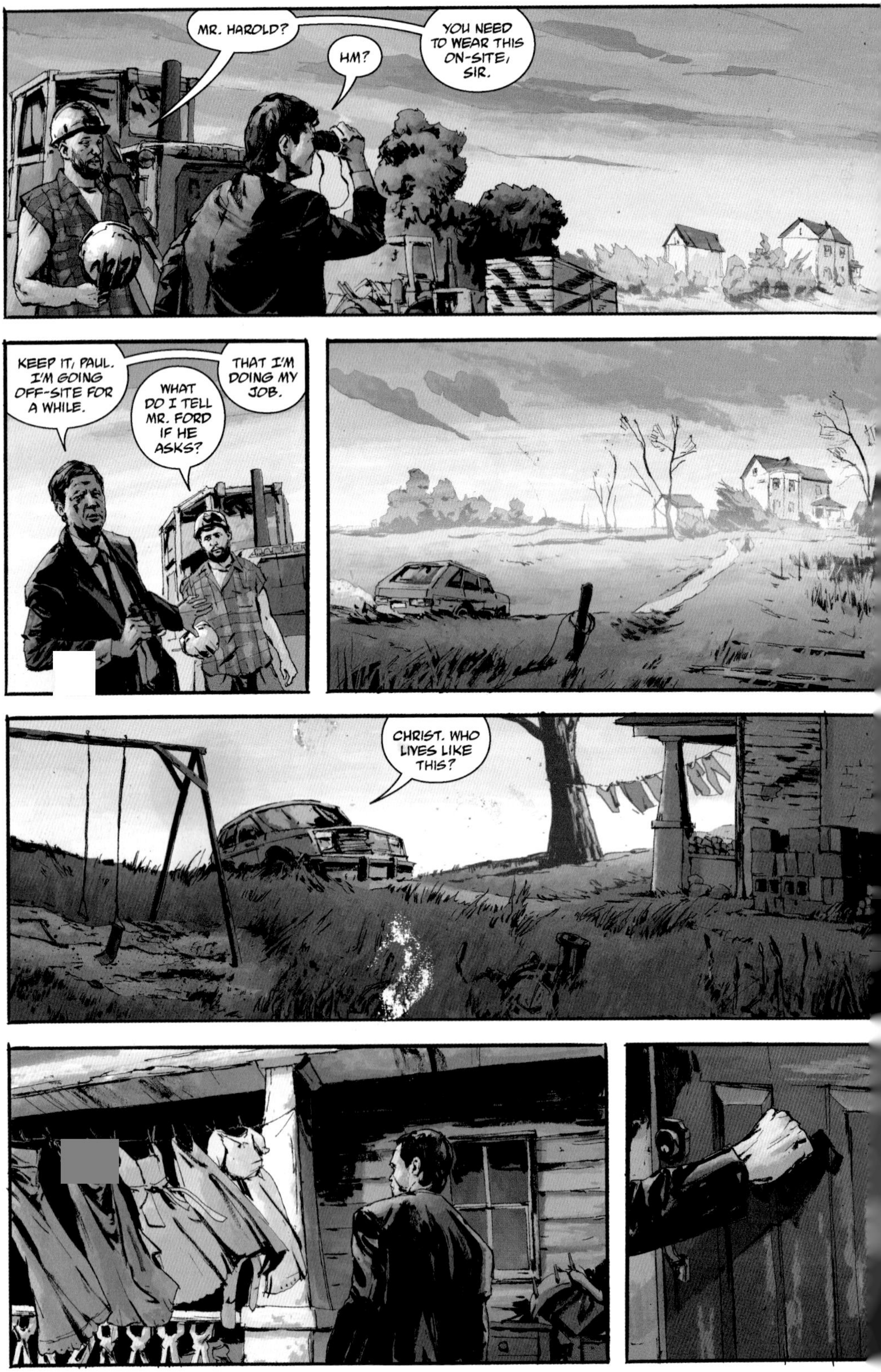
MR. HAROLD?
HM?
YOU NEED TO WEAR THIS ON-SITE, SIR.
KEEP IT, PAUL. I'M GOING OFF-SITE FOR A WHILE.
WHAT DO I TELL MR. FORD IF HE ASKS?
THAT I'M DOING MY JOB.
CHRIST. WHO LIVES LIKE THIS?

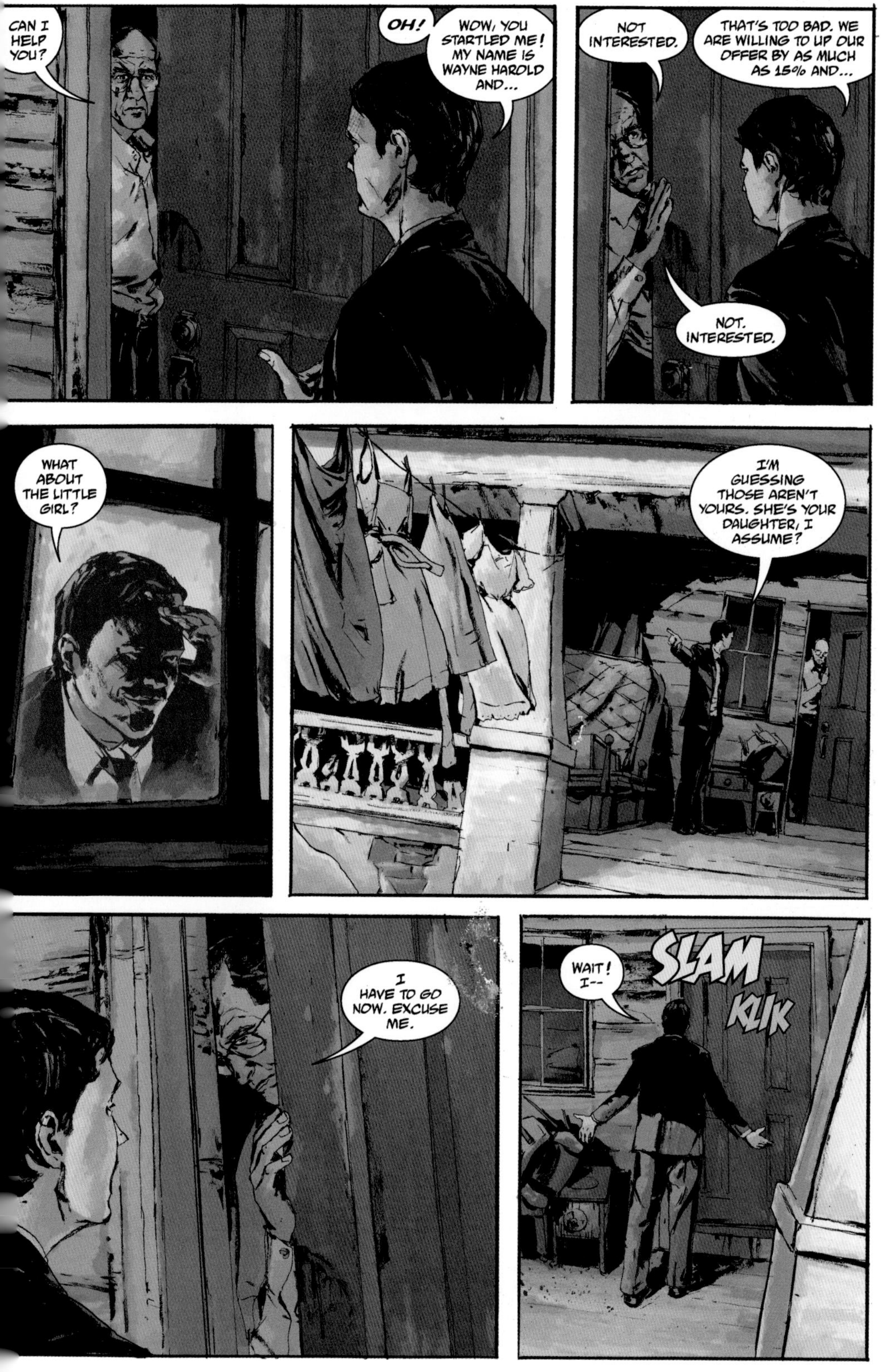
CAN I HELP YOU?
OH!
WOW, YOU STARTLED ME! MY NAME IS WAYNE HAROLD AND...
NOT INTERESTED.
THAT'S TOO BAD. WE ARE WILLING TO UP OUR OFFER BY AS MUCH AS 15% AND...
NOT. INTERESTED.
WHAT ABOUT THE LITTLE GIRL?
I'M GUESSING THOSE AREN'T YOURS. SHE'S YOUR DAUGHTER, I ASSUME?
I HAVE TO GO NOW. EXCUSE ME.
WAIT! I--
SLAM
KLIK

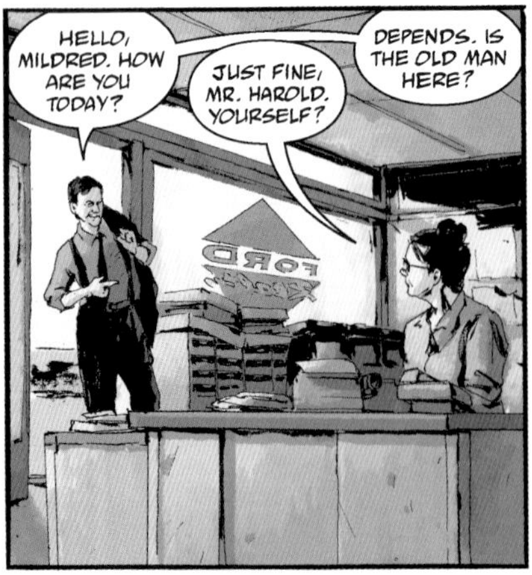
HELLO, MILDRED. HOW ARE YOU TODAY?
JUST FINE, MR. HAROLD. YOURSELF?
DEPENDS. IS THE OLD MAN HERE?

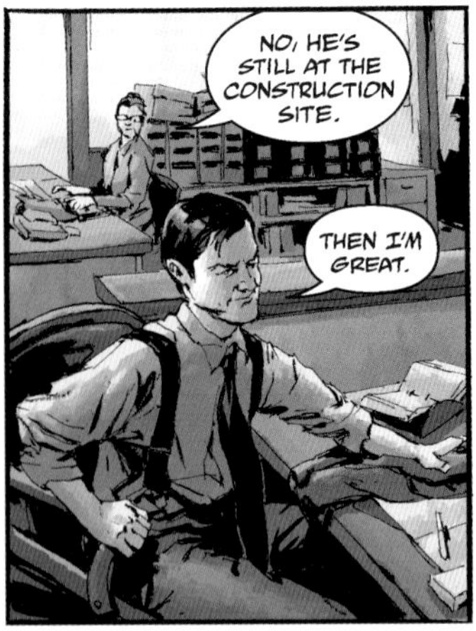
NO, HE'S STILL AT THE CONSTRUCTION SITE.
THEN I'M GREAT.

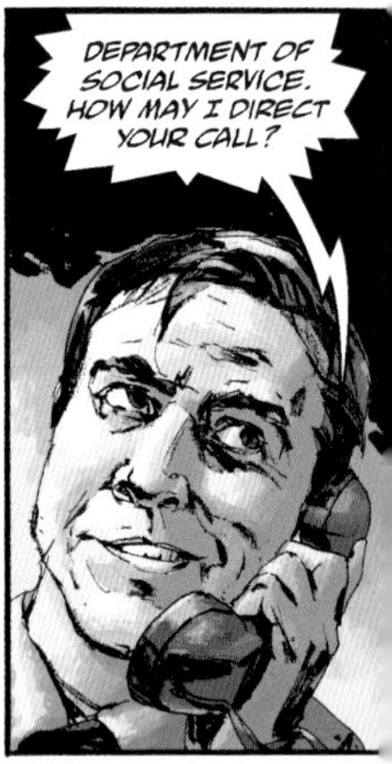
DEPARTMENT OF SOCIAL SERVICE. HOW MAY I DIRECT YOUR CALL?

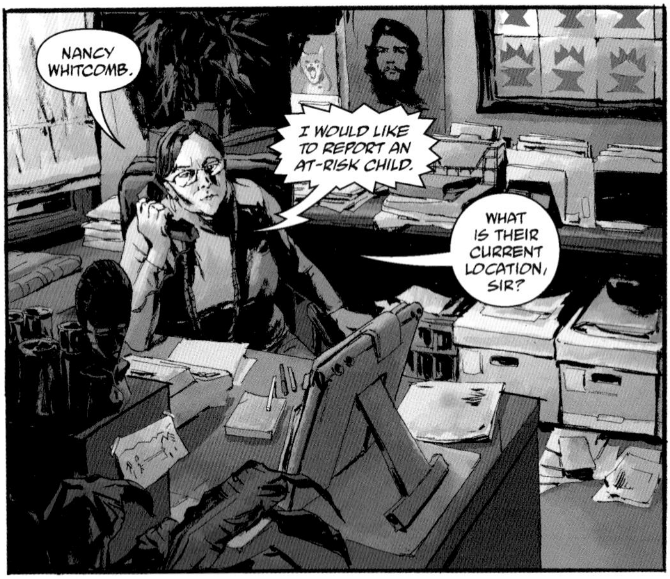
NANCY WHITCOMB.
I WOULD LIKE TO REPORT AN AT-RISK CHILD.
WHAT IS THEIR CURRENT LOCATION, SIR?

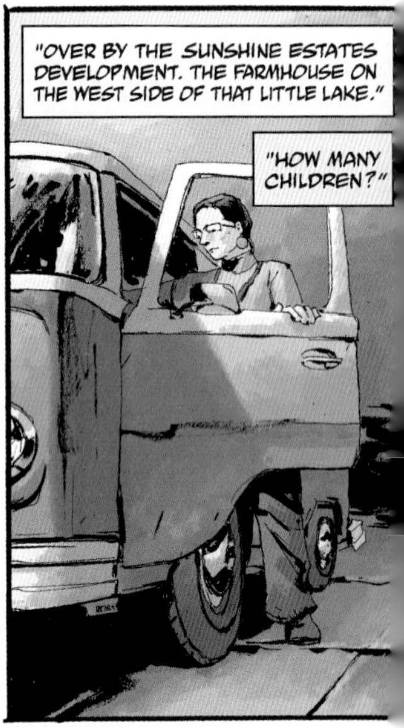
"OVER BY THE SUNSHINE ESTATES DEVELOPMENT. THE FARMHOUSE ON THE WEST SIDE OF THAT LITTLE LAKE."
"HOW MANY CHILDREN?"

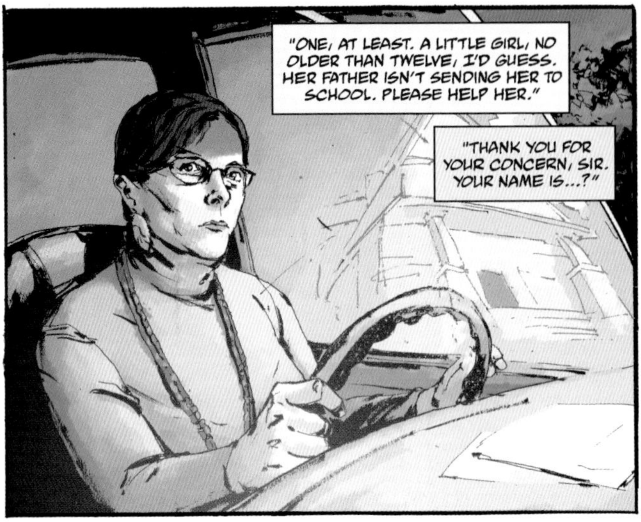
"ONE, AT LEAST. A LITTLE GIRL, NO OLDER THAN TWELVE, I'D GUESS. HER FATHER ISN'T SENDING HER TO SCHOOL. PLEASE HELP HER."
"THANK YOU FOR YOUR CONCERN, SIR. YOUR NAME IS...?"

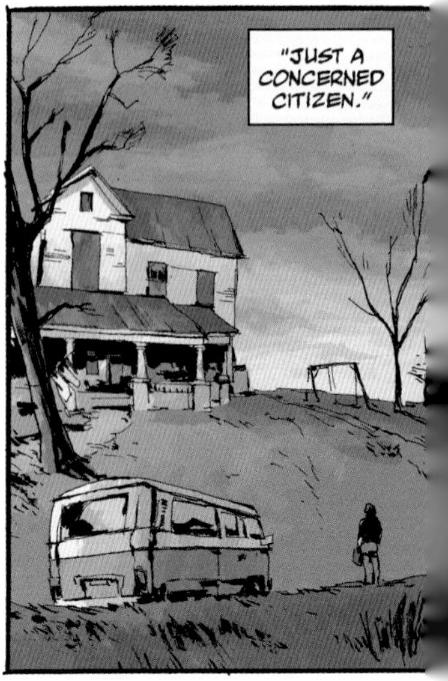
"JUST A CONCERNED CITIZEN."

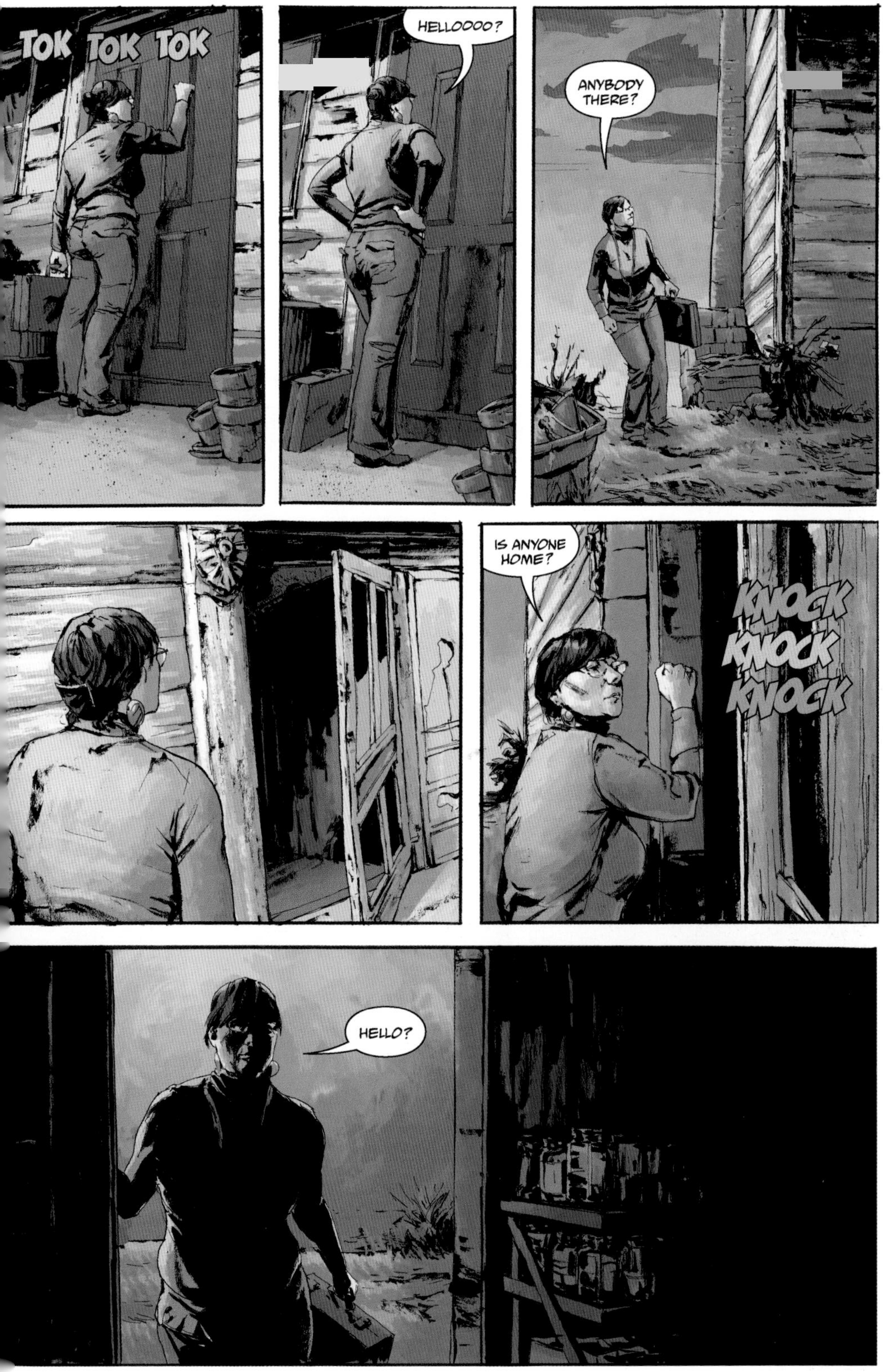
TOK TOK TOK
HELLOOOO?
ANYBODY THERE?
IS ANYONE HOME?
KNOCK KNOCK KNOCK
HELLO?

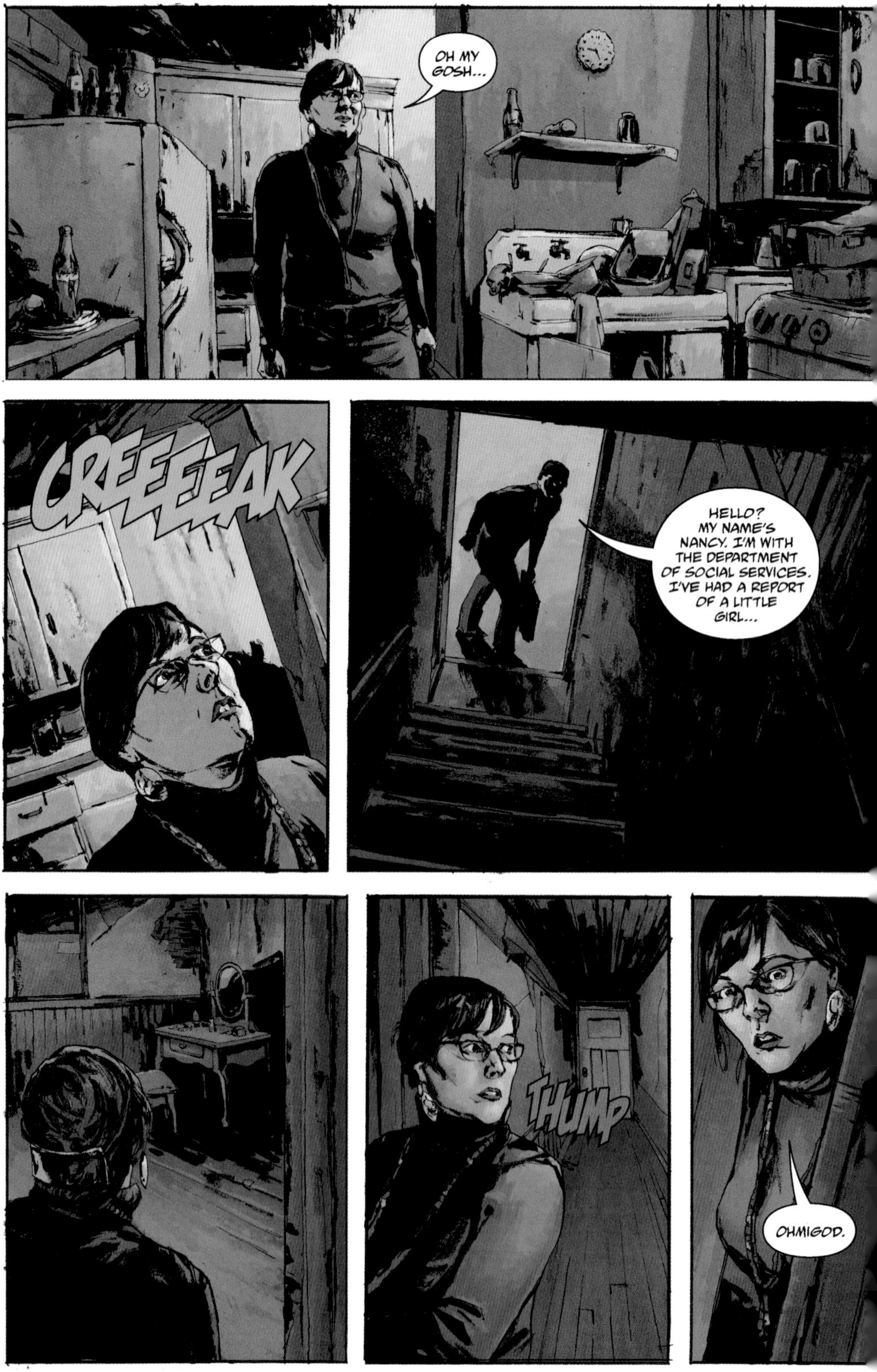
OH MY GOSH...
CREEEEAK
HELLO? MY NAME'S NANCY. I'M WITH THE DEPARTMENT OF SOCIAL SERVICES. I'VE HAD A REPORT OF A LITTLE GIRL...
THUMP
OHMIGOD.

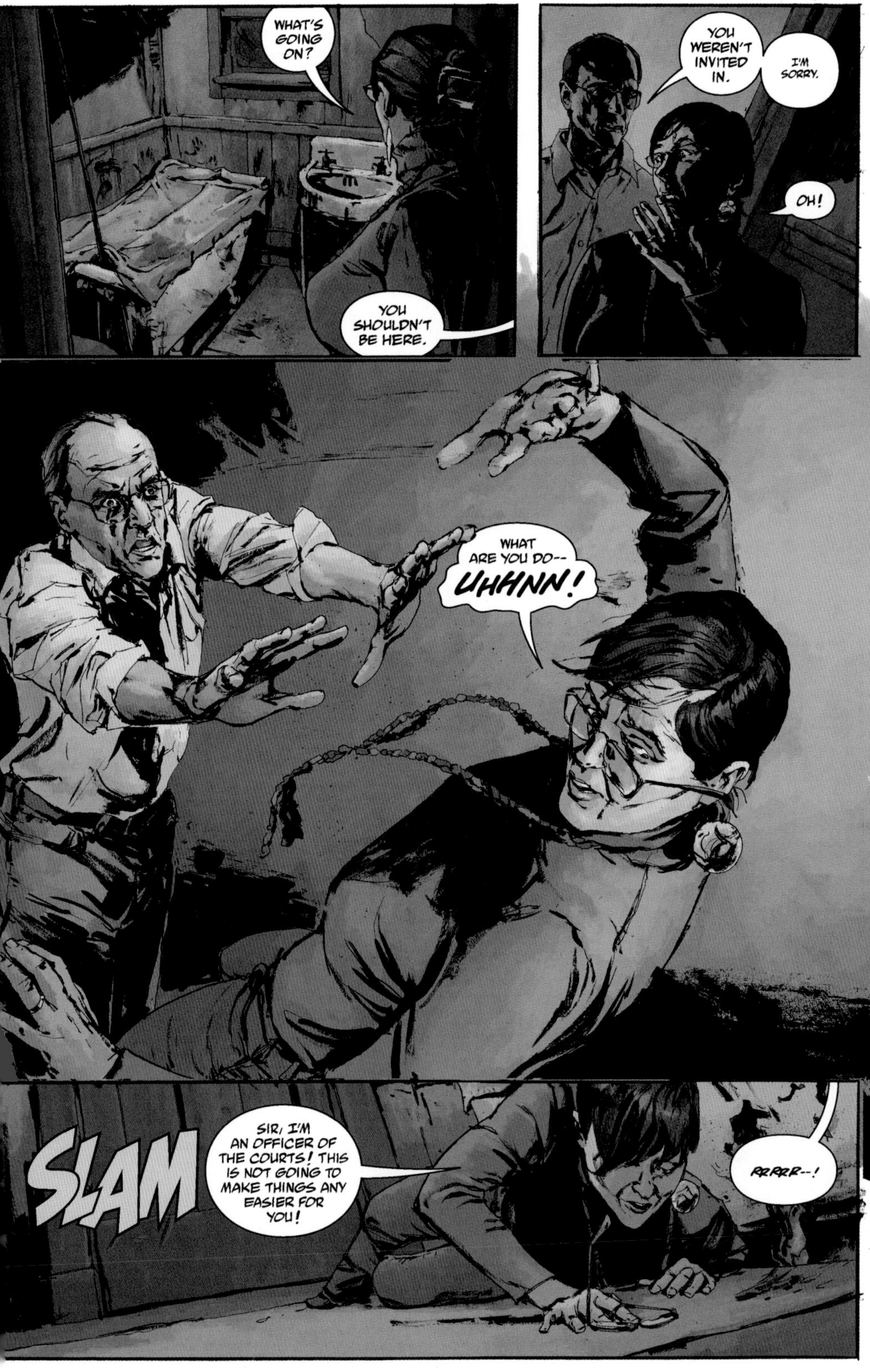
WHAT'S GOING ON?
YOU SHOULDN'T BE HERE.
YOU WEREN'T INVITED IN.
I'M SORRY.
OH!
WHAT ARE YOU DO-- UHHNN!
SLAM
SIR, I'M AN OFFICER OF THE COURTS! THIS IS NOT GOING TO MAKE THINGS ANY EASIER FOR YOU!
RRRRR--!

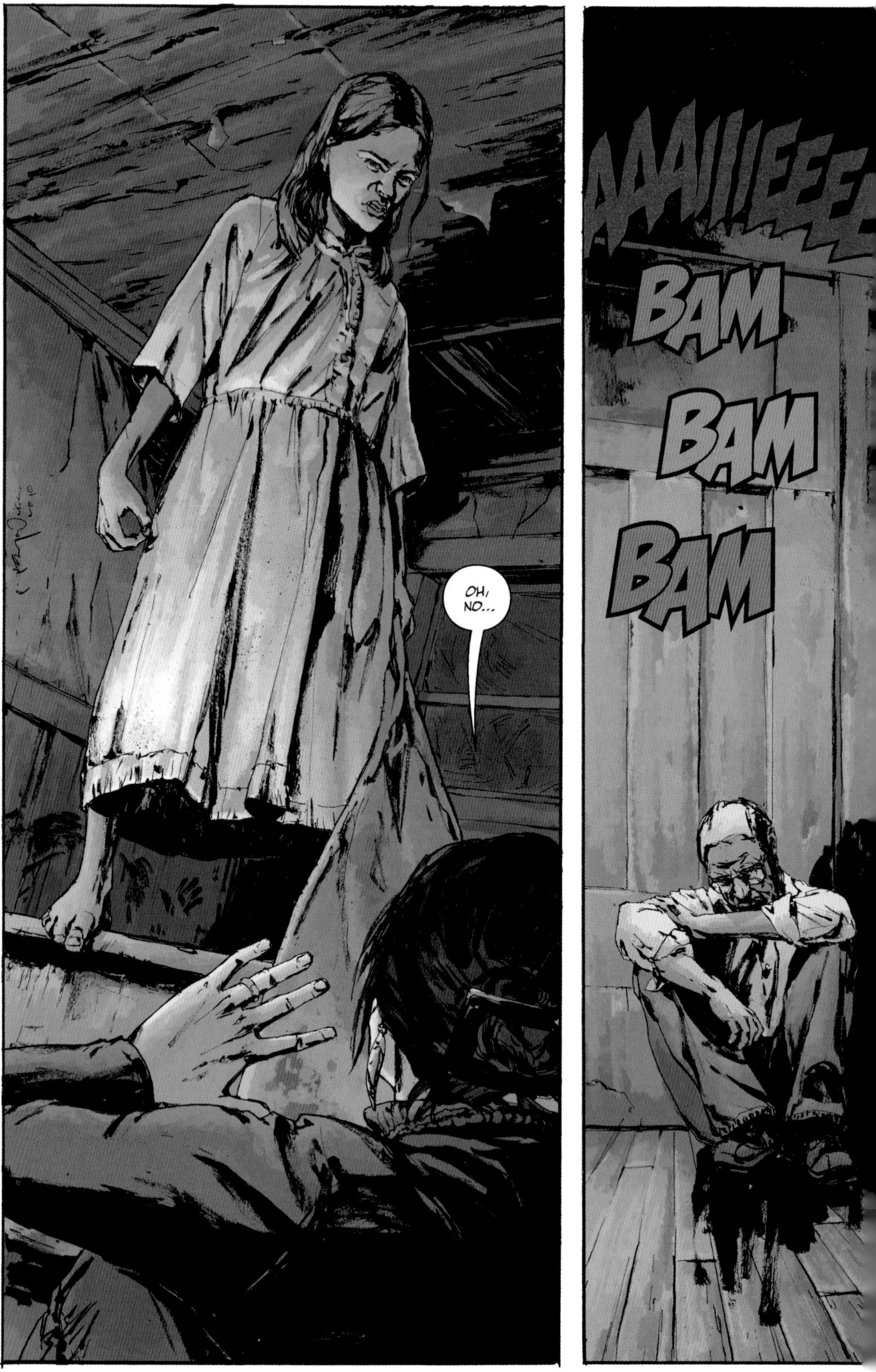
OH, NO...
AAAIIIEEEE
BAM
BAM
BAM

CHAPTER TWO

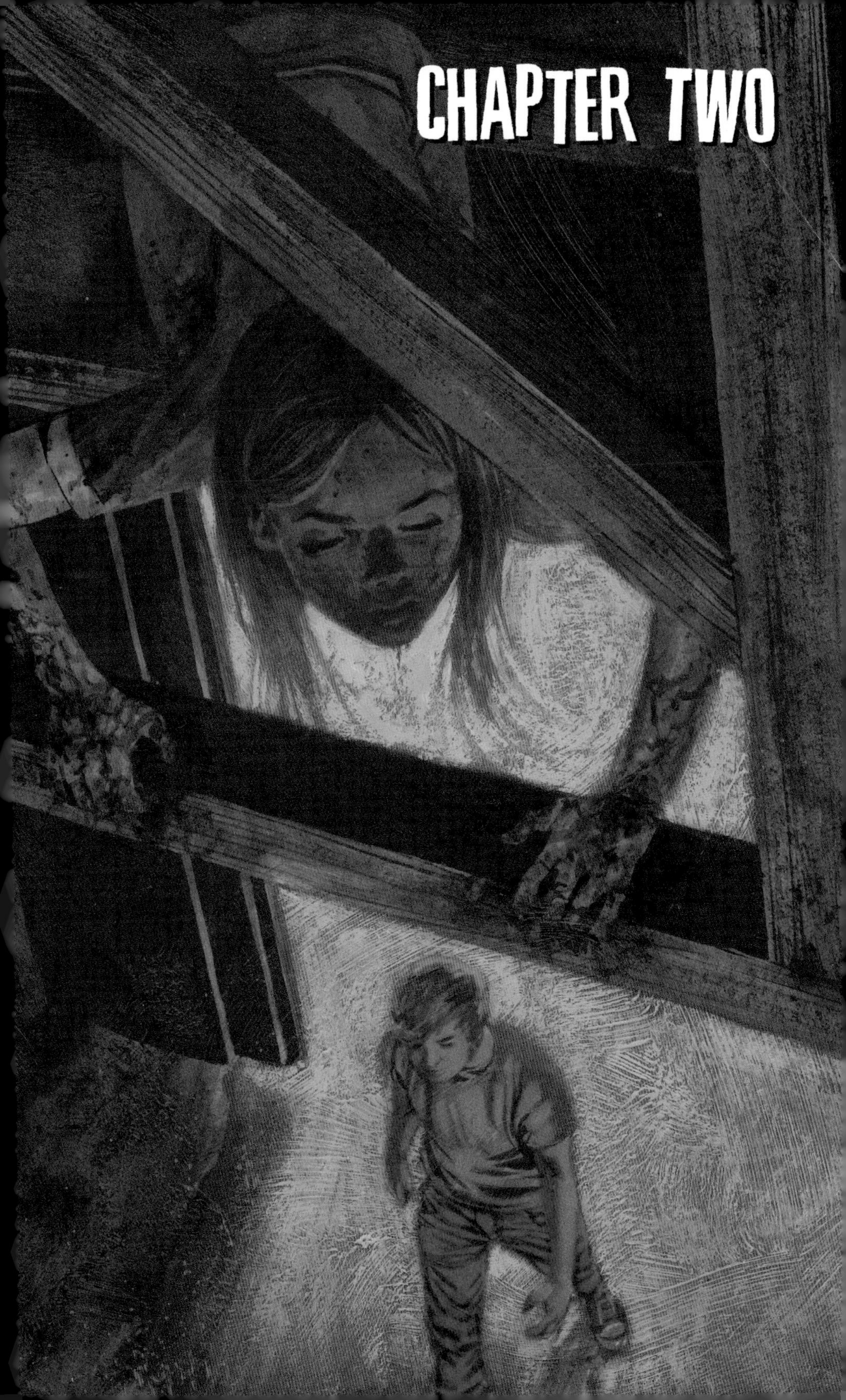

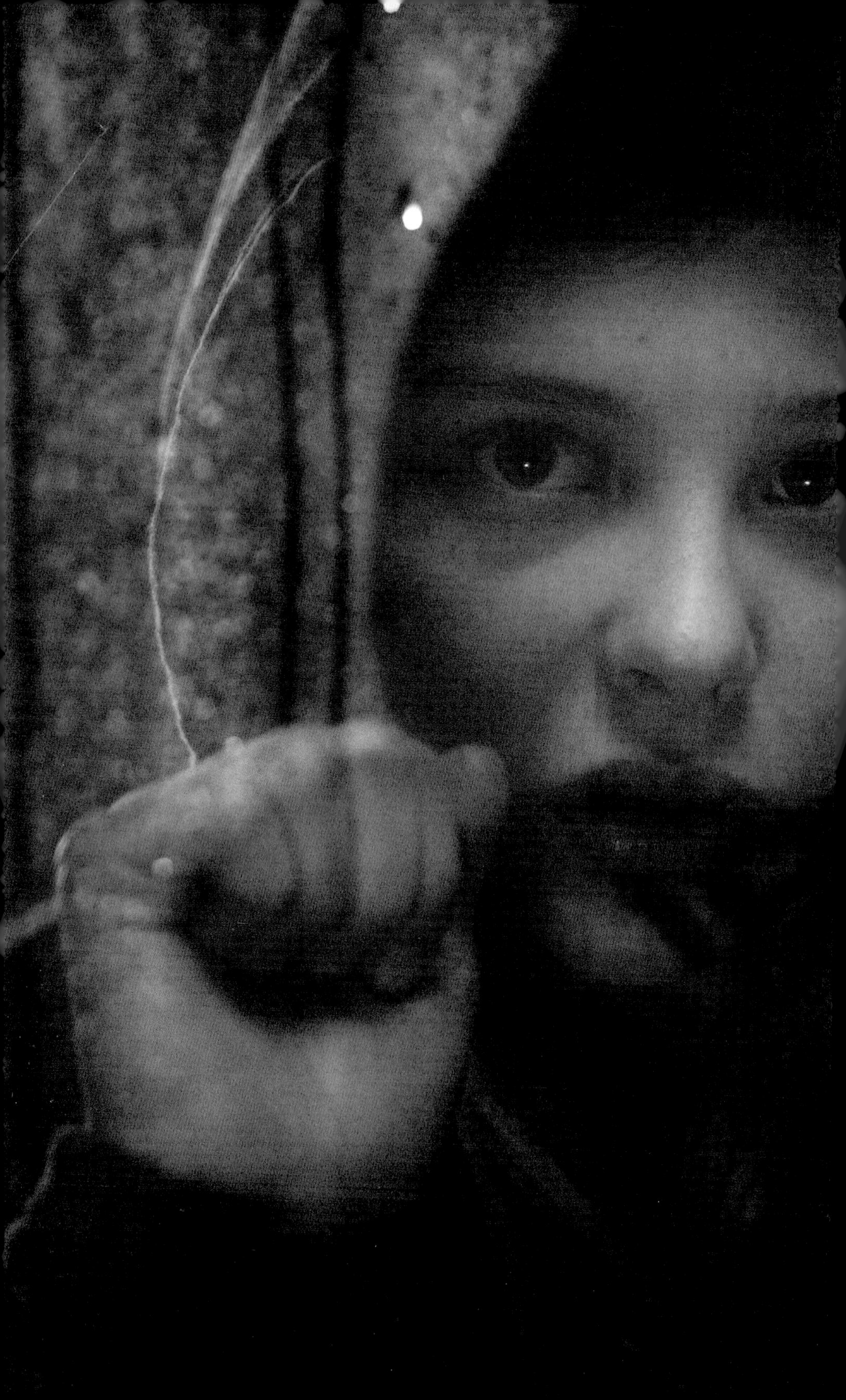

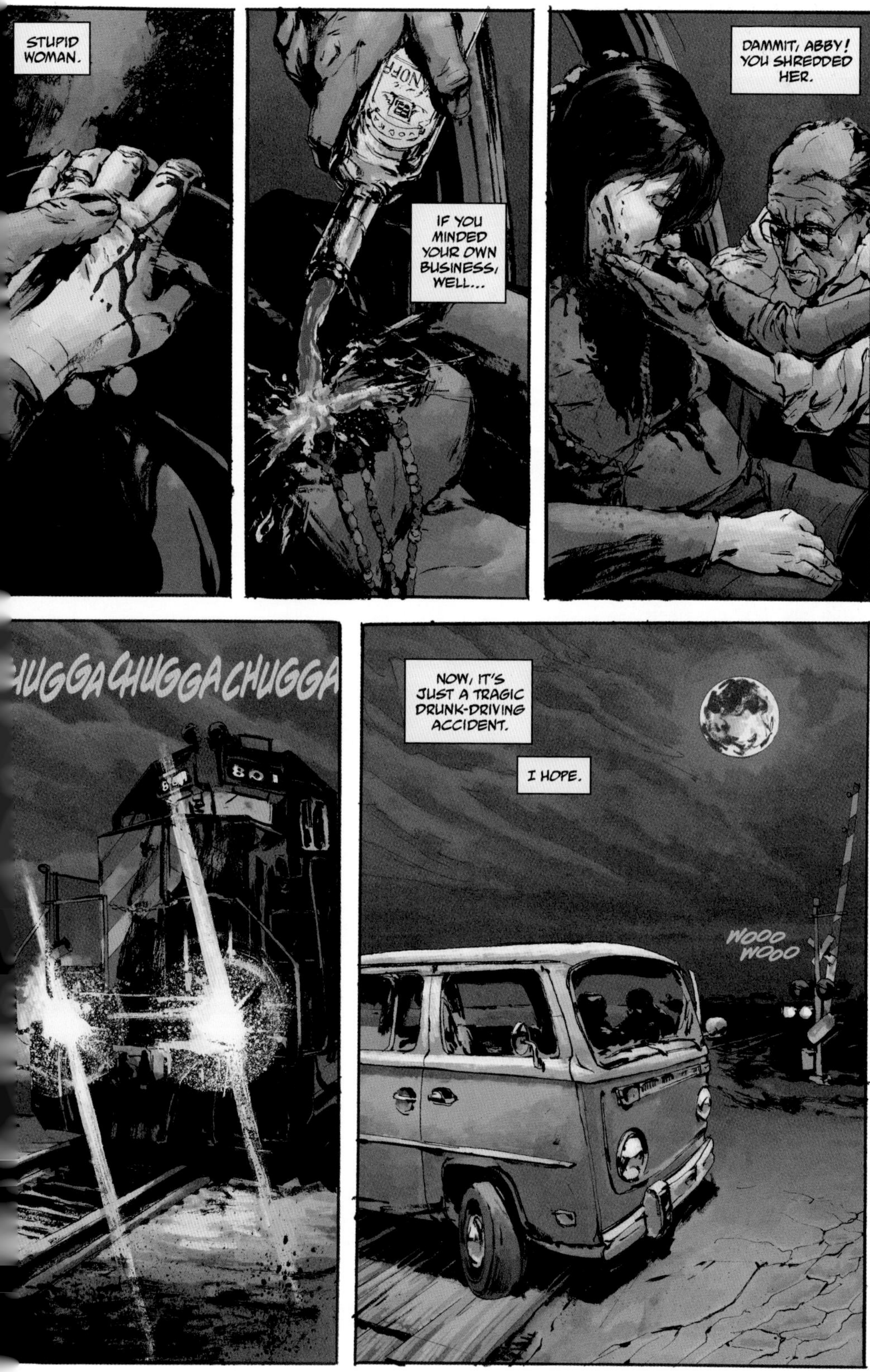
STUPID WOMAN.
IF YOU MINDED YOUR OWN BUSINESS, WELL...
DAMMIT, ABBY! YOU SHREDDED HER.
CHUGGA CHUGGA CHUGGA
NOW, IT'S JUST A TRAGIC DRUNK-DRIVING ACCIDENT.
I HOPE.
WOOO WOOO

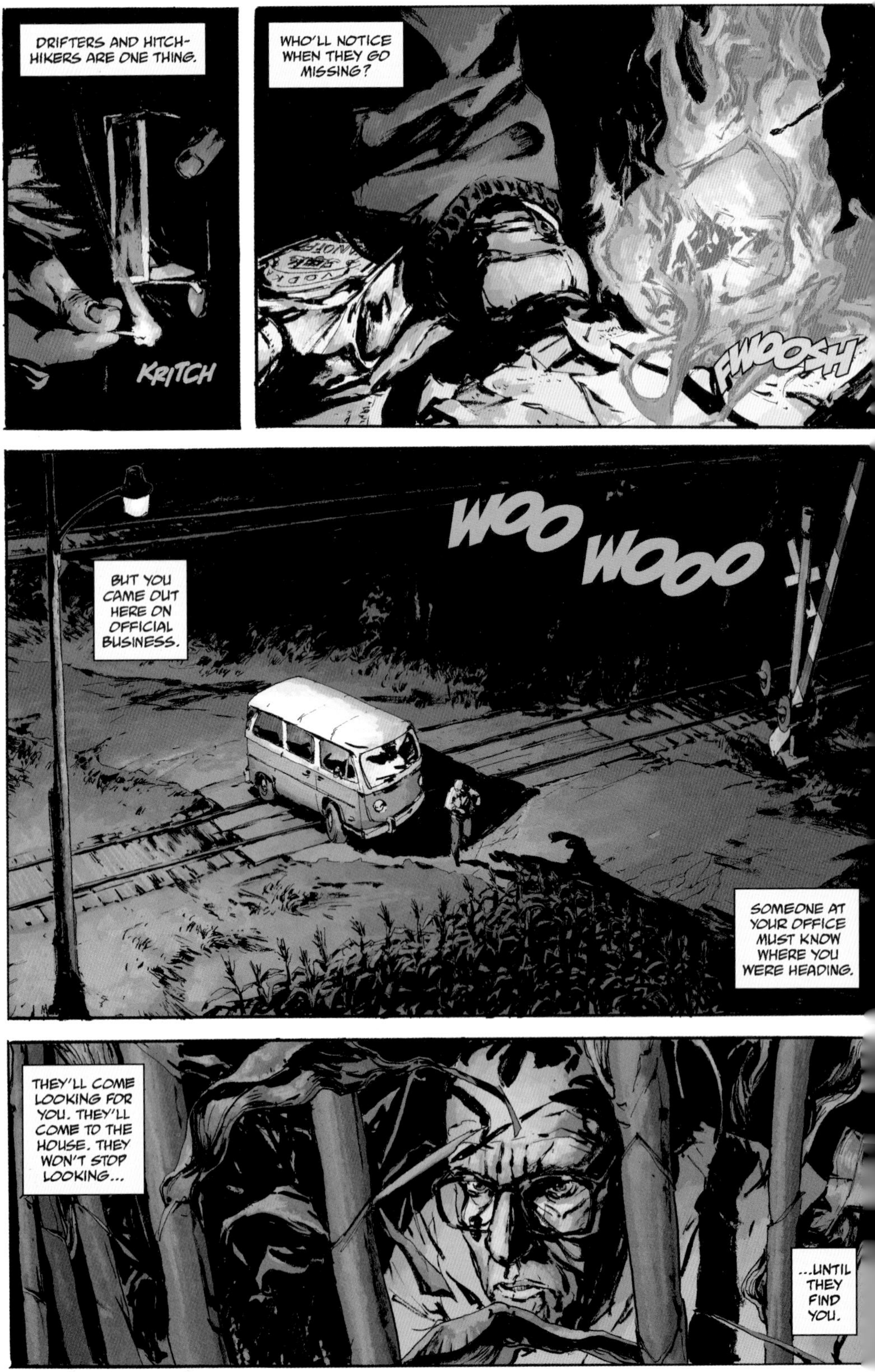
DRIFTERS AND HITCH-HIKERS ARE ONE THING.
KRITCH
WHO'LL NOTICE WHEN THEY GO MISSING?
FWOOSH
WOO WOOO
BUT YOU CAME OUT HERE ON OFFICIAL BUSINESS.
SOMEONE AT YOUR OFFICE MUST KNOW WHERE YOU WERE HEADING.
THEY'LL COME LOOKING FOR YOU. THEY'LL COME TO THE HOUSE. THEY WON'T STOP LOOKING...
...UNTIL THEY FIND YOU.

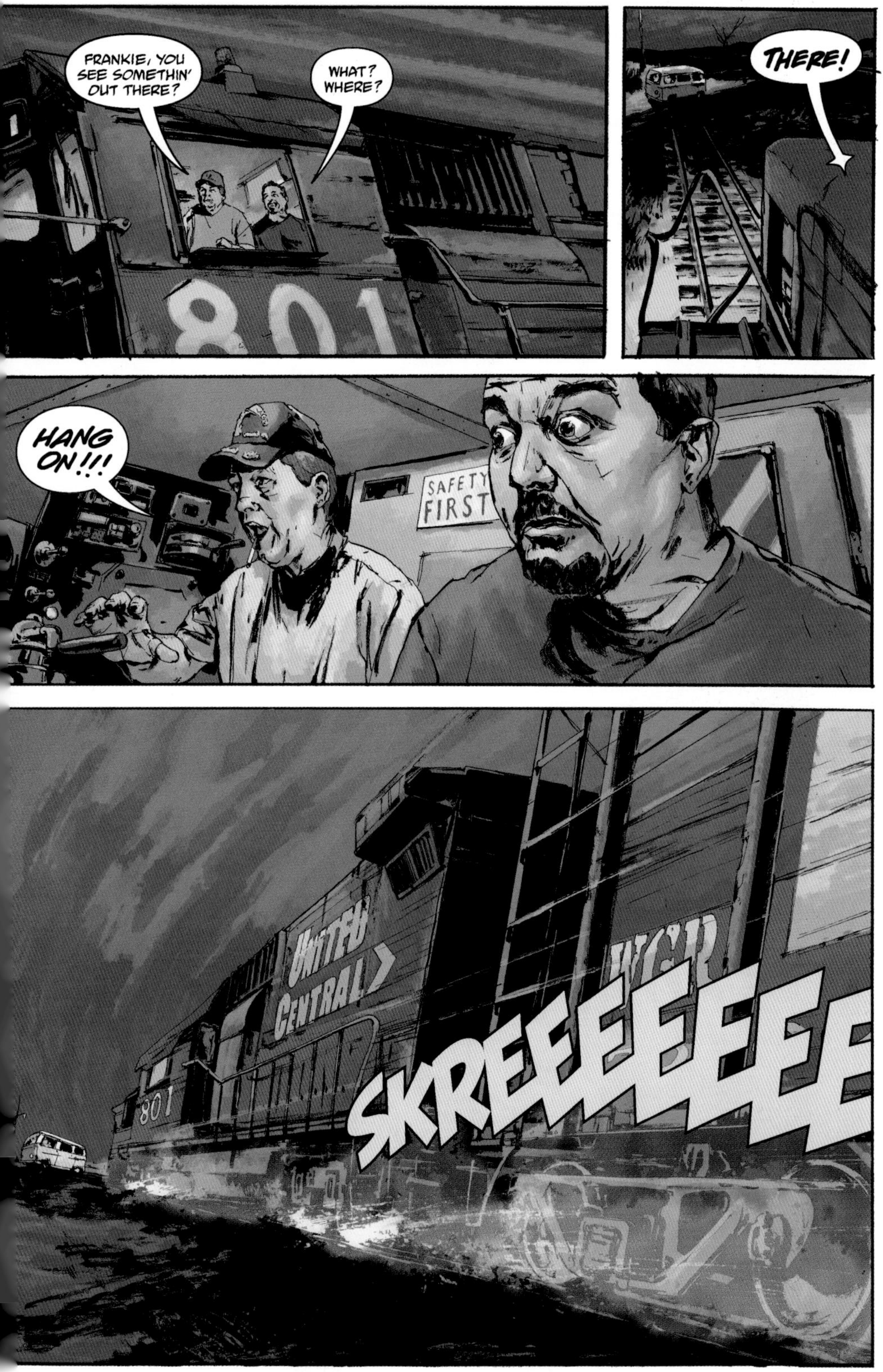
FRANKIE, YOU SEE SOMETHIN' OUT THERE?
WHAT? WHERE?
THERE!
HANG ON!!!
SAFETY FIRST
801
UNITED CENTRAL
SKREEEEEEEE

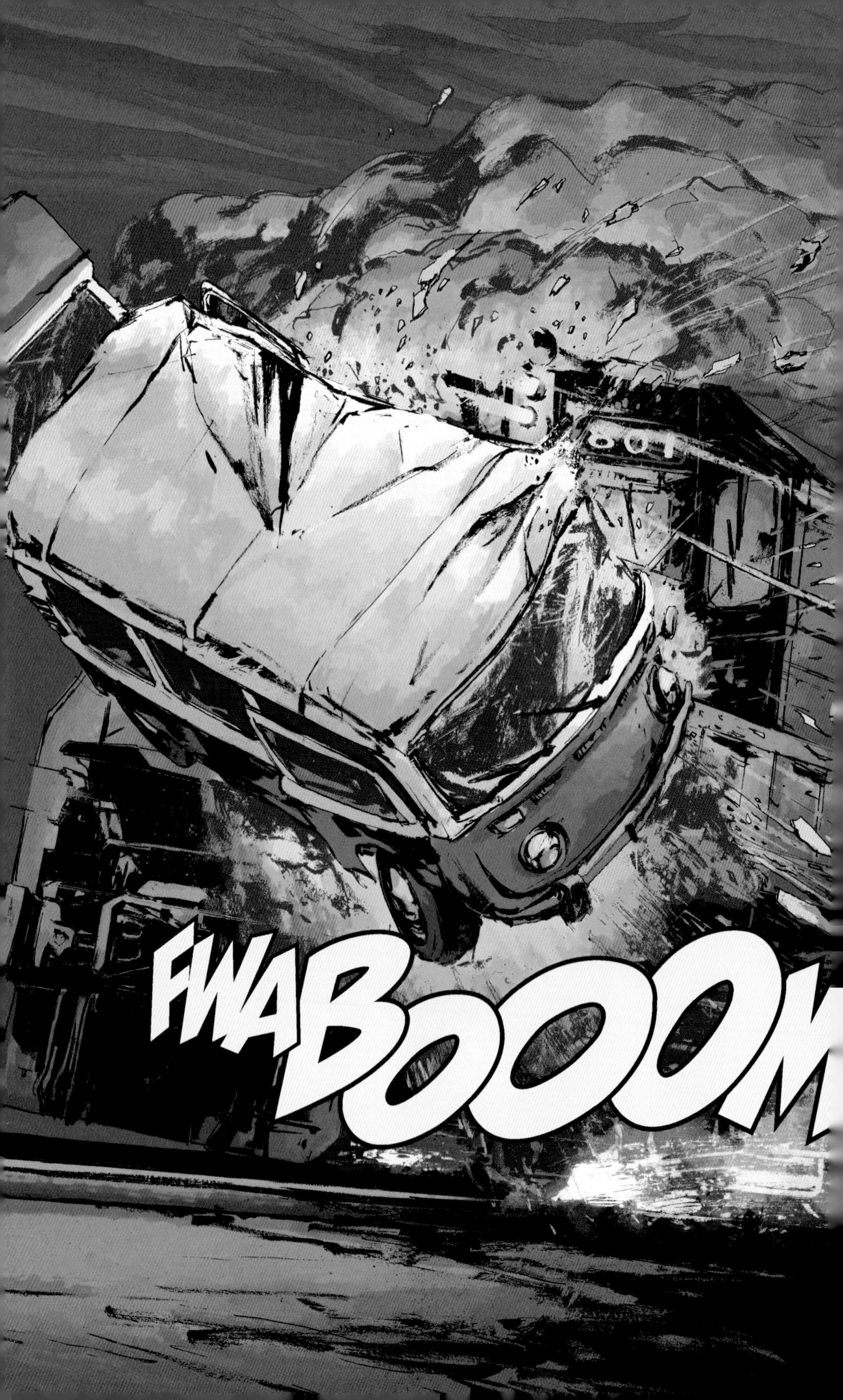
FWABOOOM

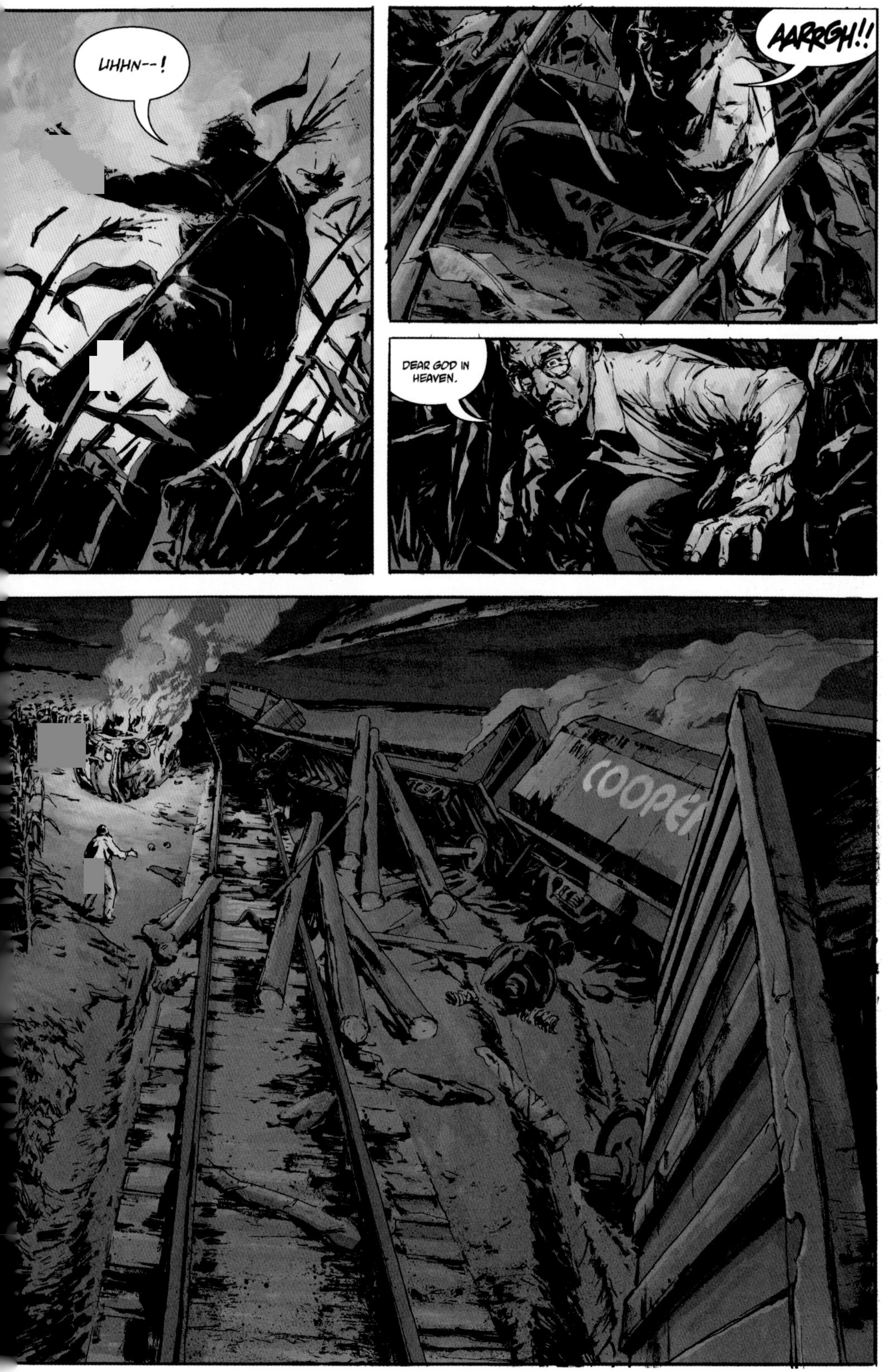
UHHN--!
AARRGH!!
DEAR GOD IN HEAVEN.
COOPER

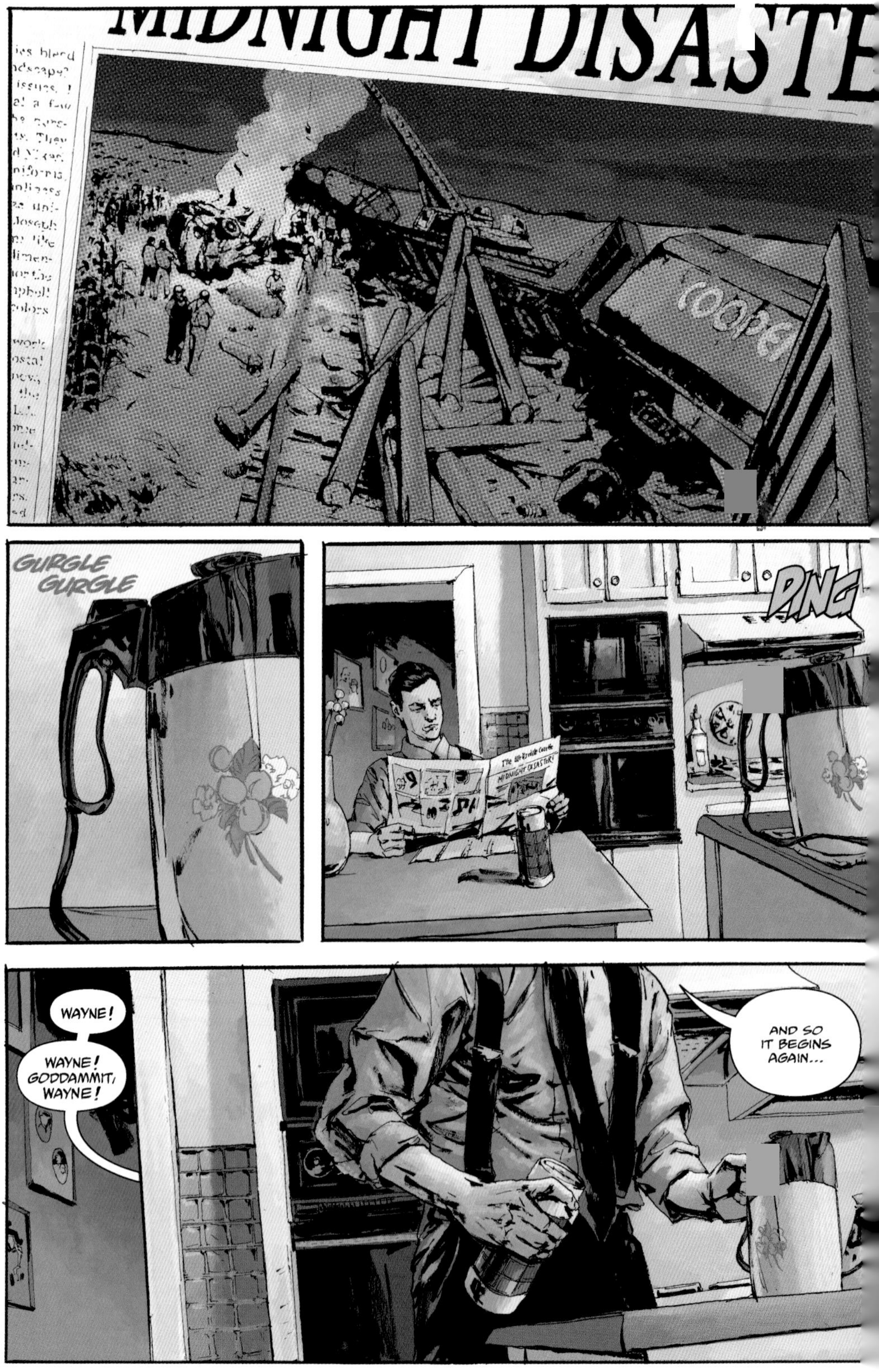
MIDNIGHT DISASTE
GURGLE GURGLE
DING
WAYNE!
WAYNE! GODDAMMIT, WAYNE!
AND SO IT BEGINS AGAIN...

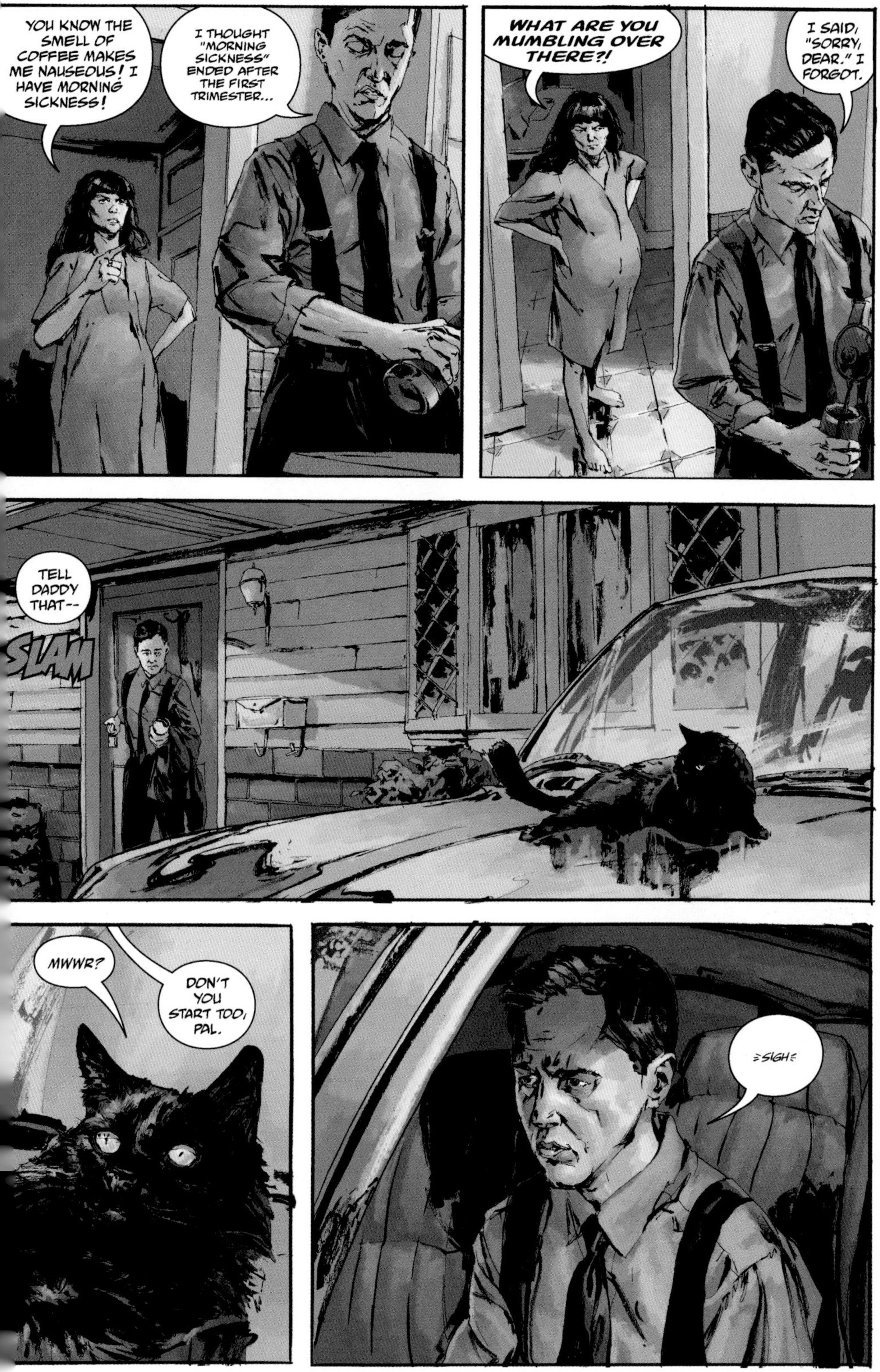
YOU KNOW THE SMELL OF COFFEE MAKES ME NAUSEOUS! I HAVE MORNING SICKNESS!
I THOUGHT "MORNING SICKNESS" ENDED AFTER THE FIRST TRIMESTER...
WHAT ARE YOU MUMBLING OVER THERE?!
I SAID, "SORRY, DEAR." I FORGOT.
TELL DADDY THAT--
SLAM
MWWR?
DON'T YOU START TOO, PAL.
SIGH

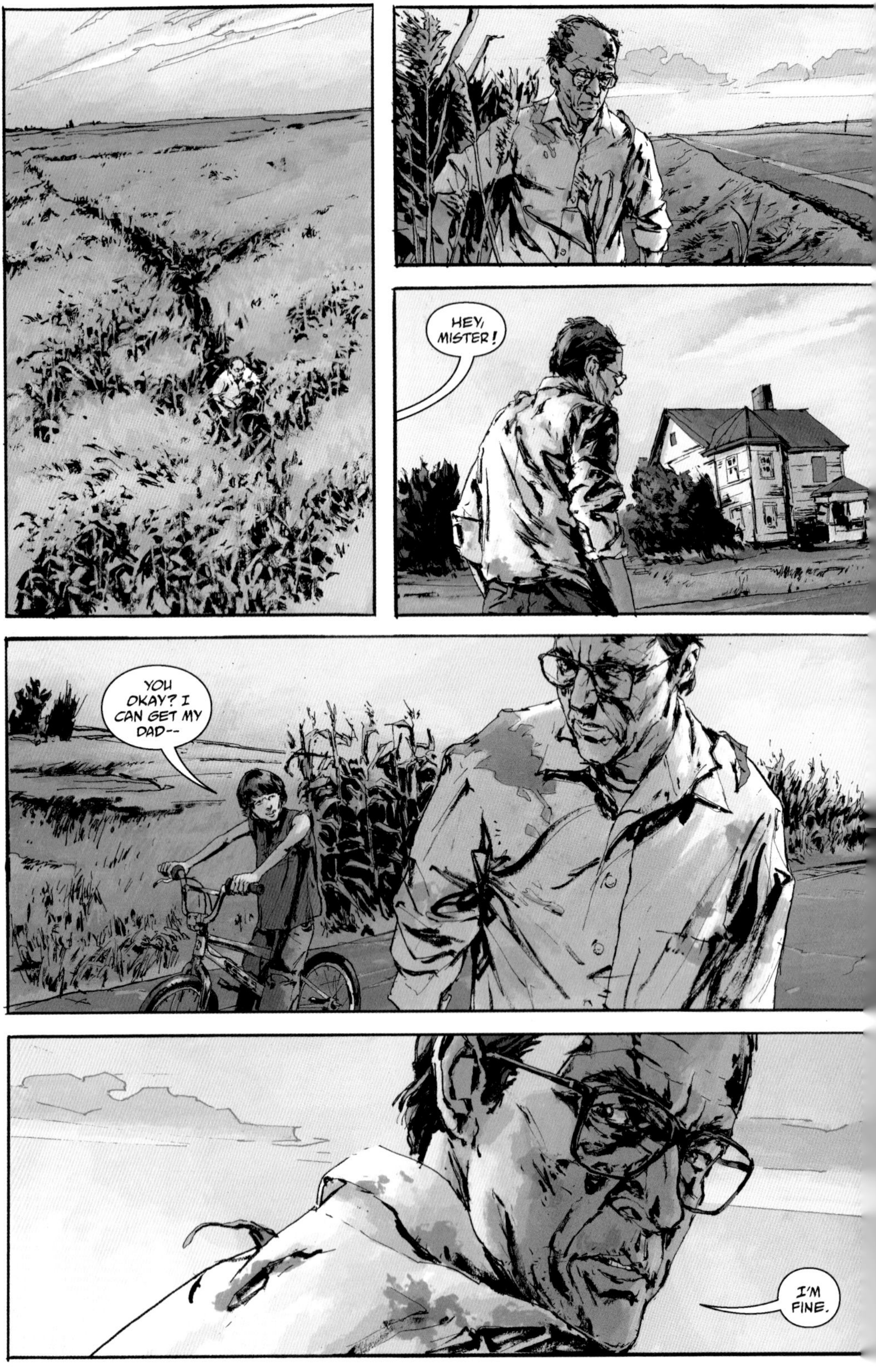
HEY, MISTER!
YOU OKAY? I CAN GET MY DAD--
I'M FINE.

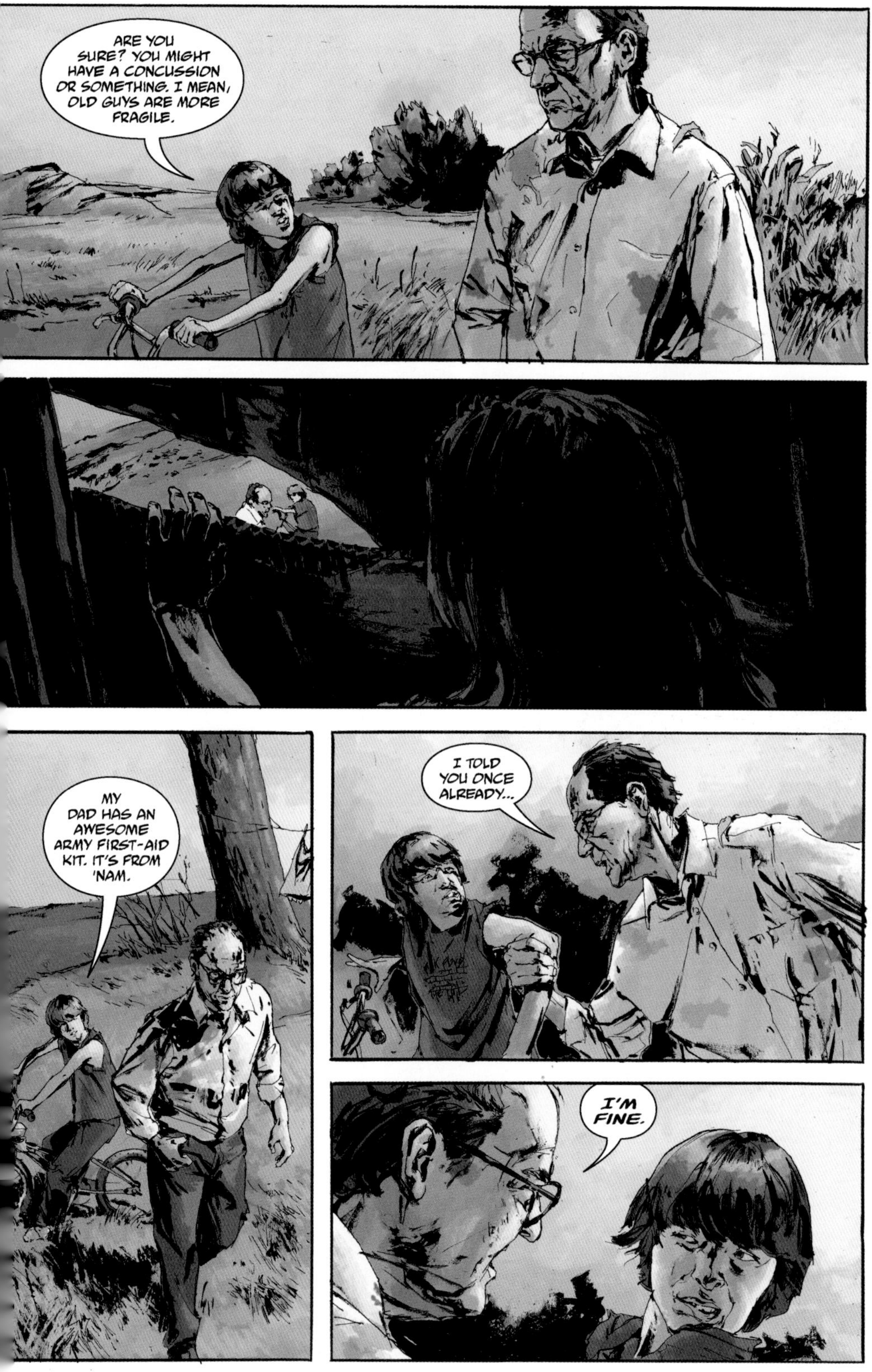
ARE YOU SURE? YOU MIGHT HAVE A CONCUSSION OR SOMETHING. I MEAN, OLD GUYS ARE MORE FRAGILE.
MY DAD HAS AN AWESOME ARMY FIRST-AID KIT. IT'S FROM 'NAM.
I TOLD YOU ONCE ALREADY...
I'M FINE.

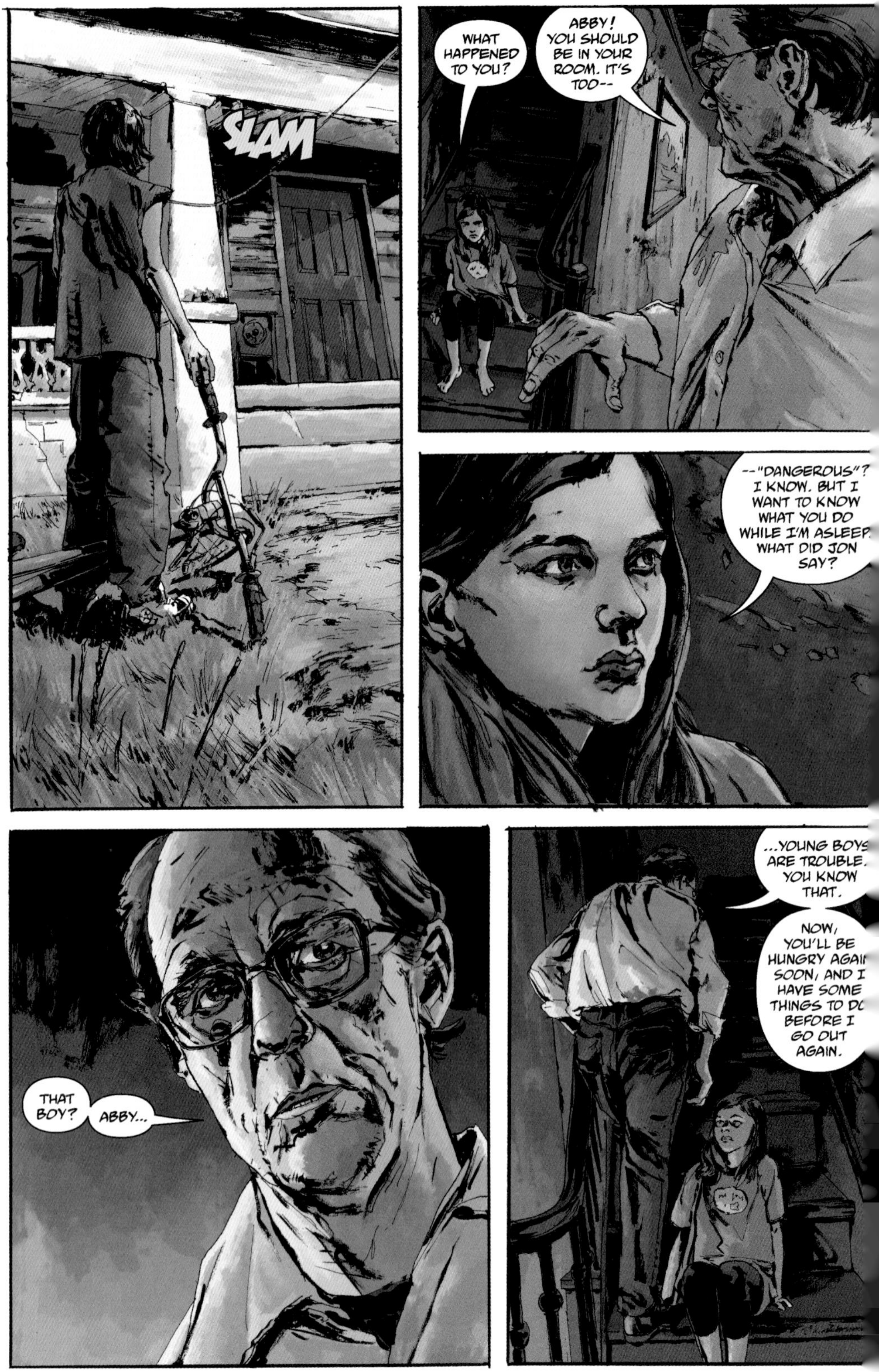
SLAM
WHAT HAPPENED TO YOU?
ABBY! YOU SHOULD BE IN YOUR ROOM. IT'S TOO--
--"DANGEROUS"? I KNOW. BUT I WANT TO KNOW WHAT YOU DO WHILE I'M ASLEEP. WHAT DID JON SAY?
THAT BOY?
ABBY...
...YOUNG BOYS ARE TROUBLE. YOU KNOW THAT.
NOW, YOU'LL BE HUNGRY AGAIN SOON, AND I HAVE SOME THINGS TO DO BEFORE I GO OUT AGAIN.

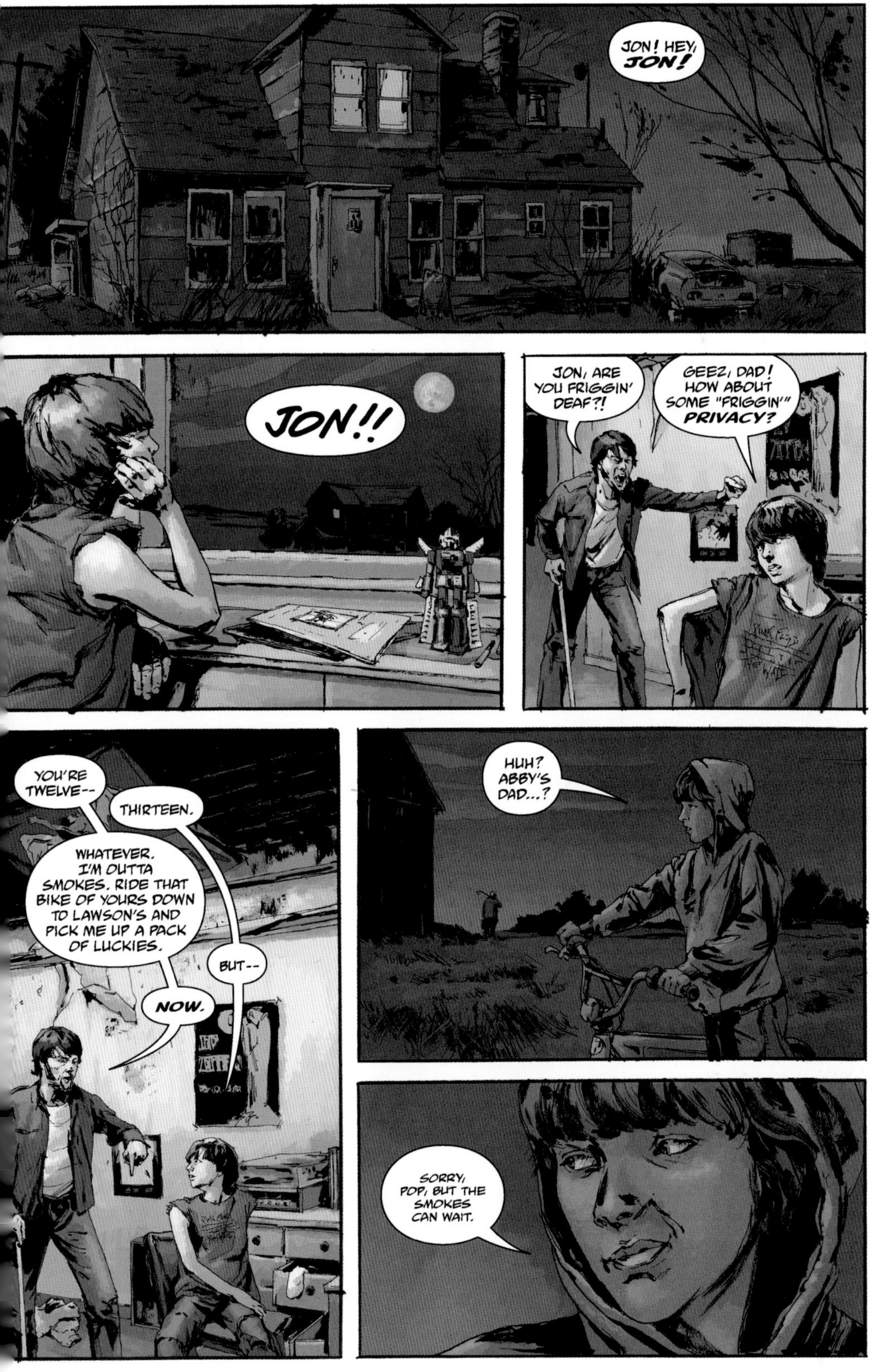
JON! HEY, JON!
JON!!
JON, ARE YOU FRIGGIN' DEAF?!
GEEZ, DAD! HOW ABOUT SOME "FRIGGIN'" PRIVACY?
YOU'RE TWELVE--
THIRTEEN.
WHATEVER. I'M OUTTA SMOKES. RIDE THAT BIKE OF YOURS DOWN TO LAWSON'S AND PICK ME UP A PACK OF LUCKIES.
BUT--
NOW.
HUH? ABBY'S DAD...?
SORRY, POP, BUT THE SMOKES CAN WAIT.

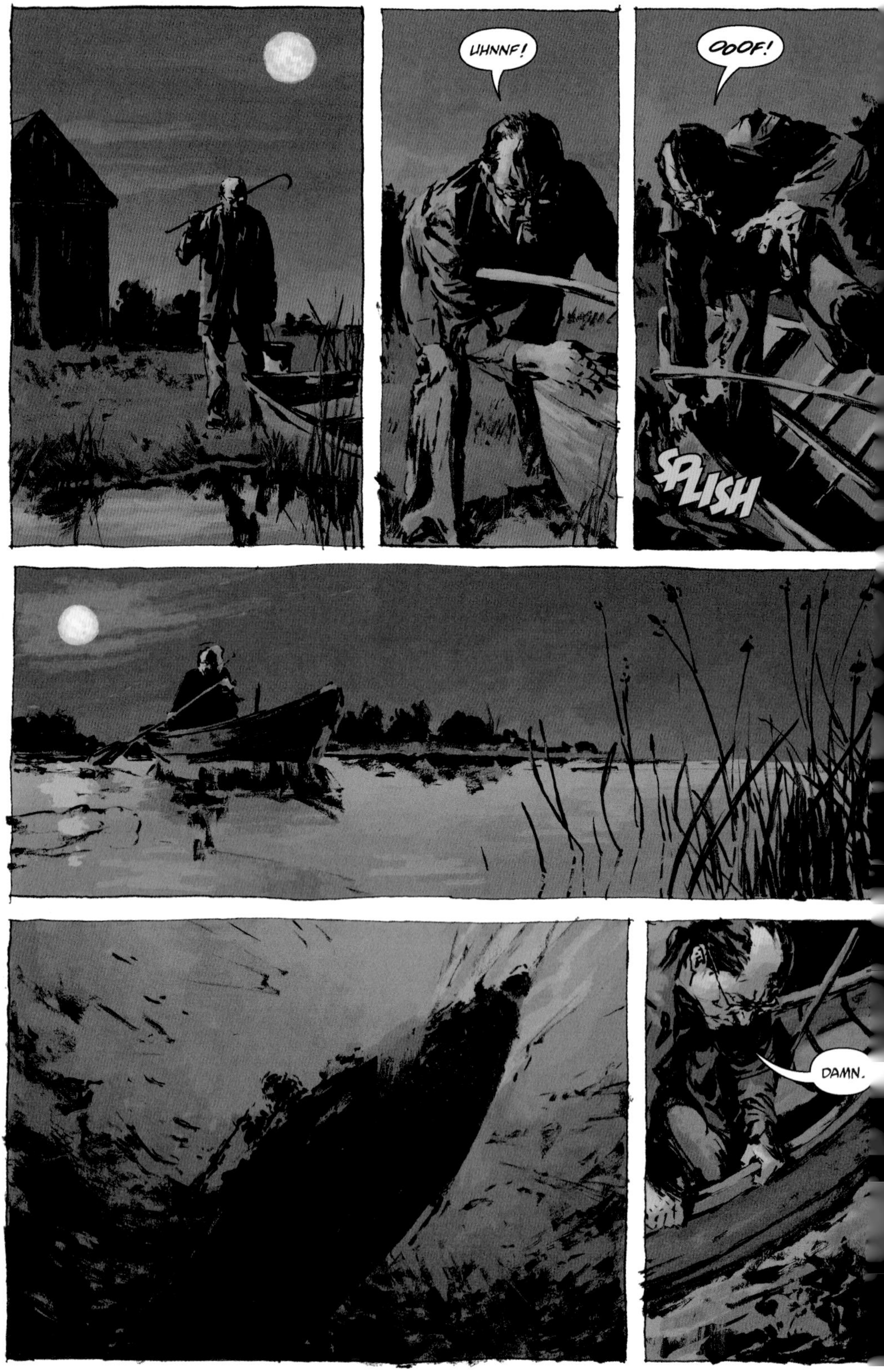
UHNNF!
OOOF!
SPLISH
DAMN.

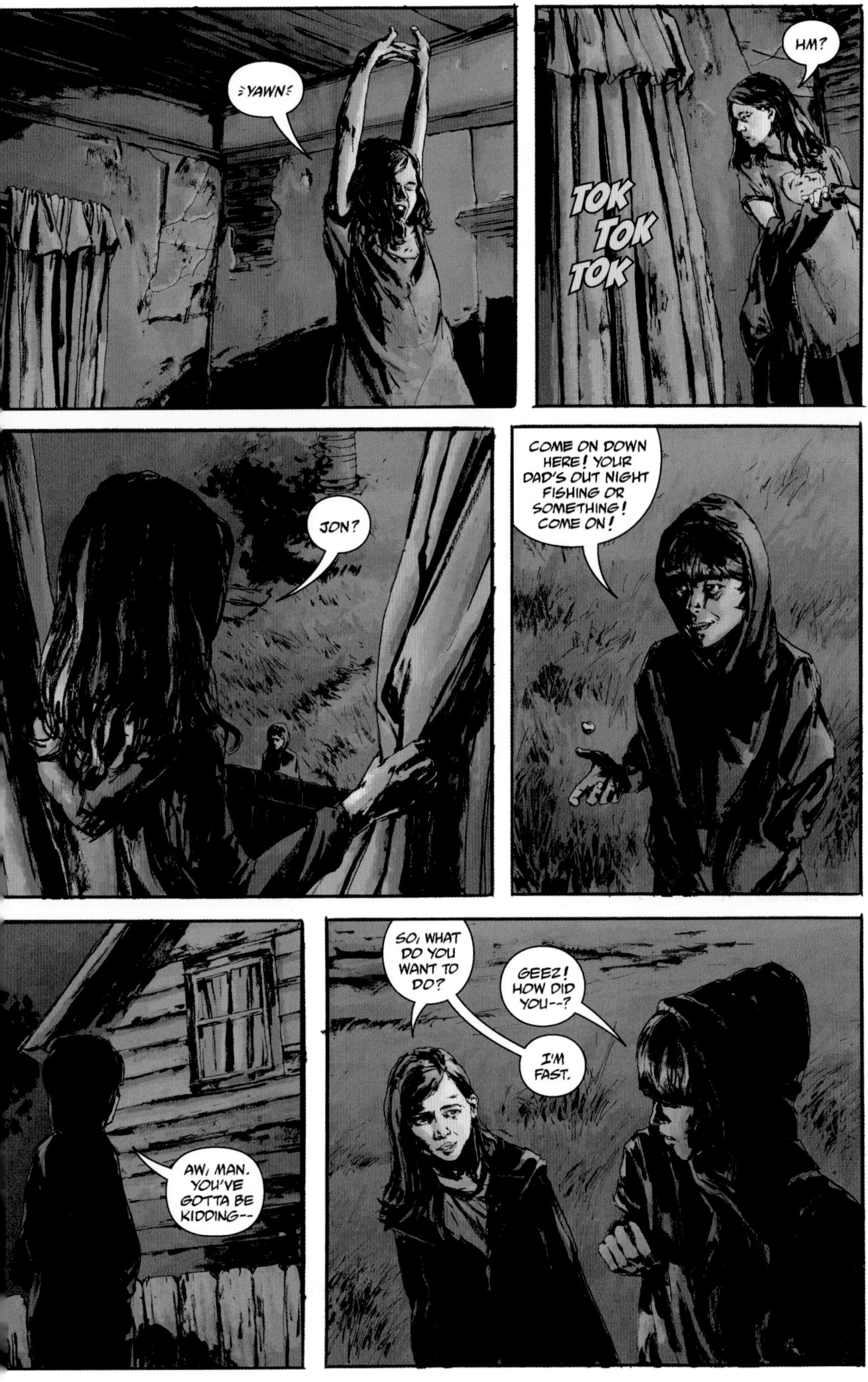

≶YAWN≷
HM?
TOK TOK TOK
JON?
COME ON DOWN HERE! YOUR DAD'S OUT NIGHT FISHING OR SOMETHING! COME ON!
AW, MAN. YOU'VE GOTTA BE KIDDING--
SO, WHAT DO YOU WANT TO DO?
GEEZ! HOW DID YOU--?
I'M FAST.

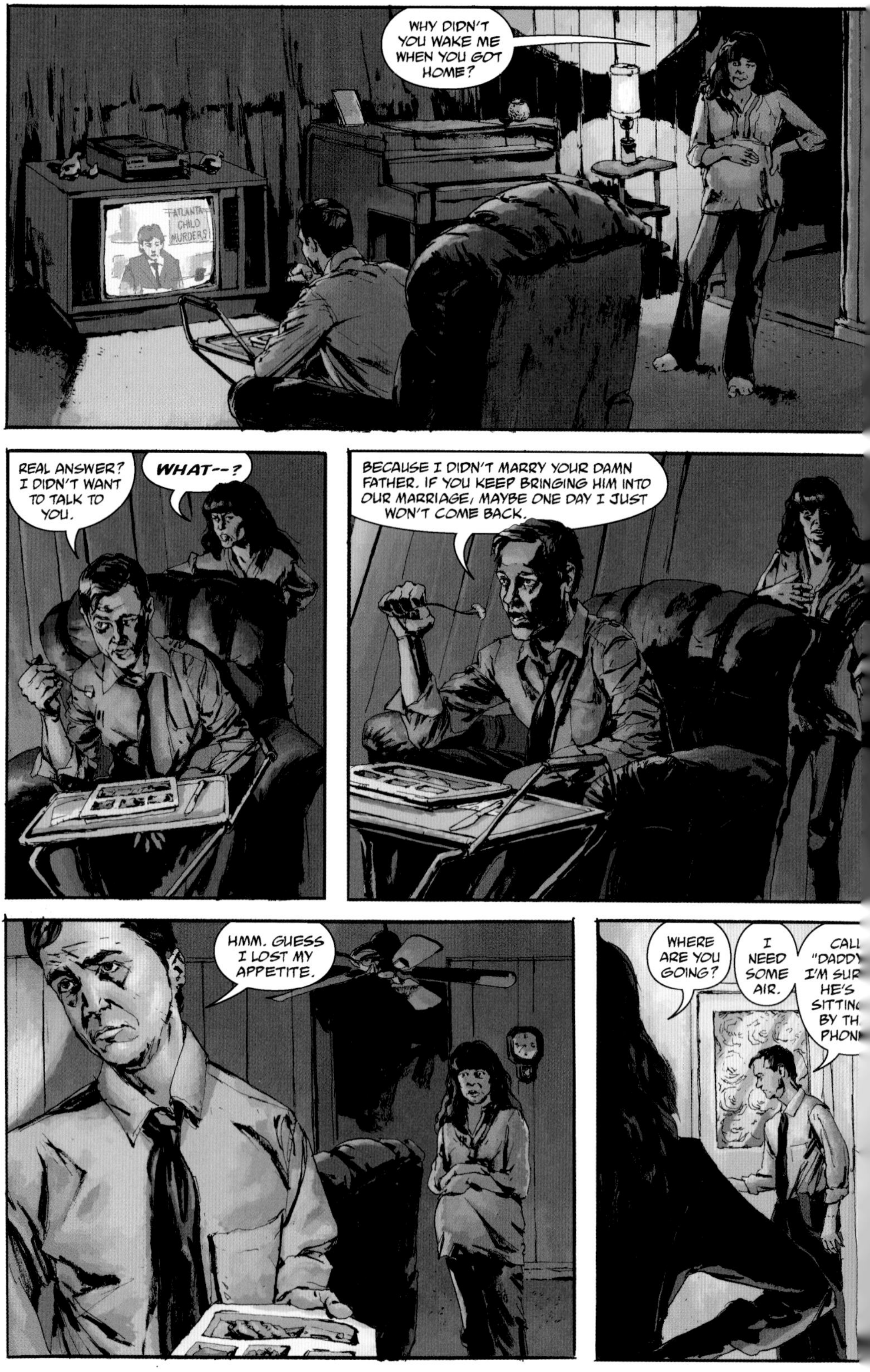
WHY DIDN'T YOU WAKE ME WHEN YOU GOT HOME?
ATLANTA CHILD MURDERS
REAL ANSWER? I DIDN'T WANT TO TALK TO YOU.
WHAT--?
BECAUSE I DIDN'T MARRY YOUR DAMN FATHER. IF YOU KEEP BRINGING HIM INTO OUR MARRIAGE, MAYBE ONE DAY I JUST WON'T COME BACK.
HMM. GUESS I LOST MY APPETITE.
WHERE ARE YOU GOING?
I NEED SOME AIR.
CALL "DADDY I'M SUR HE'S SITTIN BY TH PHON

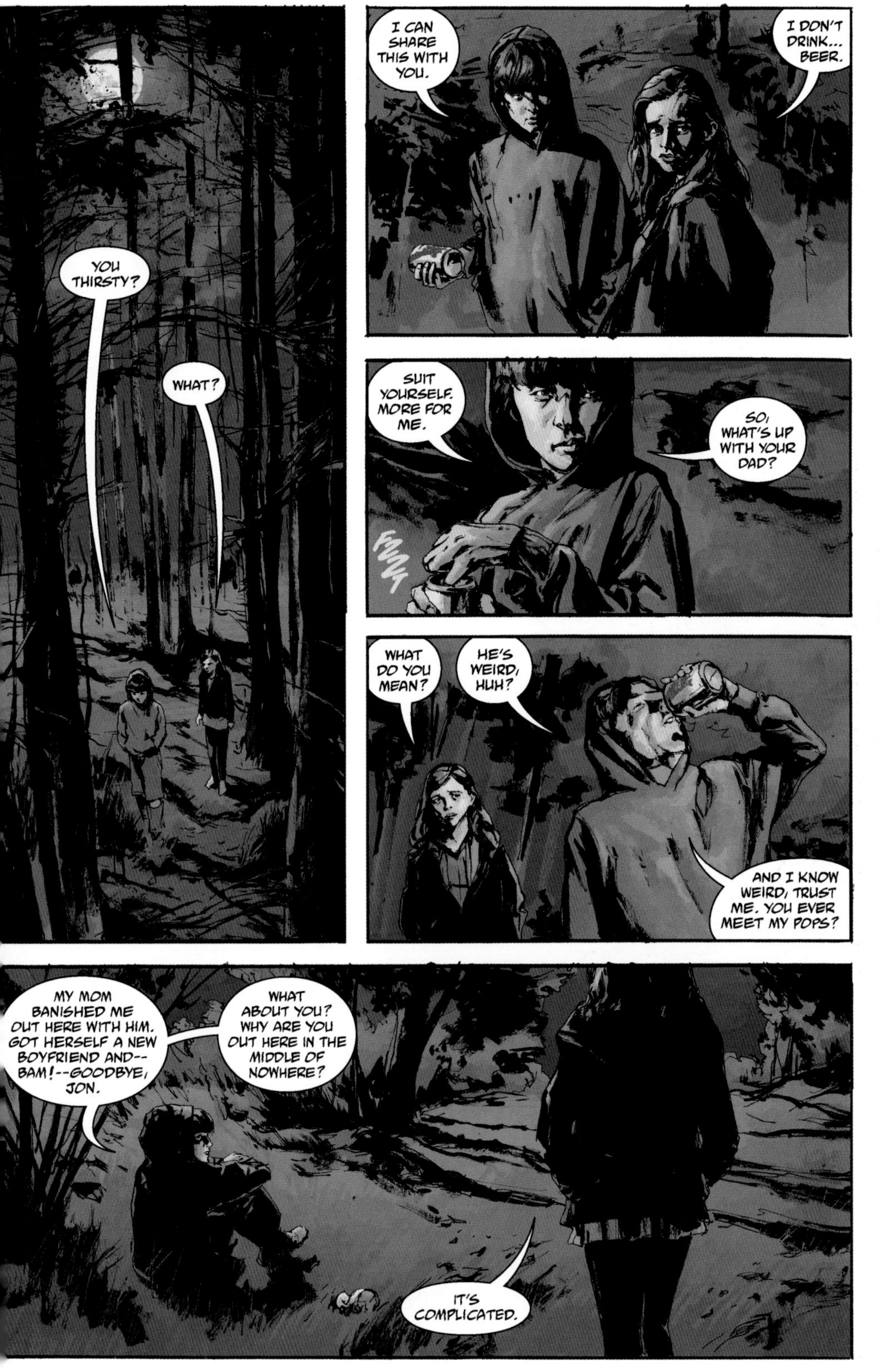
YOU THIRSTY?
WHAT?
I CAN SHARE THIS WITH YOU.
I DON'T DRINK... BEER.
SUIT YOURSELF. MORE FOR ME.
FSSSH
SO, WHAT'S UP WITH YOUR DAD?
WHAT DO YOU MEAN?
HE'S WEIRD, HUH?
AND I KNOW WEIRD, TRUST ME. YOU EVER MEET MY POPS?
MY MOM BANISHED ME OUT HERE WITH HIM. GOT HERSELF A NEW BOYFRIEND AND-- BAM!--GOODBYE, JON.
WHAT ABOUT YOU? WHY ARE YOU OUT HERE IN THE MIDDLE OF NOWHERE?
IT'S COMPLICATED.

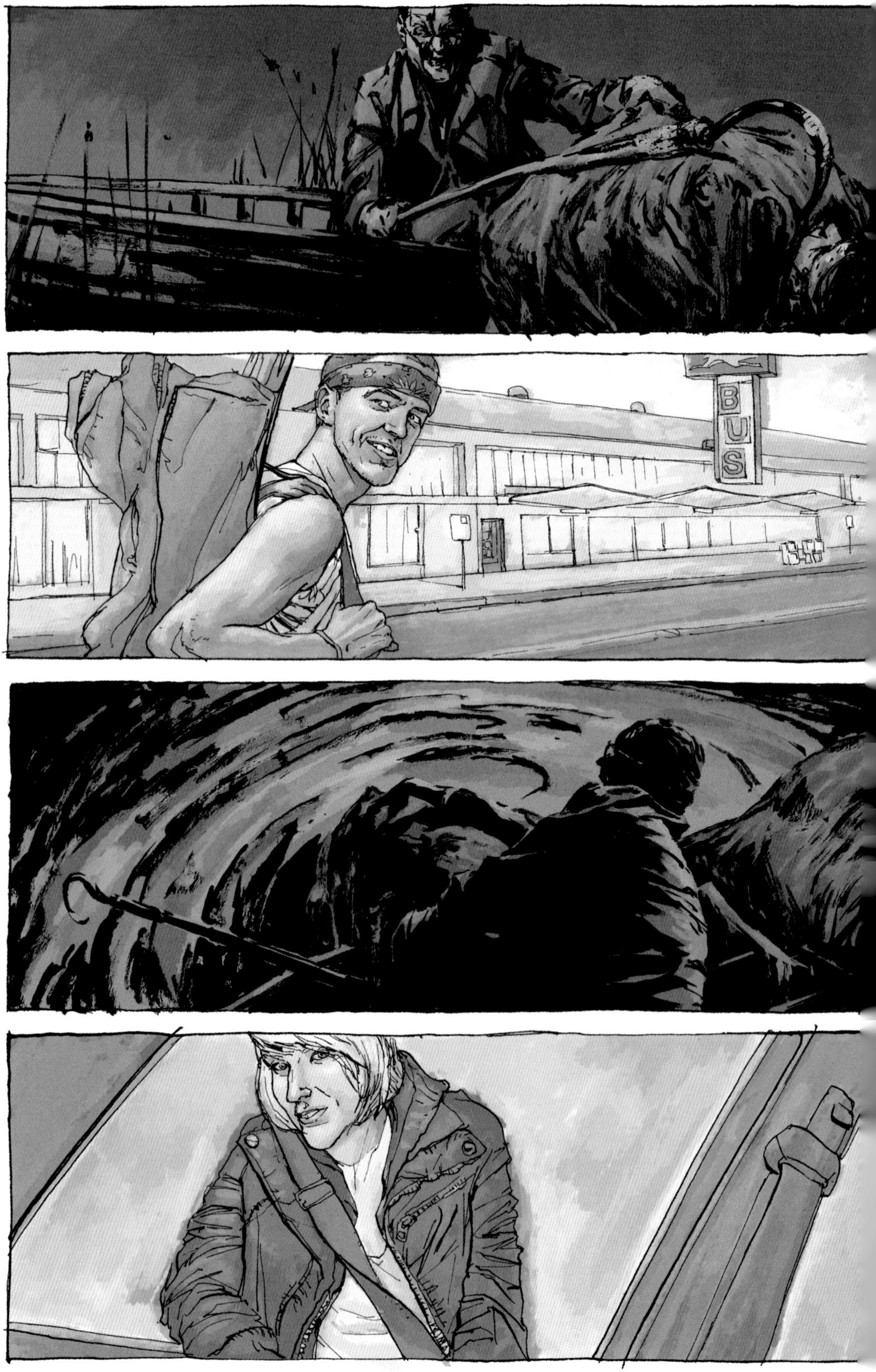
BUS

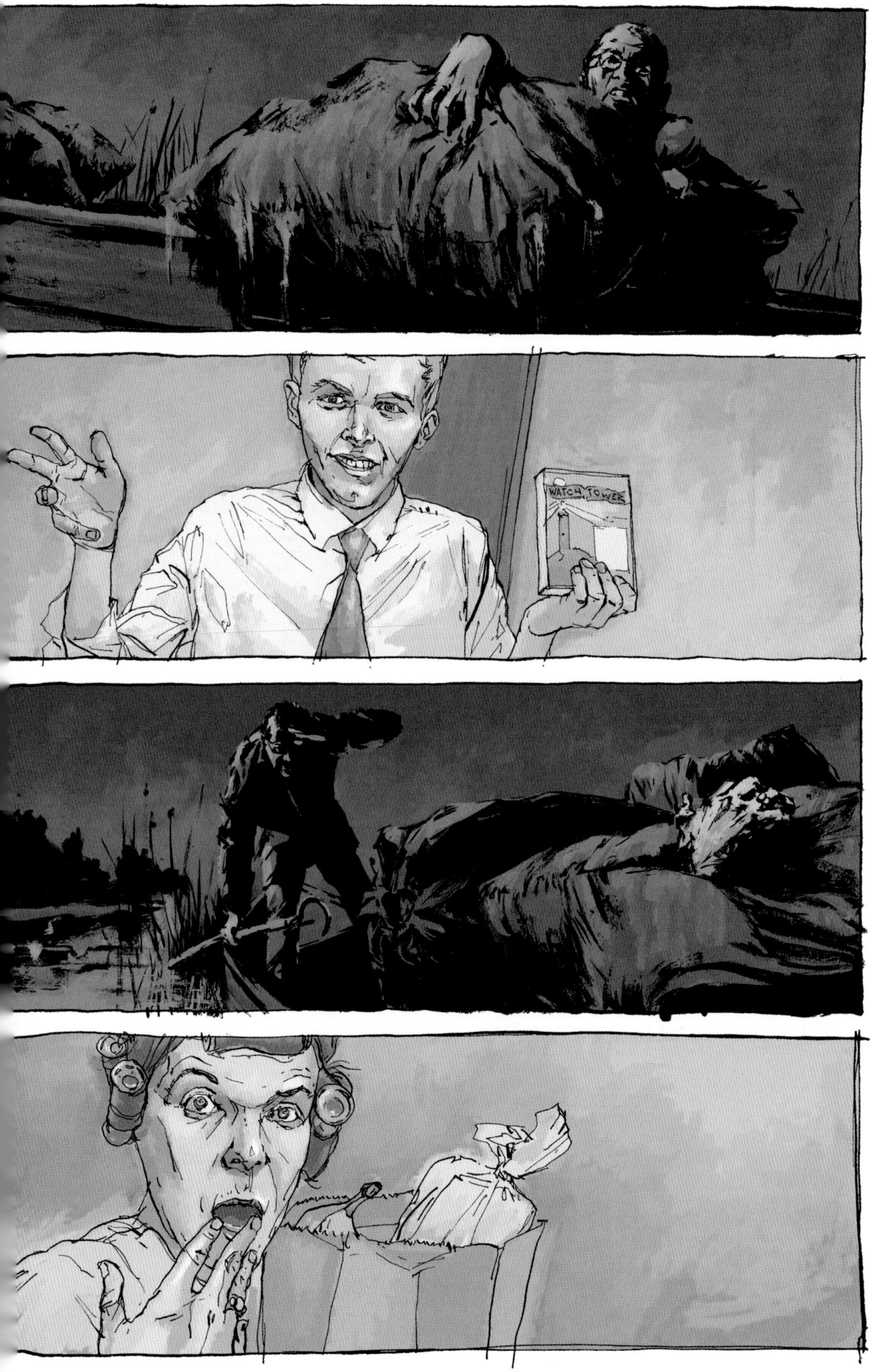
WATCHTOWER

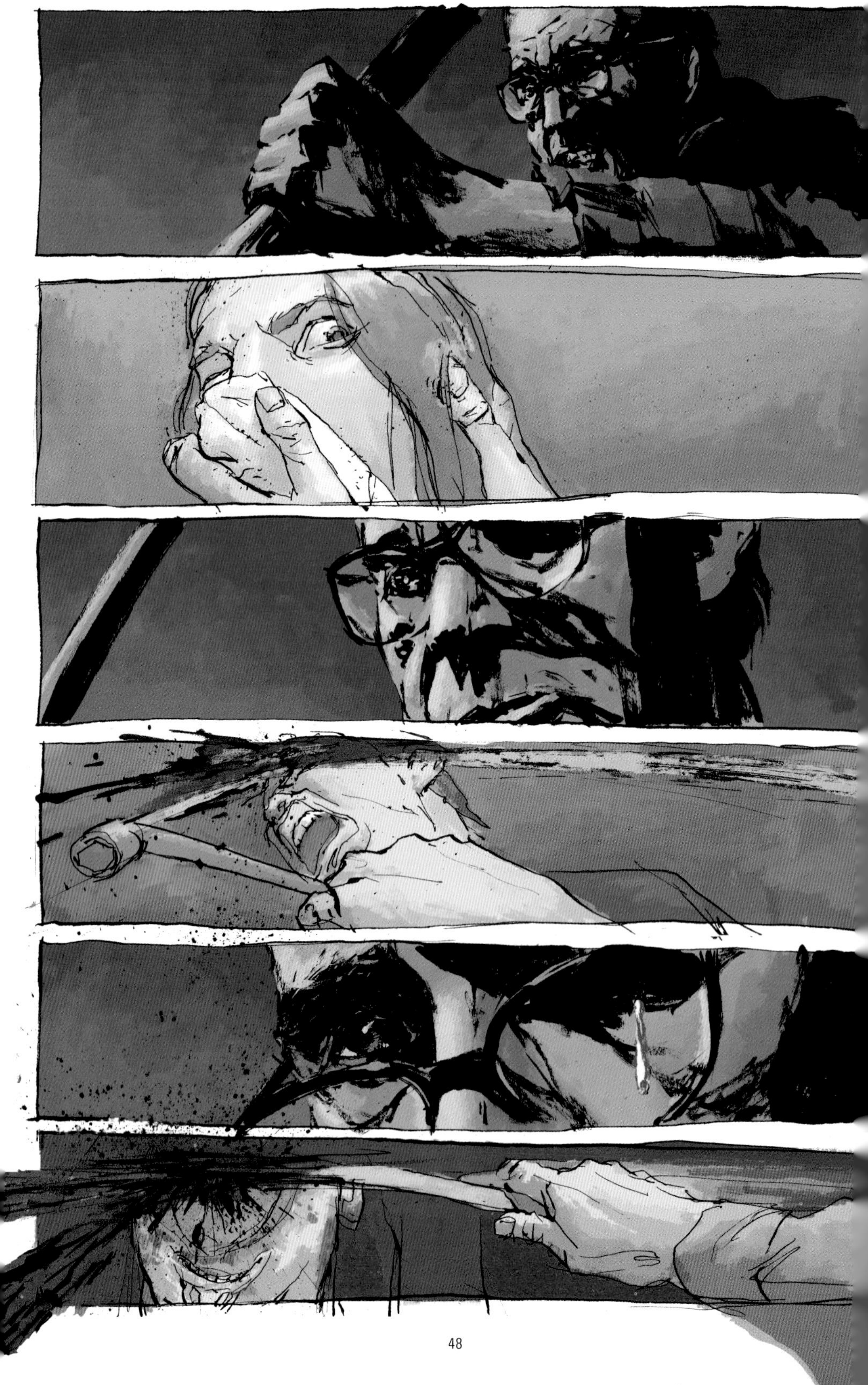

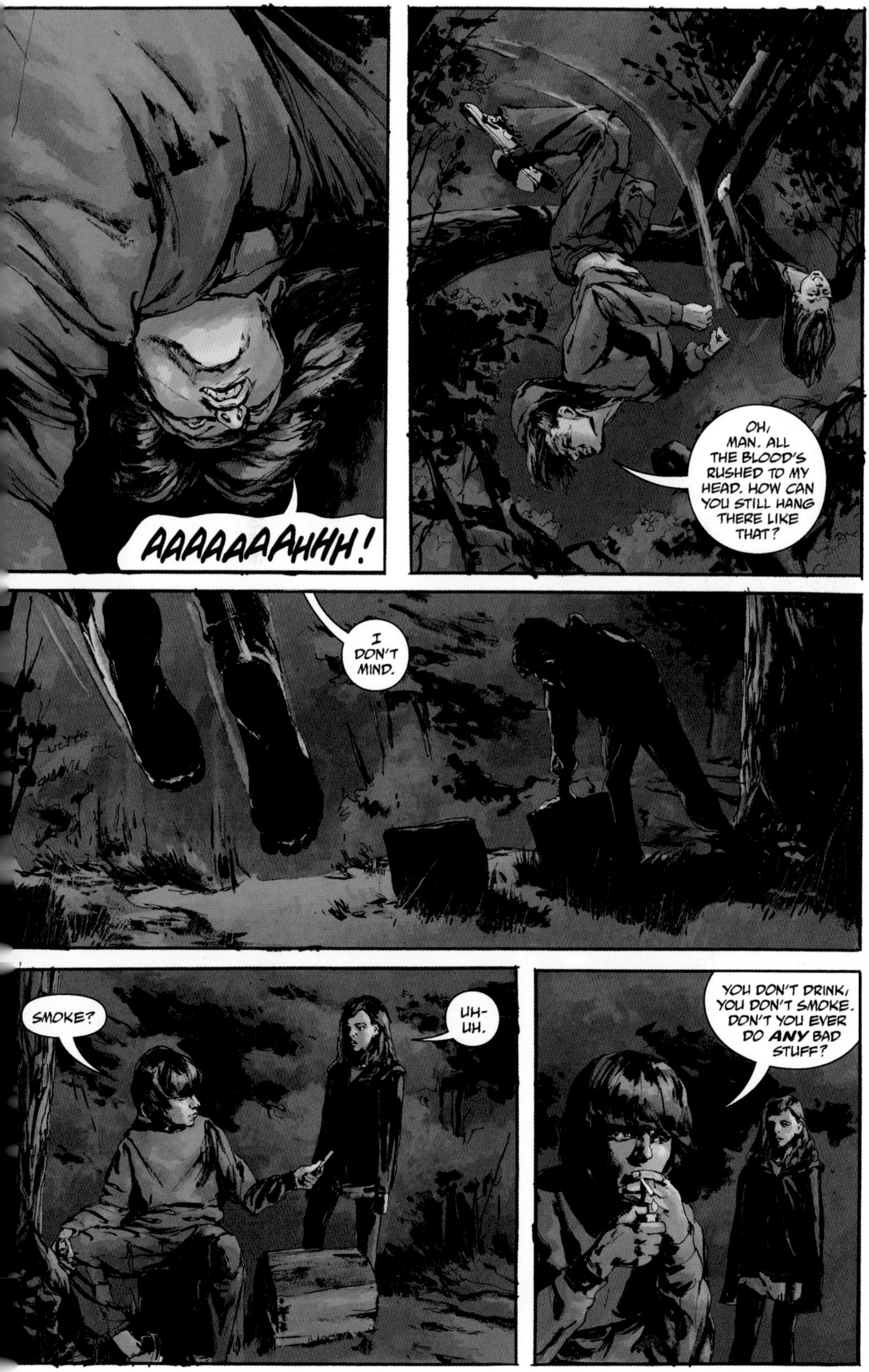
AAAAAAAHHH!
OH, MAN. ALL THE BLOOD'S RUSHED TO MY HEAD. HOW CAN YOU STILL HANG THERE LIKE THAT?
I DON'T MIND.
SMOKE?
UH-UH.
YOU DON'T DRINK, YOU DON'T SMOKE. DON'T YOU EVER DO **ANY** BAD STUFF?

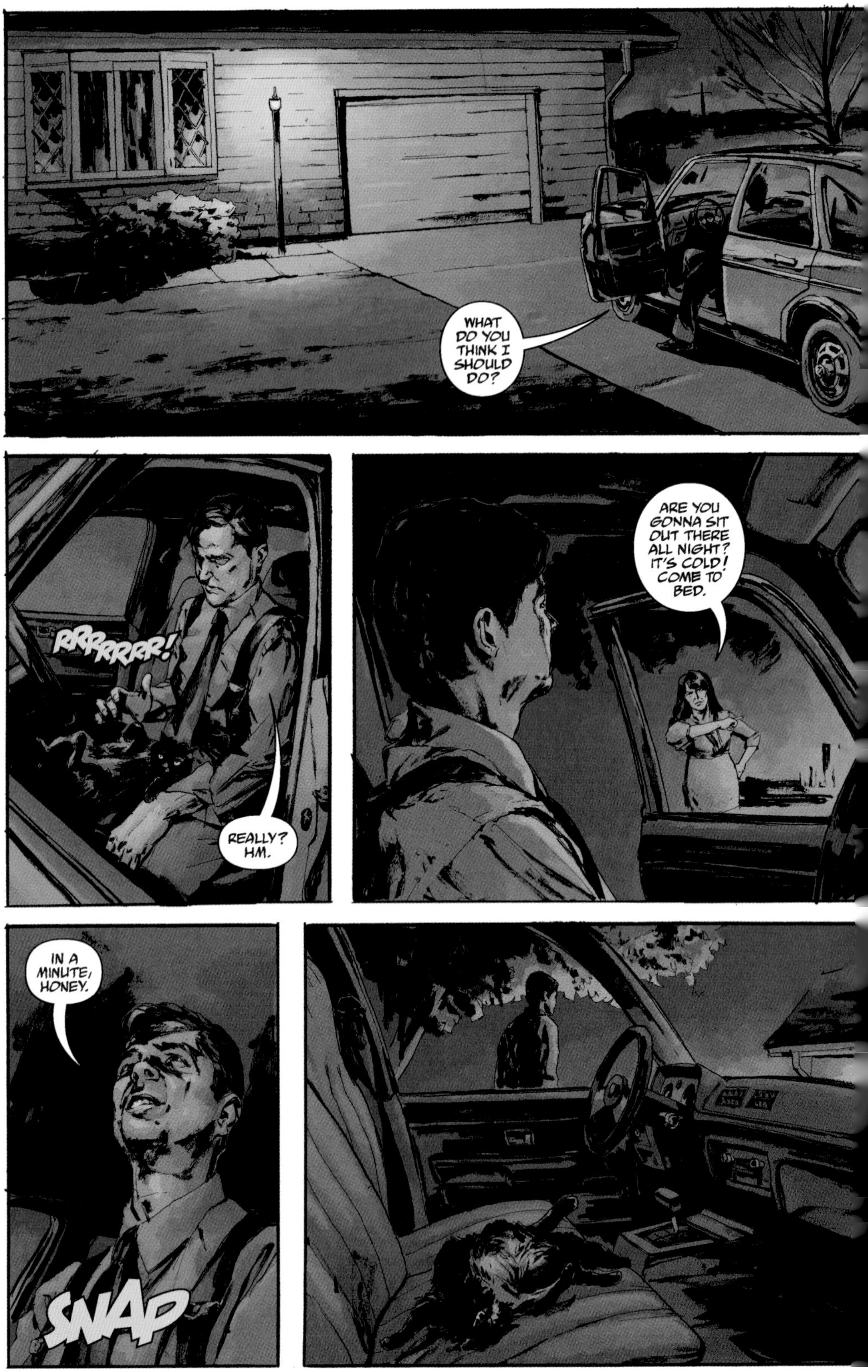
WHAT DO YOU THINK I SHOULD DO?
RRRRRRR!
REALLY? HM.
ARE YOU GONNA SIT OUT THERE ALL NIGHT? IT'S COLD! COME TO BED.
IN A MINUTE, HONEY.
SNAP

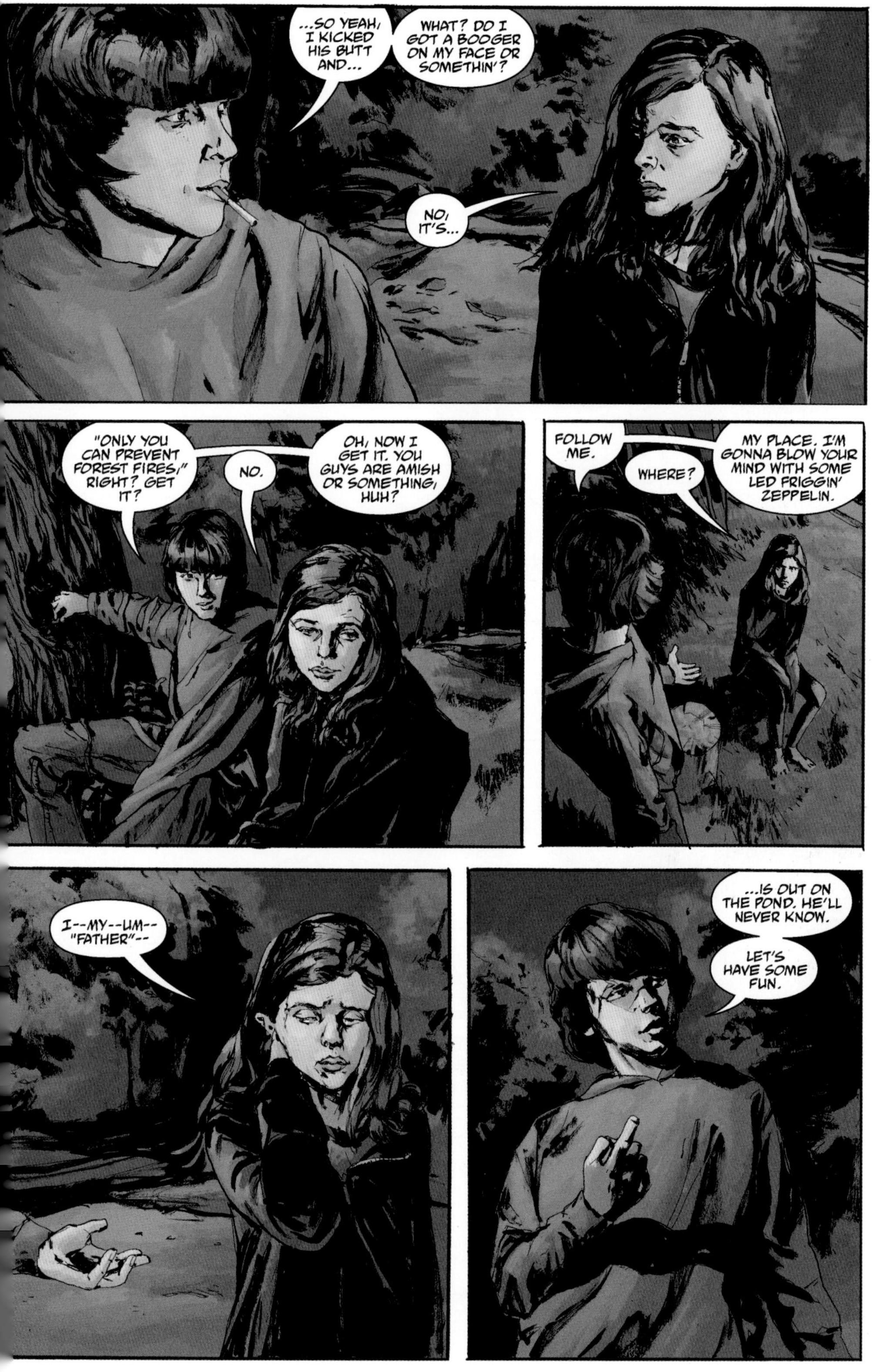
...SO YEAH, I KICKED HIS BUTT AND...
WHAT? DO I GOT A BOOGER ON MY FACE OR SOMETHIN'?
NO, IT'S...
"ONLY YOU CAN PREVENT FOREST FIRES," RIGHT? GET IT?
NO.
OH, NOW I GET IT. YOU GUYS ARE AMISH OR SOMETHING, HUH?
FOLLOW ME.
WHERE?
MY PLACE. I'M GONNA BLOW YOUR MIND WITH SOME LED FRIGGIN' ZEPPELIN.
I--MY--UM-- "FATHER"--
...IS OUT ON THE POND. HE'LL NEVER KNOW.
LET'S HAVE SOME FUN.

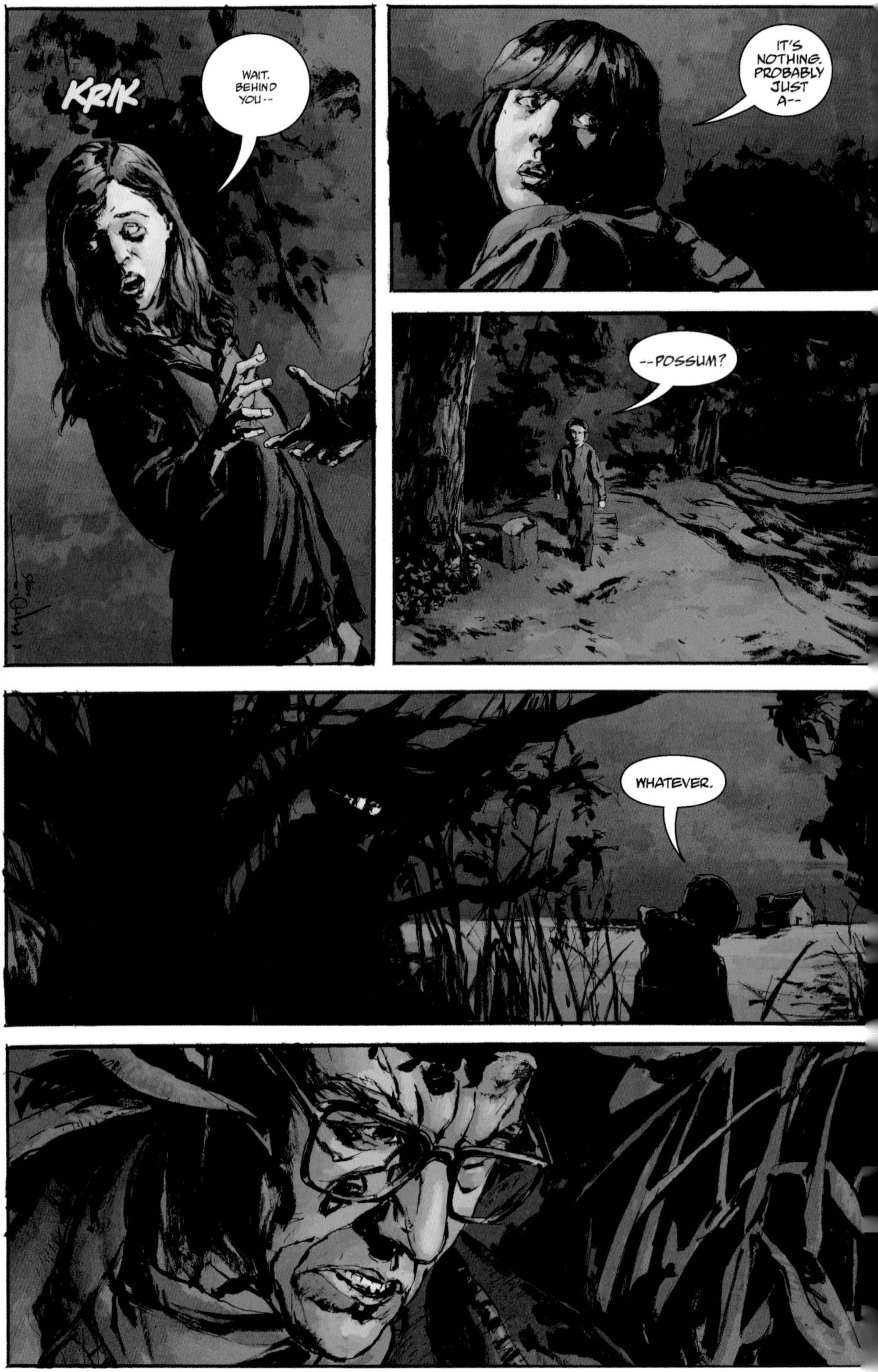
KRIK
WAIT. BEHIND YOU--
IT'S NOTHING. PROBABLY JUST A--
--POSSUM?
WHATEVER.

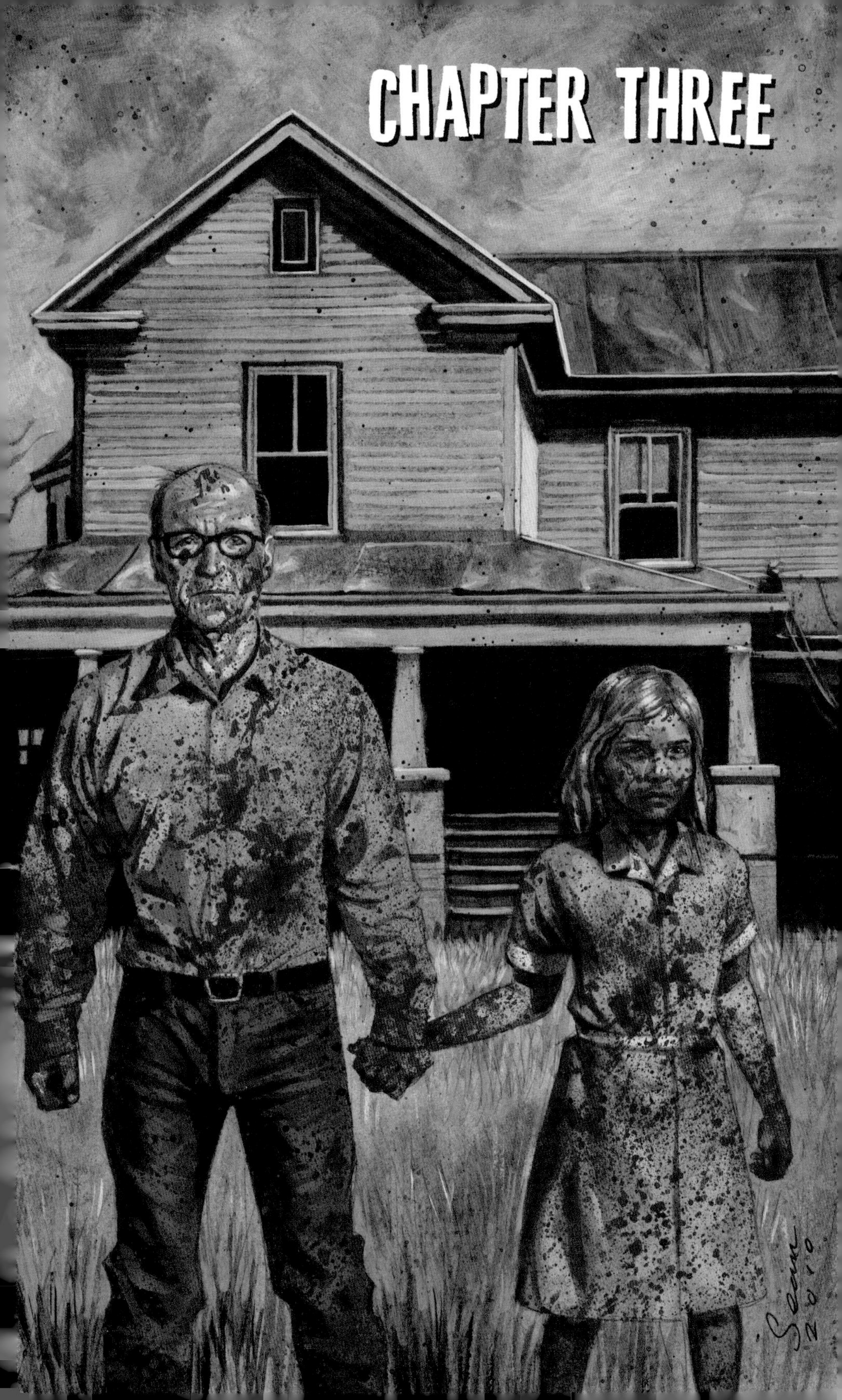
CHAPTER THREE
Sean 2010

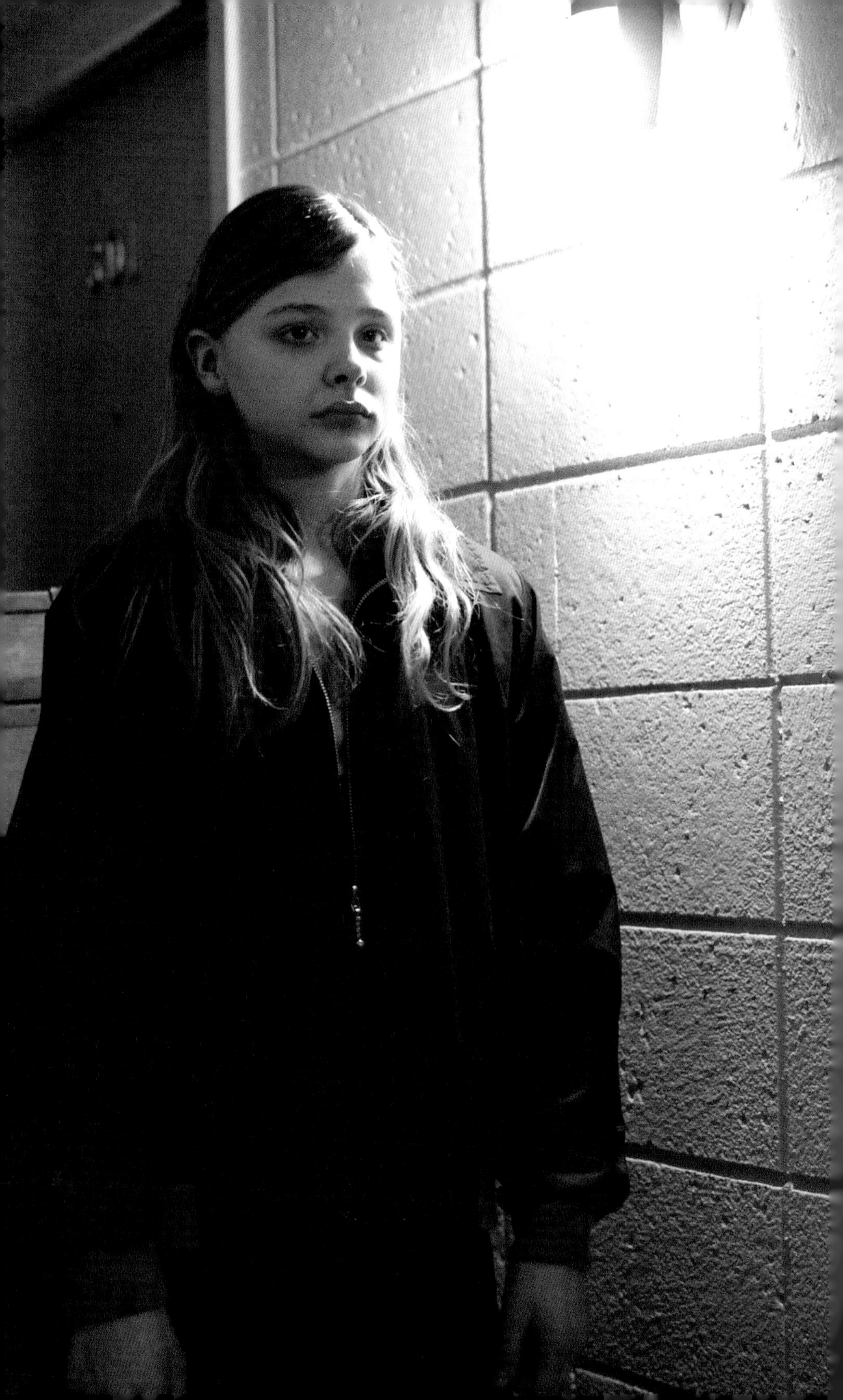

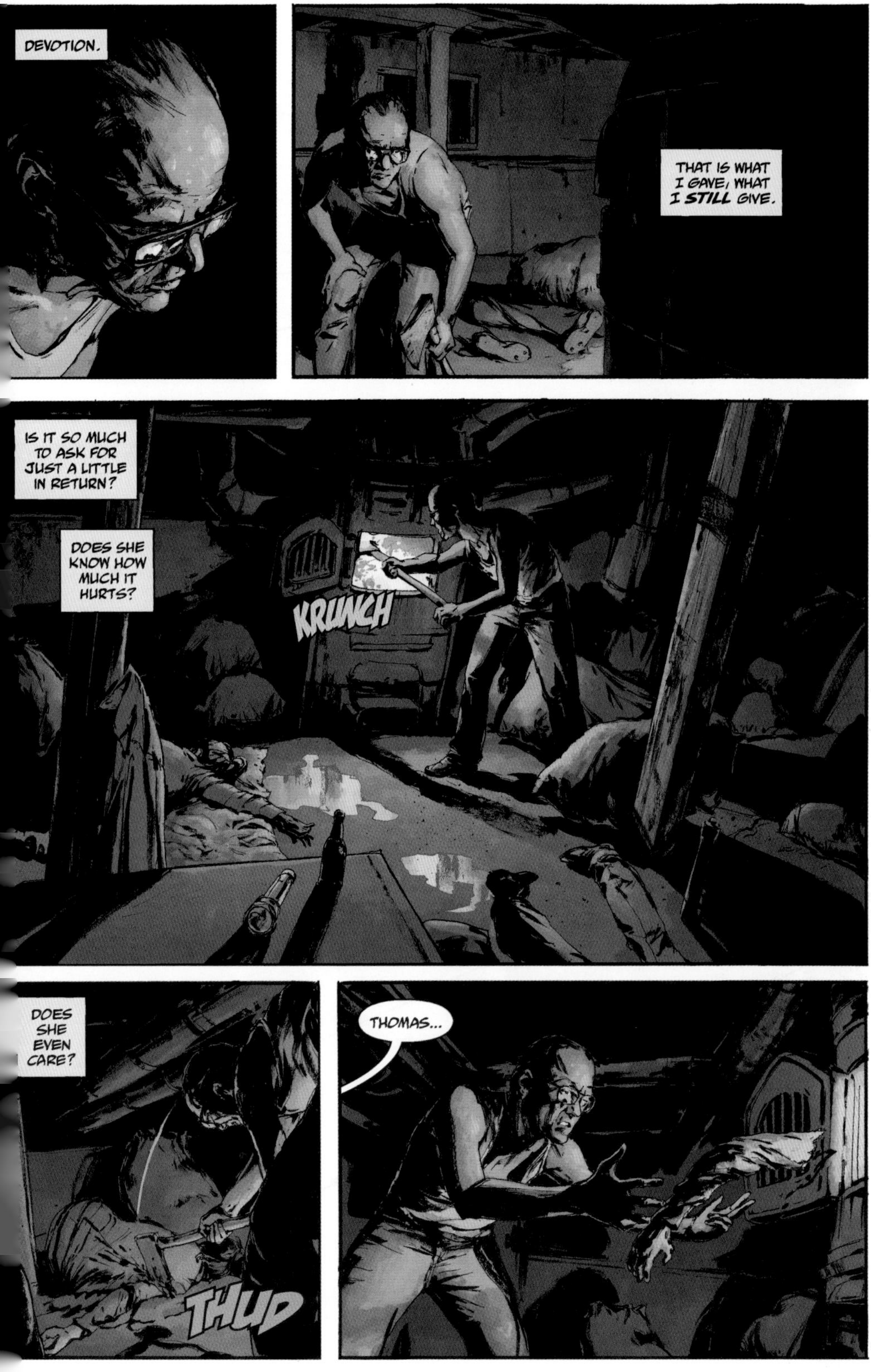
DEVOTION.
THAT IS WHAT I GAVE, WHAT I STILL GIVE.
IS IT SO MUCH TO ASK FOR JUST A LITTLE IN RETURN?
DOES SHE KNOW HOW MUCH IT HURTS?
KRUNCH
DOES SHE EVEN CARE?
THUD
THOMAS...

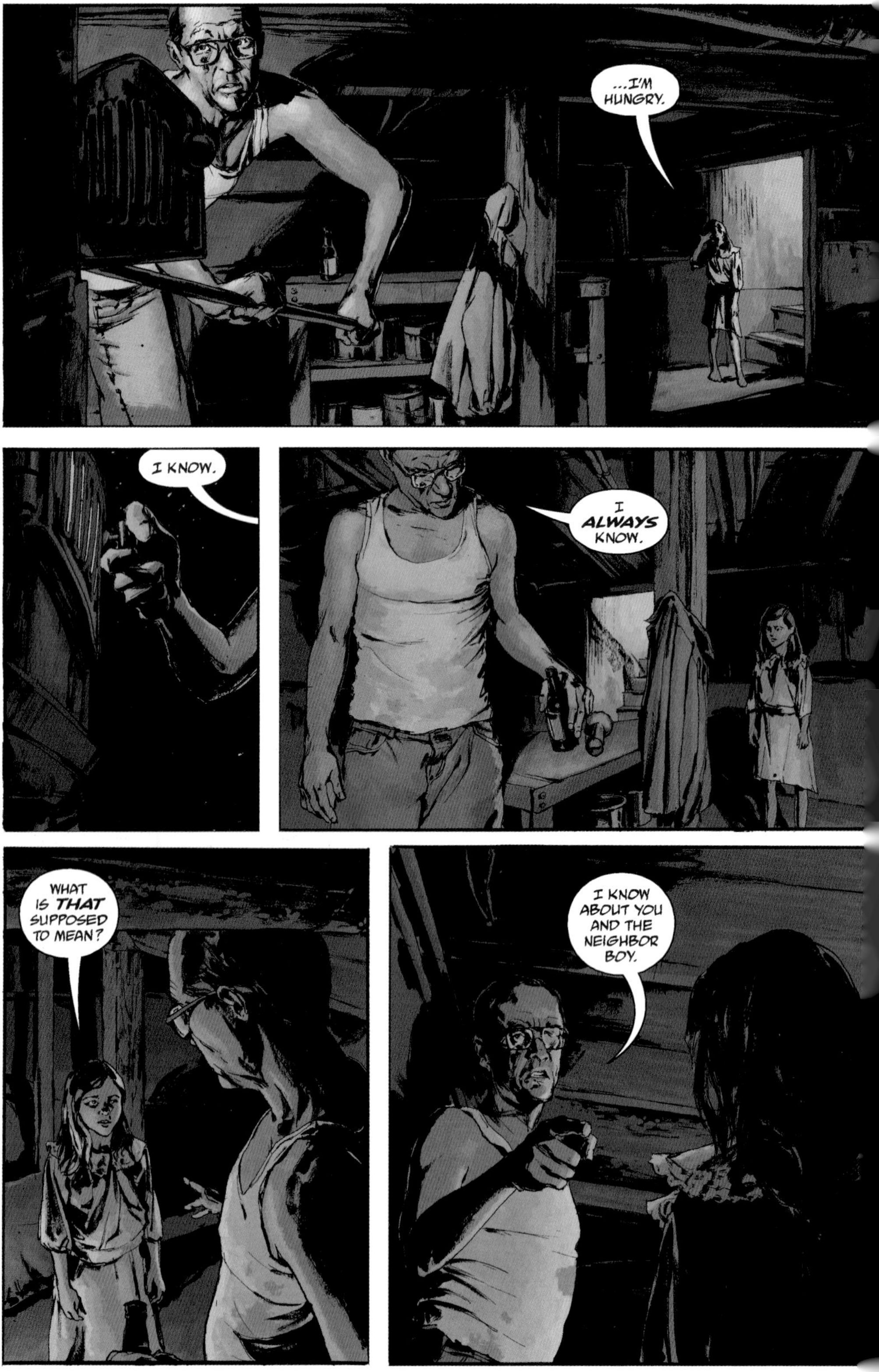
...I'M HUNGRY.
I KNOW.
I ALWAYS KNOW.
WHAT IS THAT SUPPOSED TO MEAN?
I KNOW ABOUT YOU AND THE NEIGHBOR BOY.

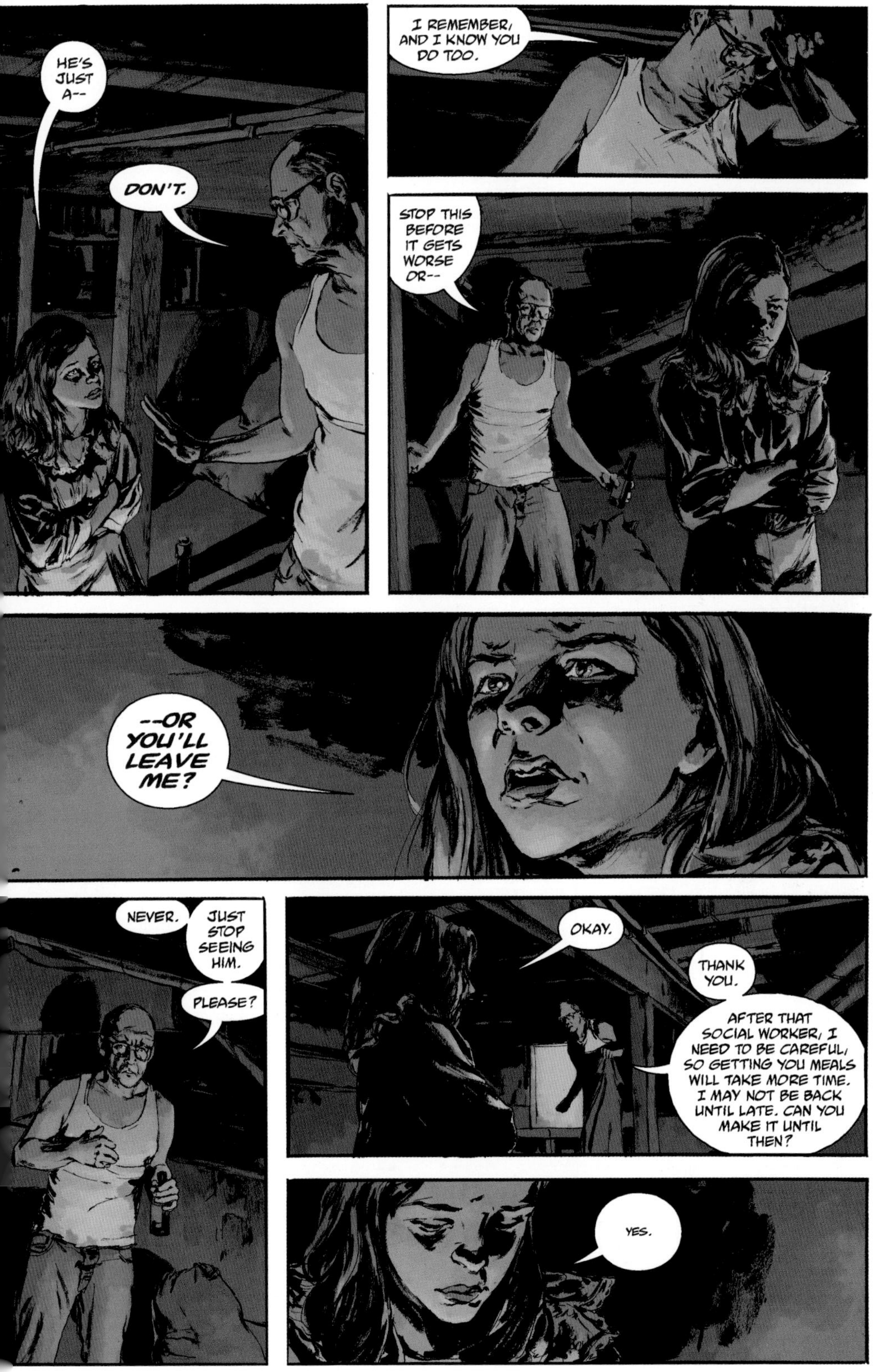
HE'S JUST A--
DON'T.
I REMEMBER, AND I KNOW YOU DO TOO.
STOP THIS BEFORE IT GETS WORSE OR--
--OR YOU'LL LEAVE ME?
NEVER.
JUST STOP SEEING HIM.
PLEASE?
OKAY.
THANK YOU.
AFTER THAT SOCIAL WORKER, I NEED TO BE CAREFUL, SO GETTING YOU MEALS WILL TAKE MORE TIME. I MAY NOT BE BACK UNTIL LATE. CAN YOU MAKE IT UNTIL THEN?
YES.

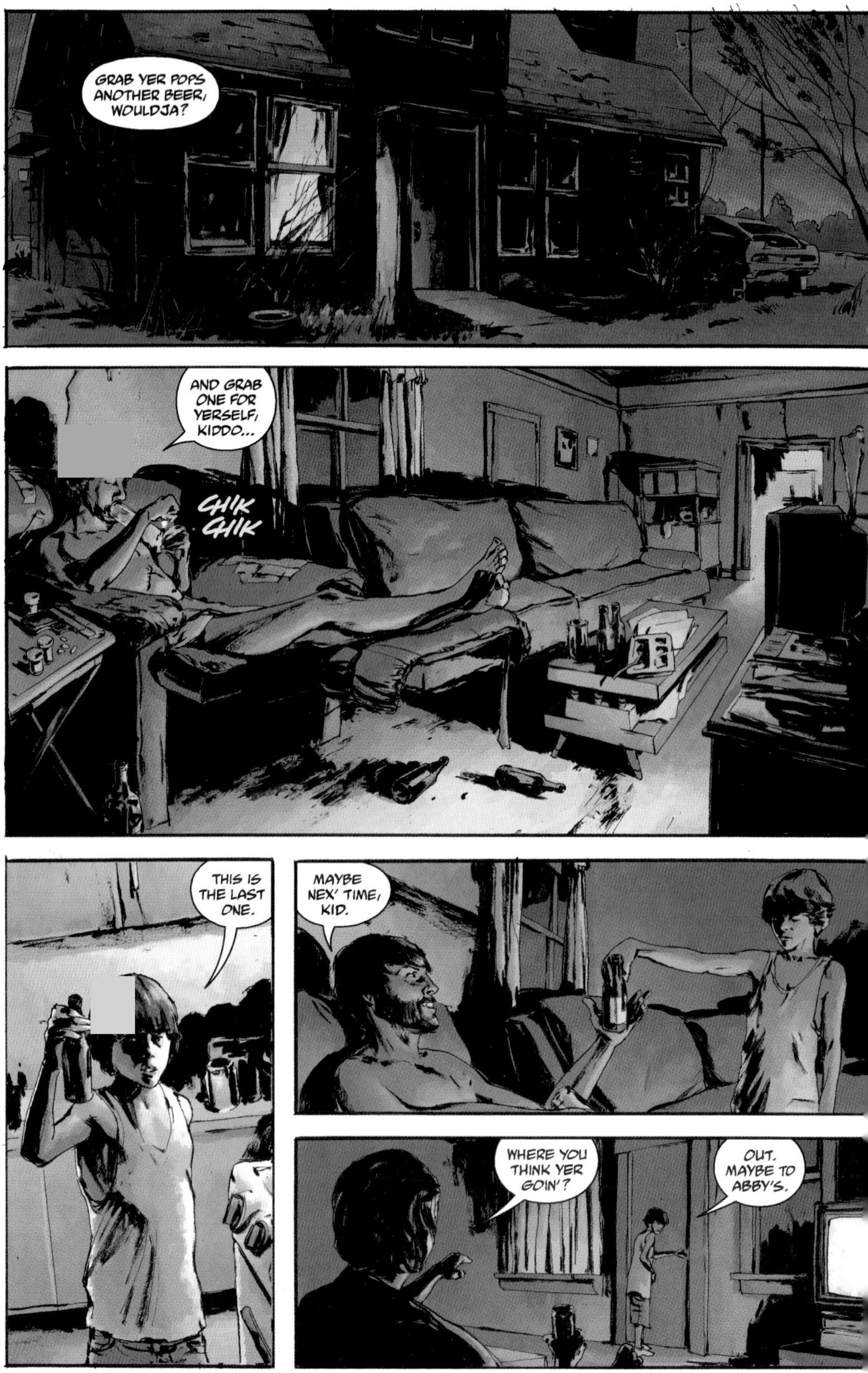
GRAB YER POPS ANOTHER BEER, WOULDJA?
AND GRAB ONE FOR YERSELF, KIDDO...
CHIK CHIK
THIS IS THE LAST ONE.
MAYBE NEX' TIME, KID.
WHERE YOU THINK YER GOIN'?
OUT. MAYBE TO ABBY'S.

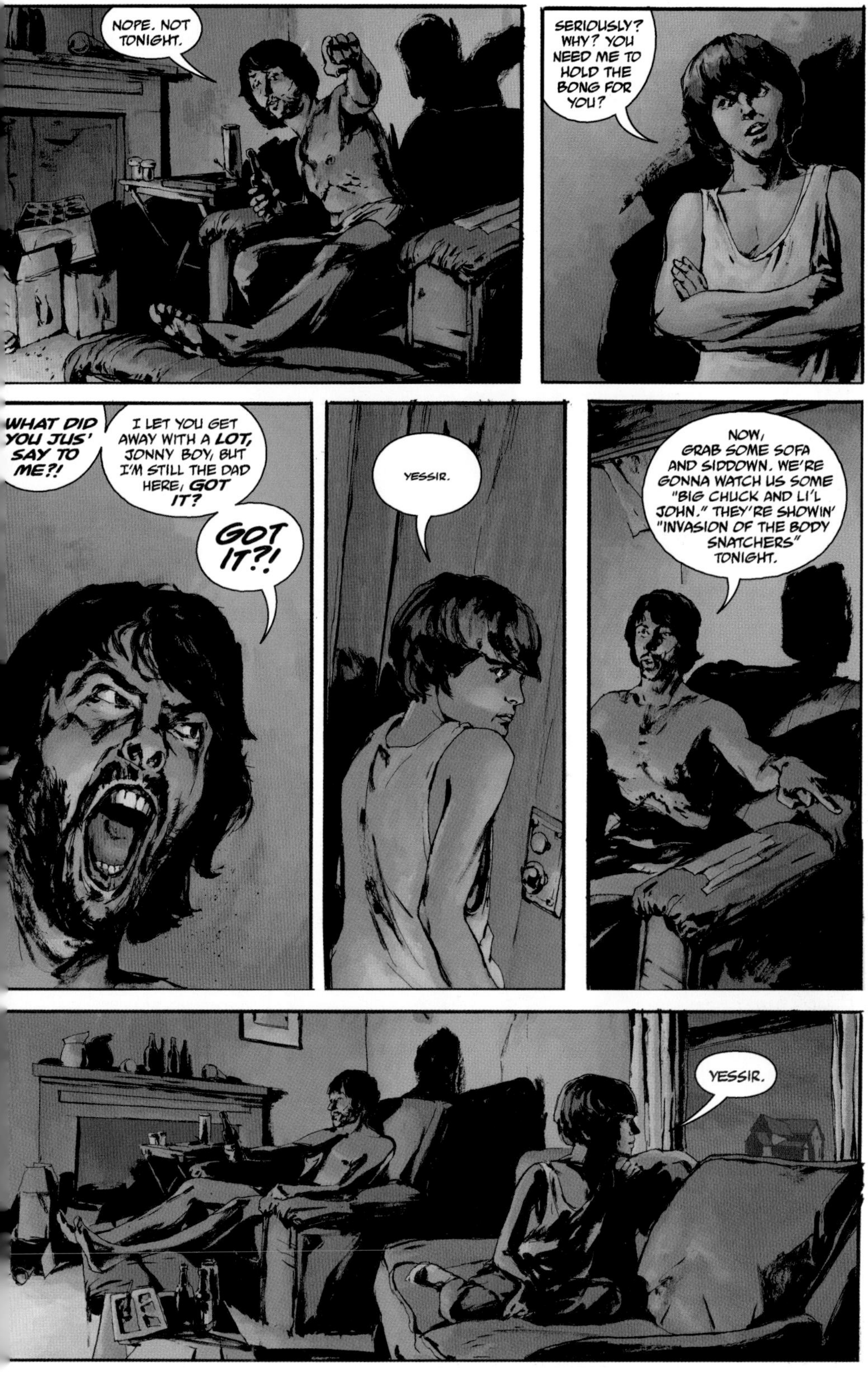
NOPE. NOT TONIGHT.
SERIOUSLY? WHY? YOU NEED ME TO HOLD THE BONG FOR YOU?
WHAT DID YOU JUS' SAY TO ME?!
I LET YOU GET AWAY WITH A LOT, JONNY BOY, BUT I'M STILL THE DAD HERE, GOT IT?
GOT IT?!
YESSIR.
NOW, GRAB SOME SOFA AND SIDDOWN. WE'RE GONNA WATCH US SOME "BIG CHUCK AND LI'L JOHN." THEY'RE SHOWIN' "INVASION OF THE BODY SNATCHERS" TONIGHT.
YESSIR.

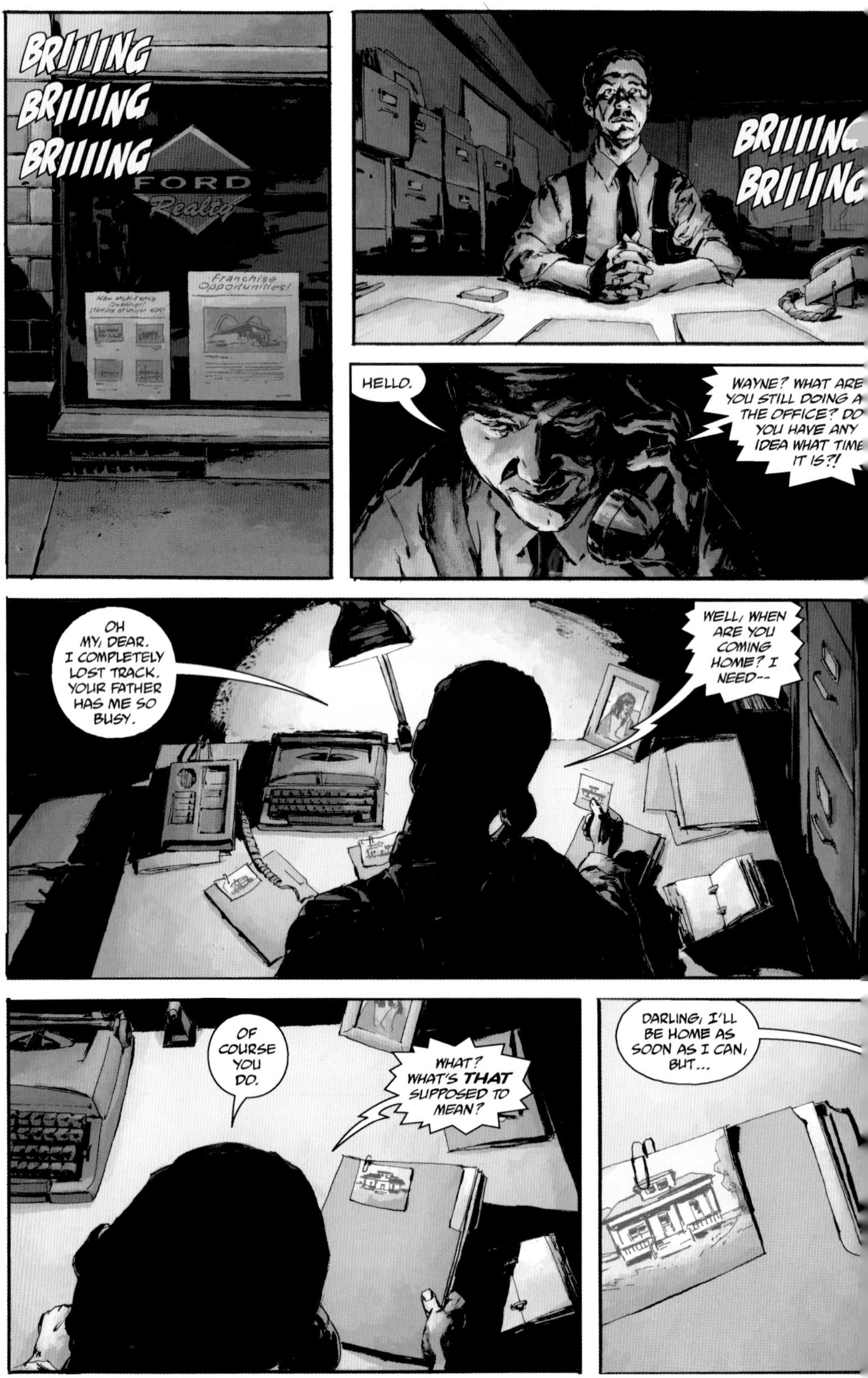
BRIIIING
BRIIIING
BRIIIING
FORD Realty
Franchise Opportunities!
BRIIIIN
BRIIIN
HELLO.
WAYNE? WHAT ARE YOU STILL DOING A THE OFFICE? DO YOU HAVE ANY IDEA WHAT TIME IT IS?!
OH MY, DEAR. I COMPLETELY LOST TRACK. YOUR FATHER HAS ME SO BUSY.
WELL, WHEN ARE YOU COMING HOME? I NEED--
OF COURSE YOU DO.
WHAT? WHAT'S THAT SUPPOSED TO MEAN?
DARLING, I'LL BE HOME AS SOON AS I CAN, BUT...

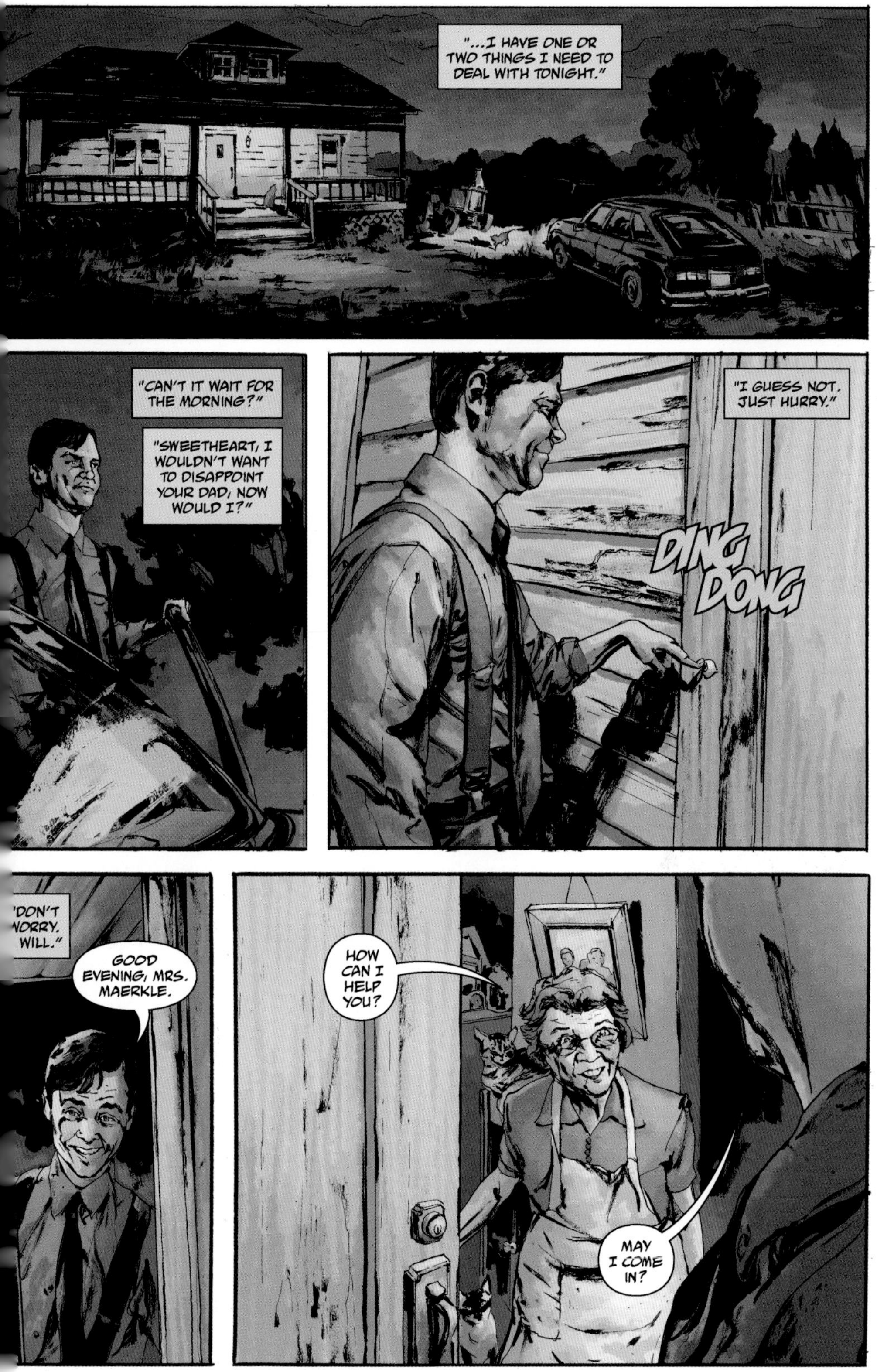
"...I HAVE ONE OR TWO THINGS I NEED TO DEAL WITH TONIGHT."
"CAN'T IT WAIT FOR THE MORNING?"
"SWEETHEART, I WOULDN'T WANT TO DISAPPOINT YOUR DAD, NOW WOULD I?"
"I GUESS NOT. JUST HURRY."
DING DONG
'DON'T WORRY. WILL."
GOOD EVENING, MRS. MAERKLE.
HOW CAN I HELP YOU?
MAY I COME IN?

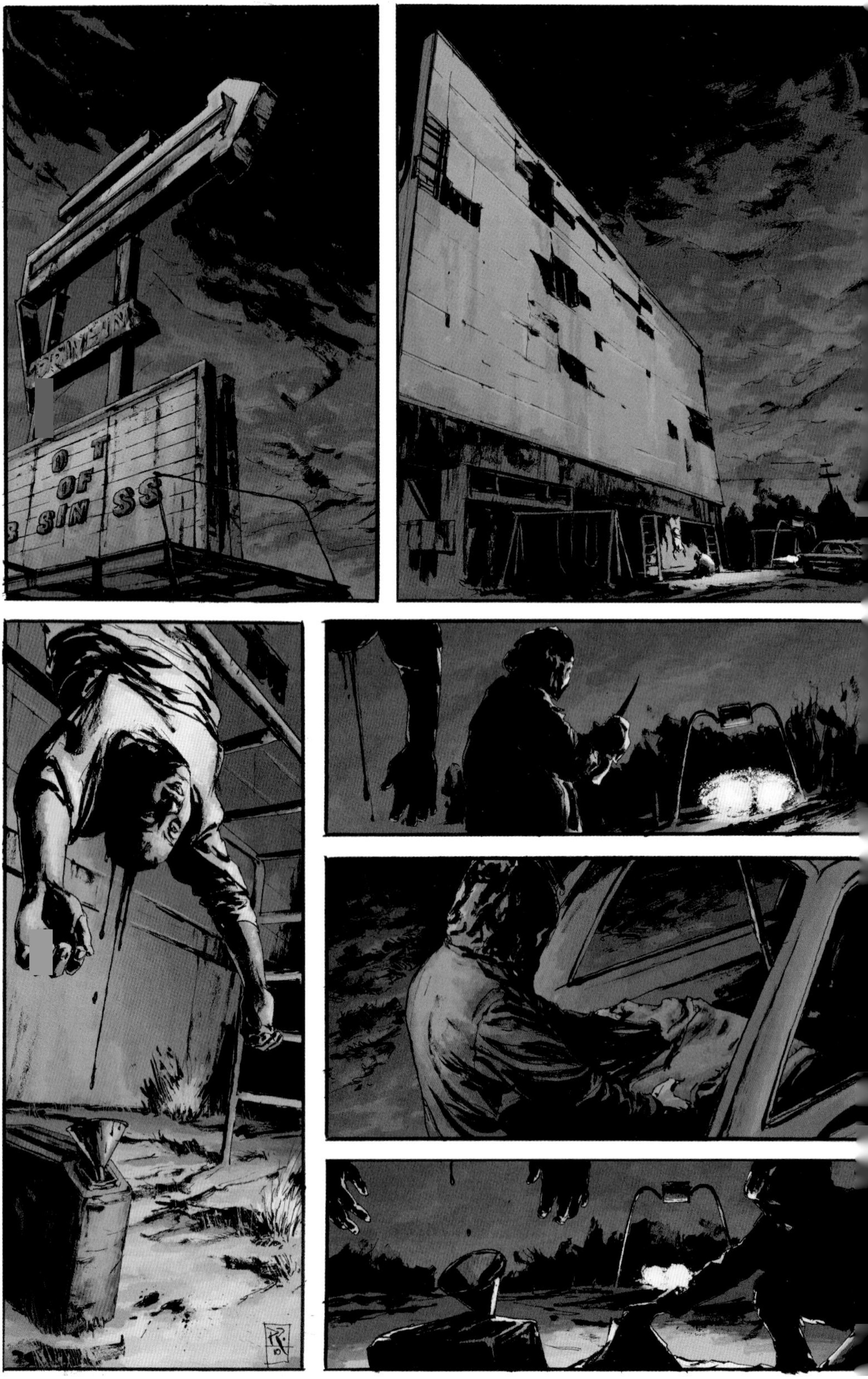
O T
OF
SIN SS

THUMP

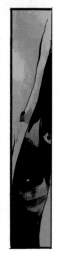

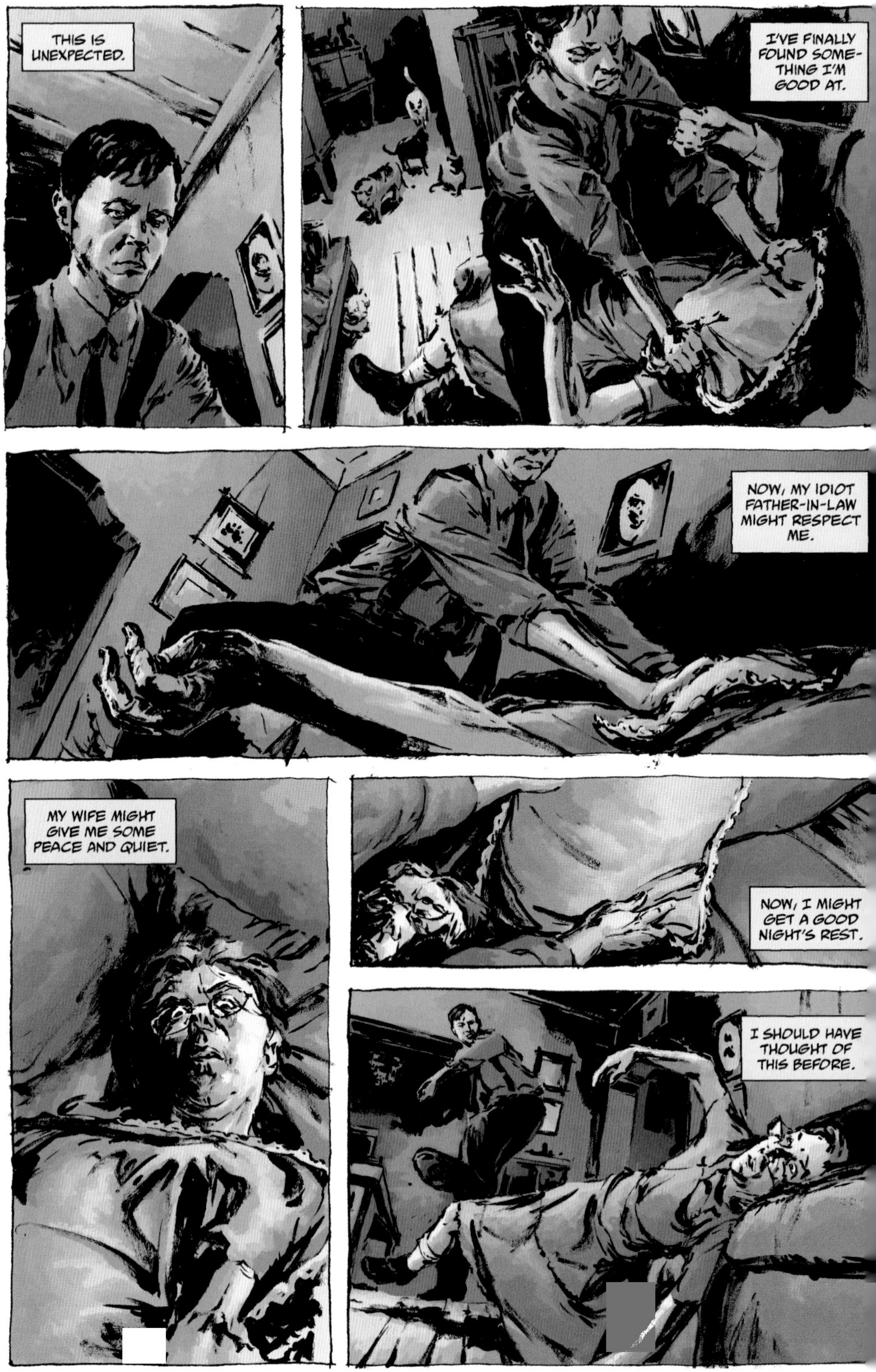
THIS IS UNEXPECTED.
I'VE FINALLY FOUND SOMETHING I'M GOOD AT.
NOW, MY IDIOT FATHER-IN-LAW MIGHT RESPECT ME.
MY WIFE MIGHT GIVE ME SOME PEACE AND QUIET.
NOW, I MIGHT GET A GOOD NIGHT'S REST.
I SHOULD HAVE THOUGHT OF THIS BEFORE.

TOK
TOK

TOK
TOK

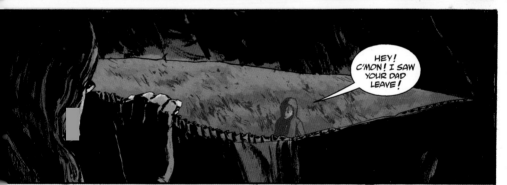

HEY! C'MON! I SAW YOUR DAD LEAVE!

HEY! HOW THE HELL DID YOU--?

COME WITH ME.

HURRY.

RELAX, WILL YA?

DAMN, GIRL, YOU'VE GOT A GRIP ON YOU!

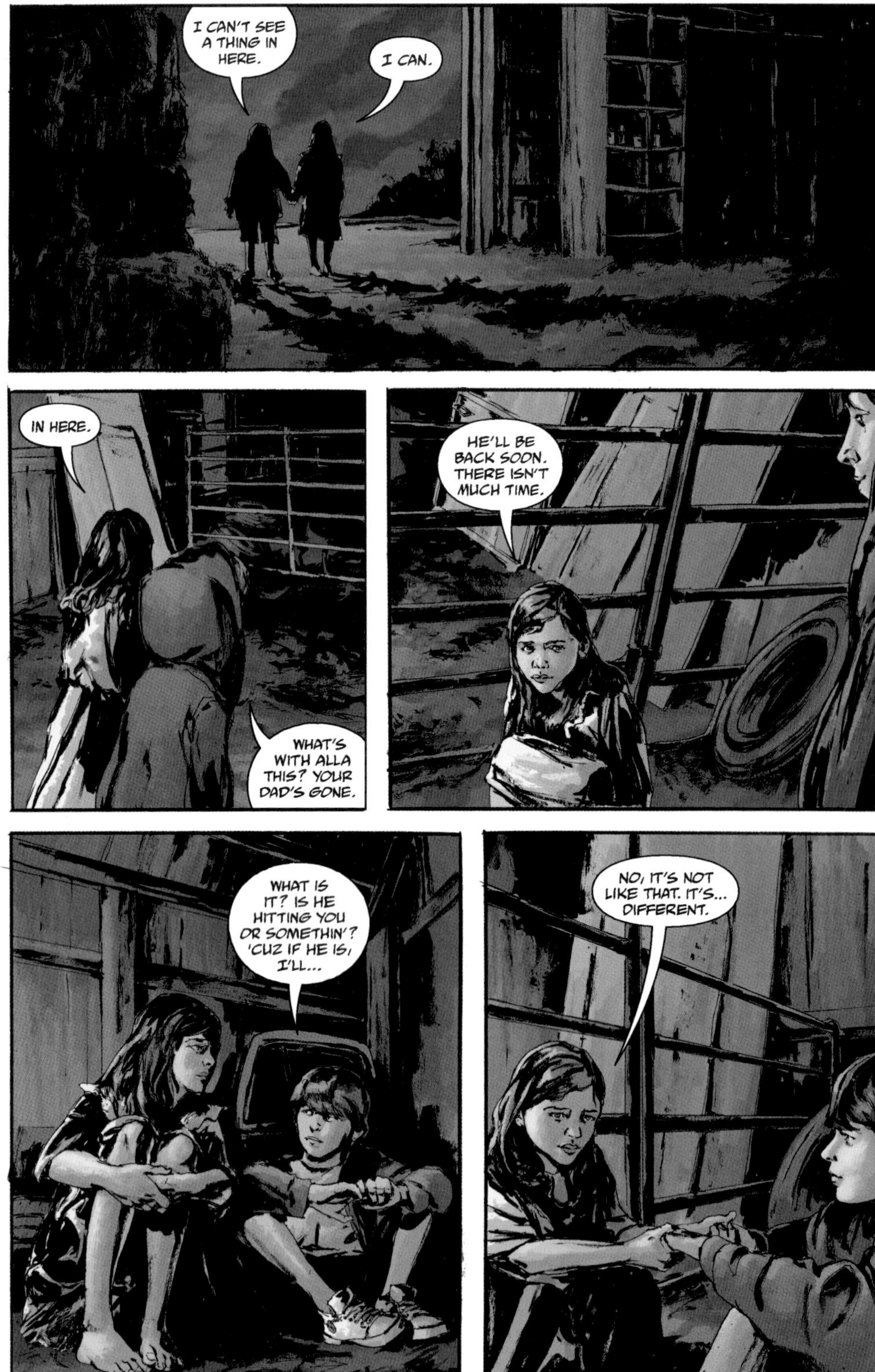
I CAN'T SEE A THING IN HERE.
I CAN.
IN HERE.
WHAT'S WITH ALLA THIS? YOUR DAD'S GONE.
HE'LL BE BACK SOON. THERE ISN'T MUCH TIME.
WHAT IS IT? IS HE HITTING YOU OR SOMETHIN'? 'CUZ IF HE IS, I'LL...
NO, IT'S NOT LIKE THAT. IT'S... DIFFERENT.

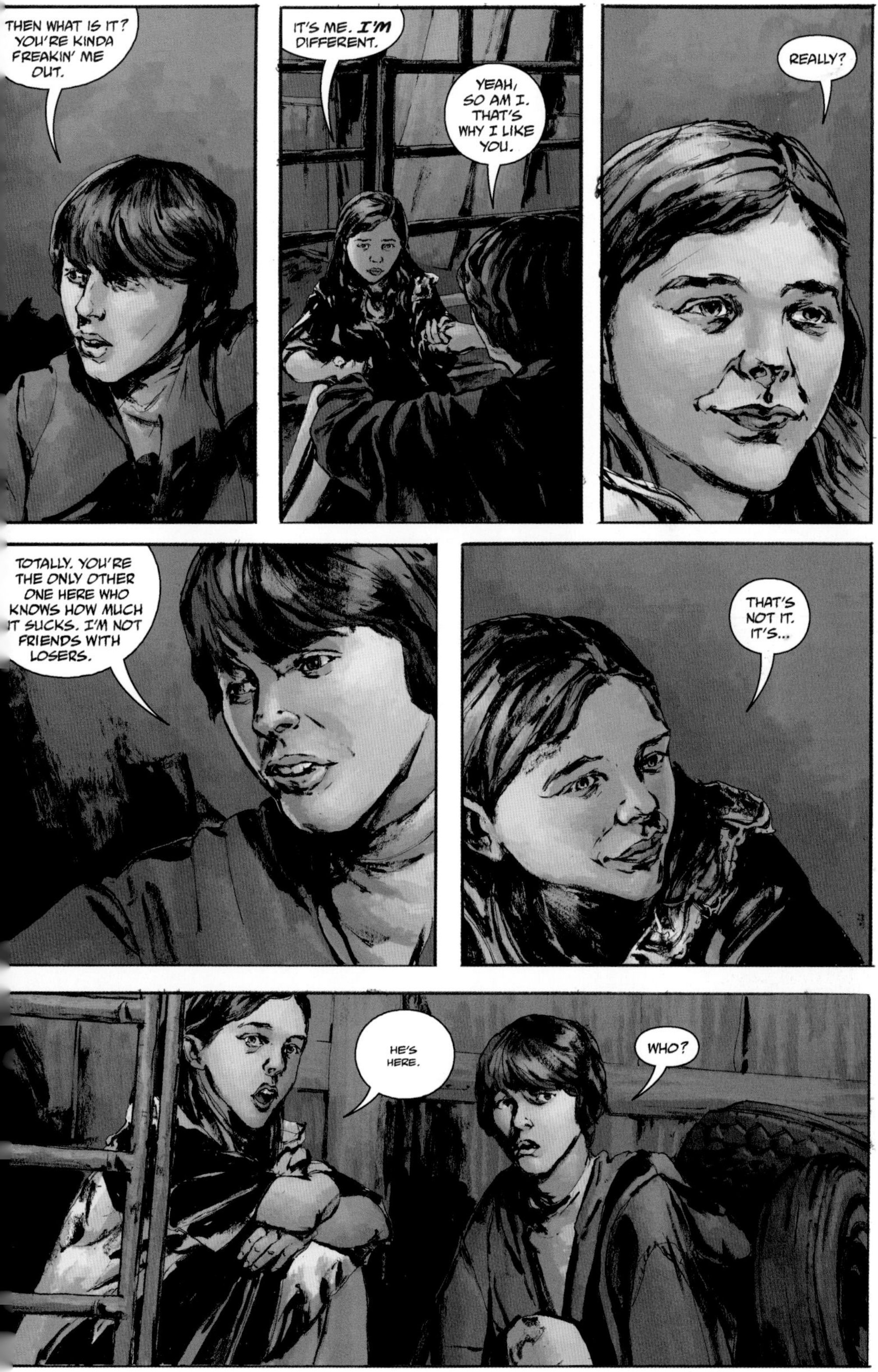
THEN WHAT IS IT? YOU'RE KINDA FREAKIN' ME OUT.
IT'S ME. I'M DIFFERENT.
YEAH, SO AM I. THAT'S WHY I LIKE YOU.
REALLY?
TOTALLY. YOU'RE THE ONLY OTHER ONE HERE WHO KNOWS HOW MUCH IT SUCKS. I'M NOT FRIENDS WITH LOSERS.
THAT'S NOT IT. IT'S...
HE'S HERE.
WHO?

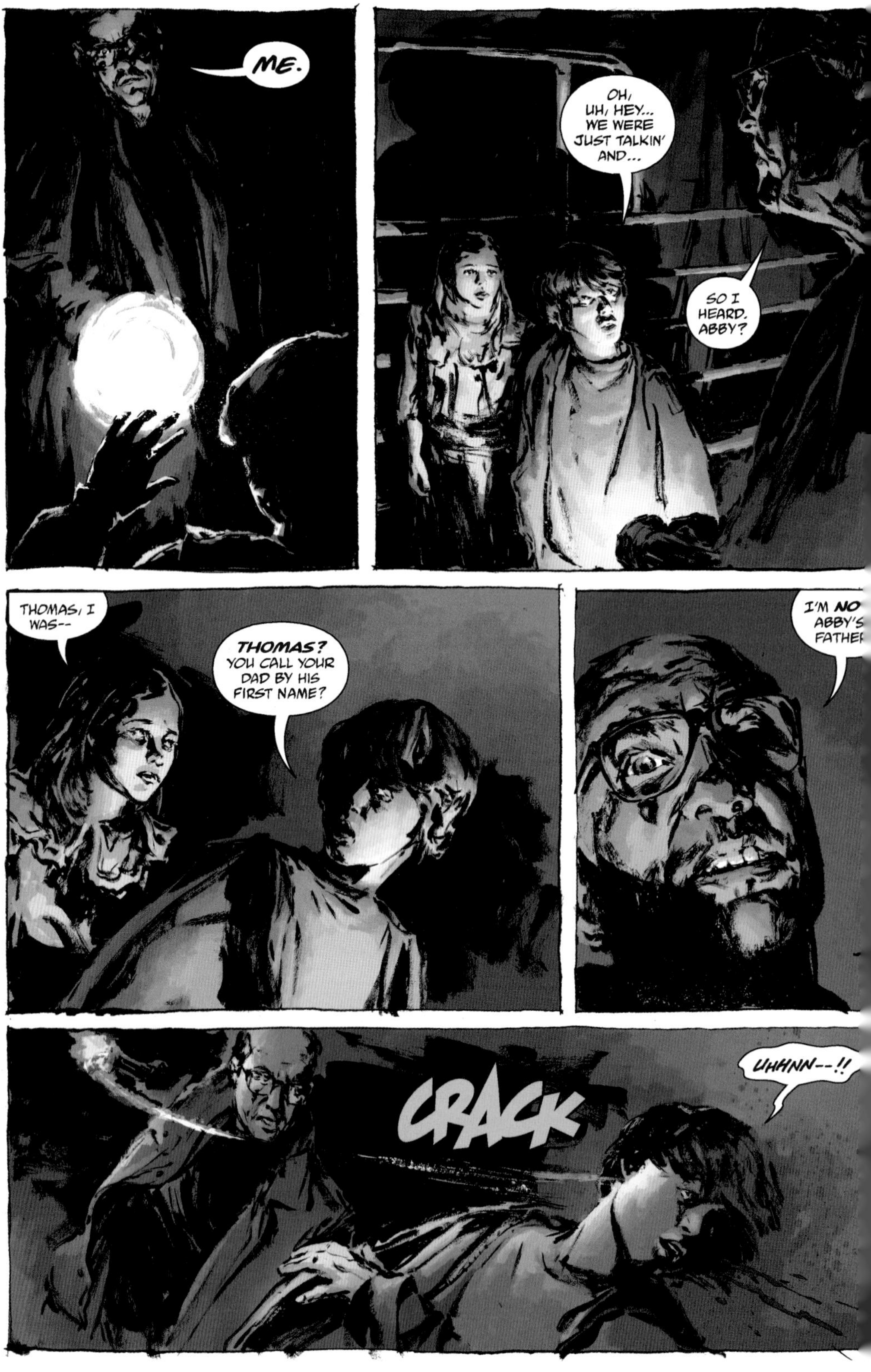

ME.
OH, UH, HEY... WE WERE JUST TALKIN' AND...
SO I HEARD. ABBY?
THOMAS, I WAS--
THOMAS? YOU CALL YOUR DAD BY HIS FIRST NAME?
I'M NO
ABBY'S
FATHE
CRACK
UHHNN--!!

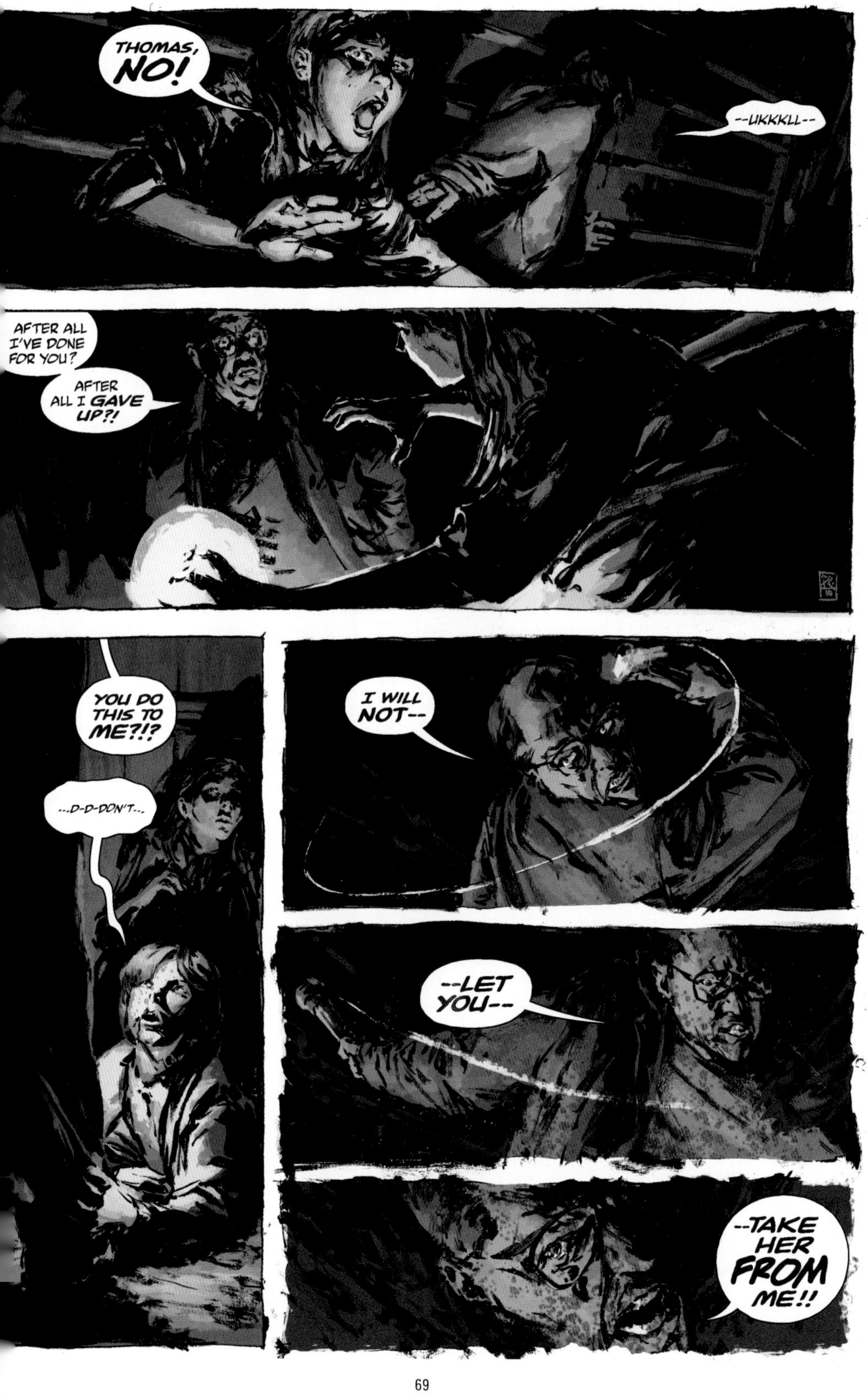
THOMAS, NO!
--UKKKLL--
AFTER ALL I'VE DONE FOR YOU?
AFTER ALL I GAVE UP?!
YOU DO THIS TO ME?!?
...D-D-DON'T...
I WILL NOT--
--LET YOU--
--TAKE HER FROM ME!!

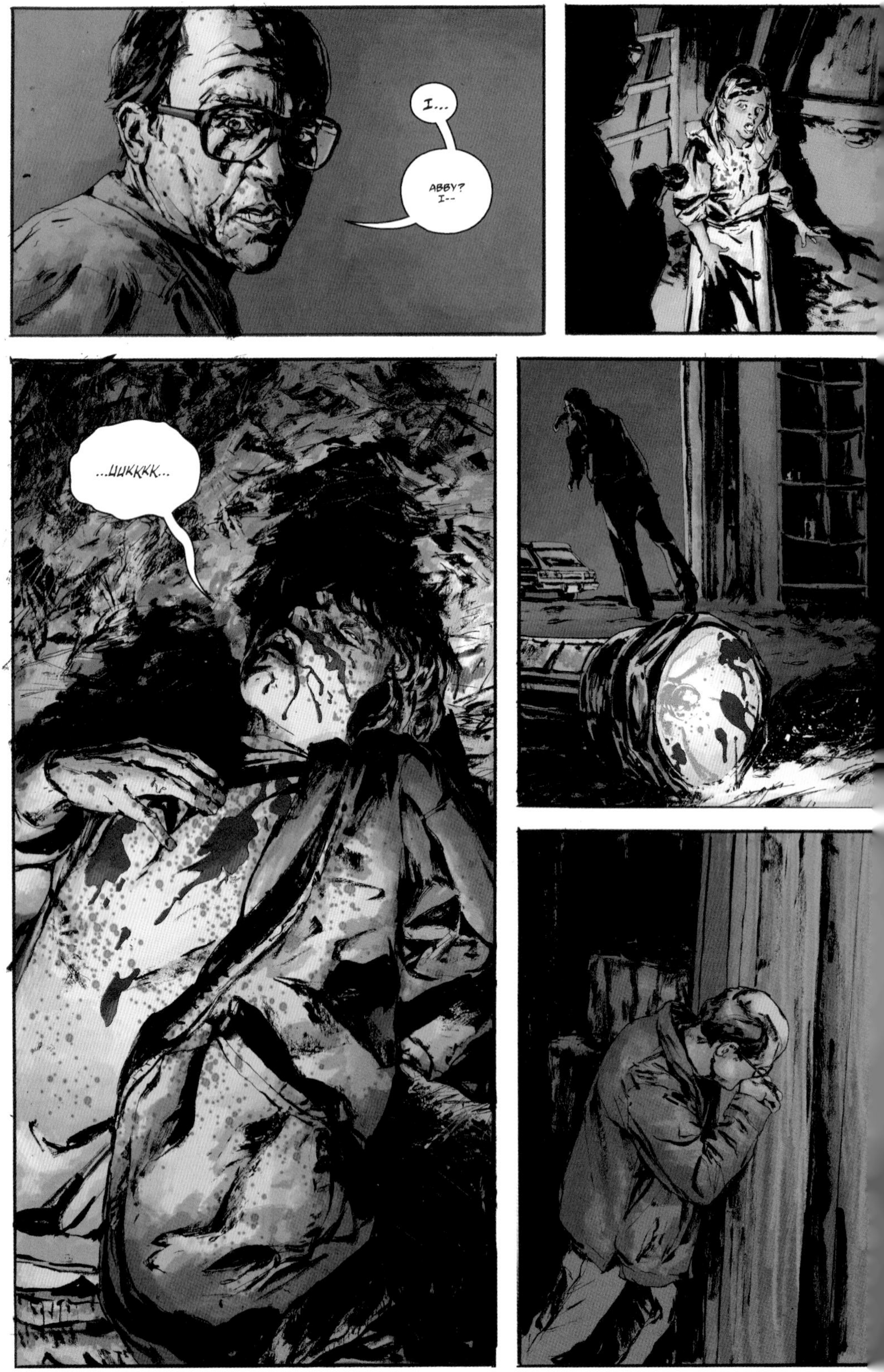
I...
ABBY? I--
...UUKKKK...

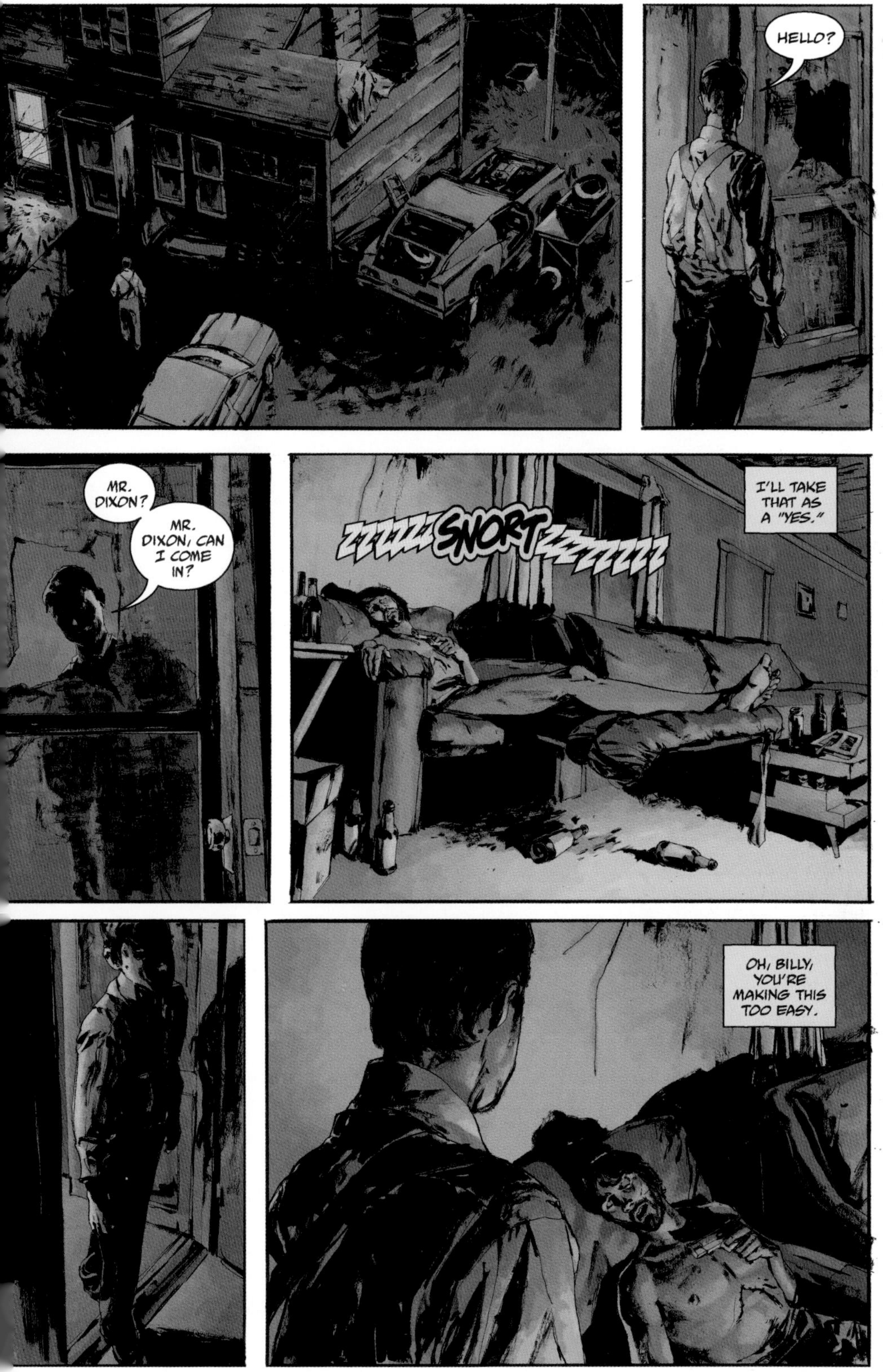
HELLO?
MR. DIXON?
MR. DIXON, CAN I COME IN?
I'LL TAKE THAT AS A "YES."
ZZZZZZ SNORT ZZZZZZZZ
OH, BILLY, YOU'RE MAKING THIS TOO EASY.

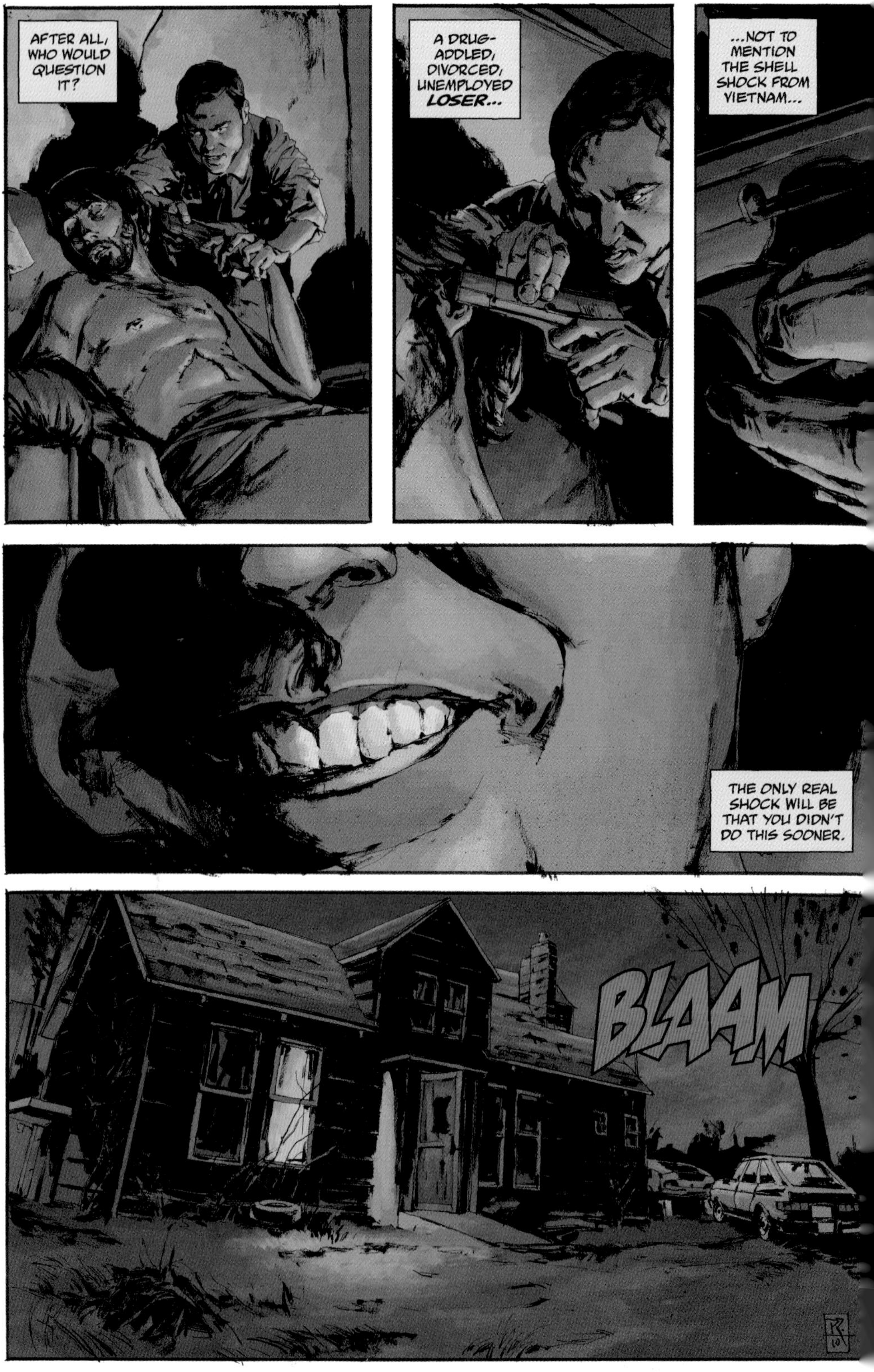
AFTER ALL, WHO WOULD QUESTION IT?
A DRUG-ADDLED, DIVORCED, UNEMPLOYED **LOSER...**
...NOT TO MENTION THE SHELL SHOCK FROM VIETNAM...
THE ONLY REAL SHOCK WILL BE THAT YOU DIDN'T DO THIS SOONER.
BLAAM

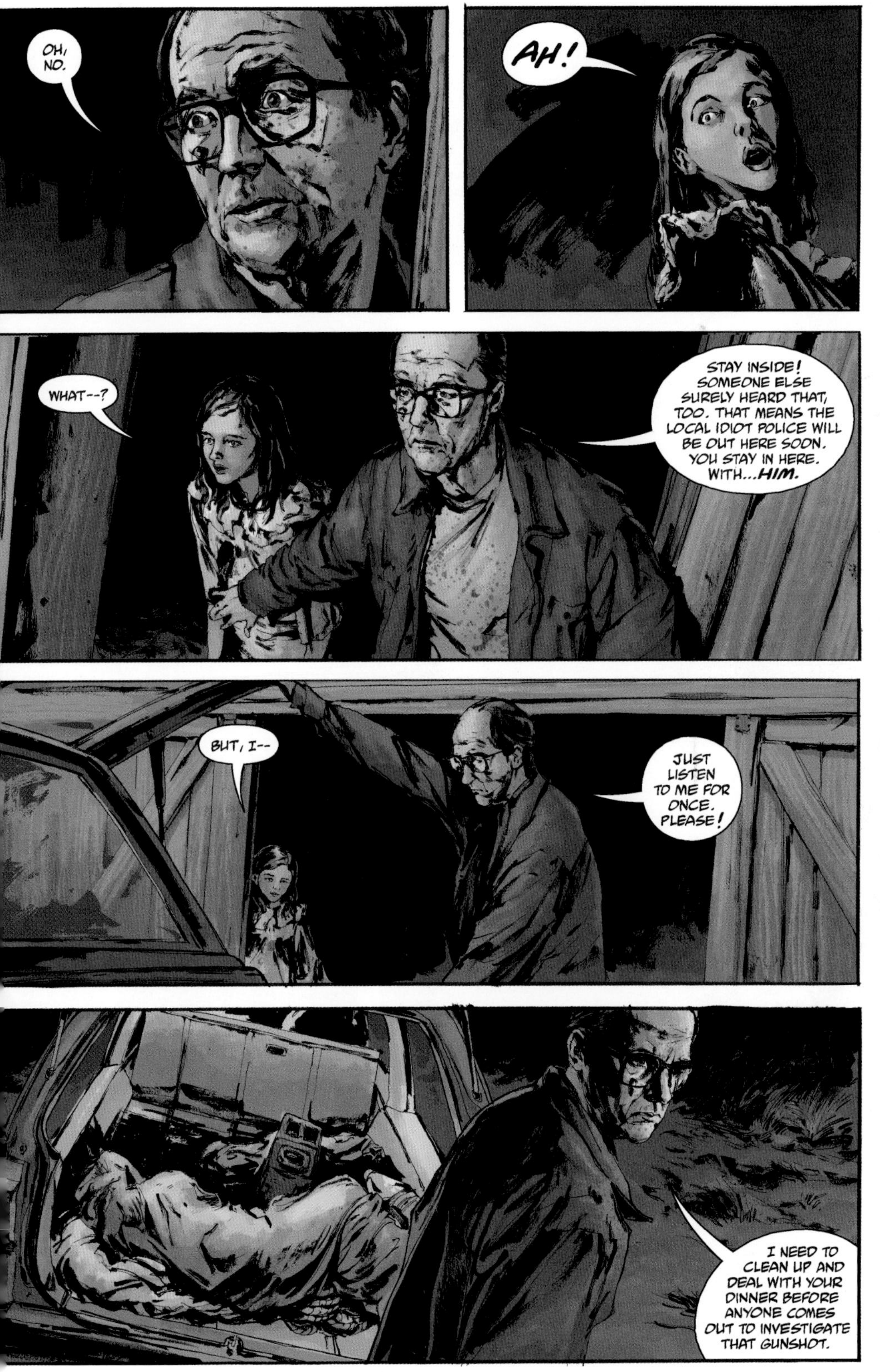

OH, NO.
AH!
WHAT--?
STAY INSIDE! SOMEONE ELSE SURELY HEARD THAT, TOO. THAT MEANS THE LOCAL IDIOT POLICE WILL BE OUT HERE SOON. YOU STAY IN HERE. WITH...HIM.
BUT, I--
JUST LISTEN TO ME FOR ONCE. PLEASE!
I NEED TO CLEAN UP AND DEAL WITH YOUR DINNER BEFORE ANYONE COMES OUT TO INVESTIGATE THAT GUNSHOT.

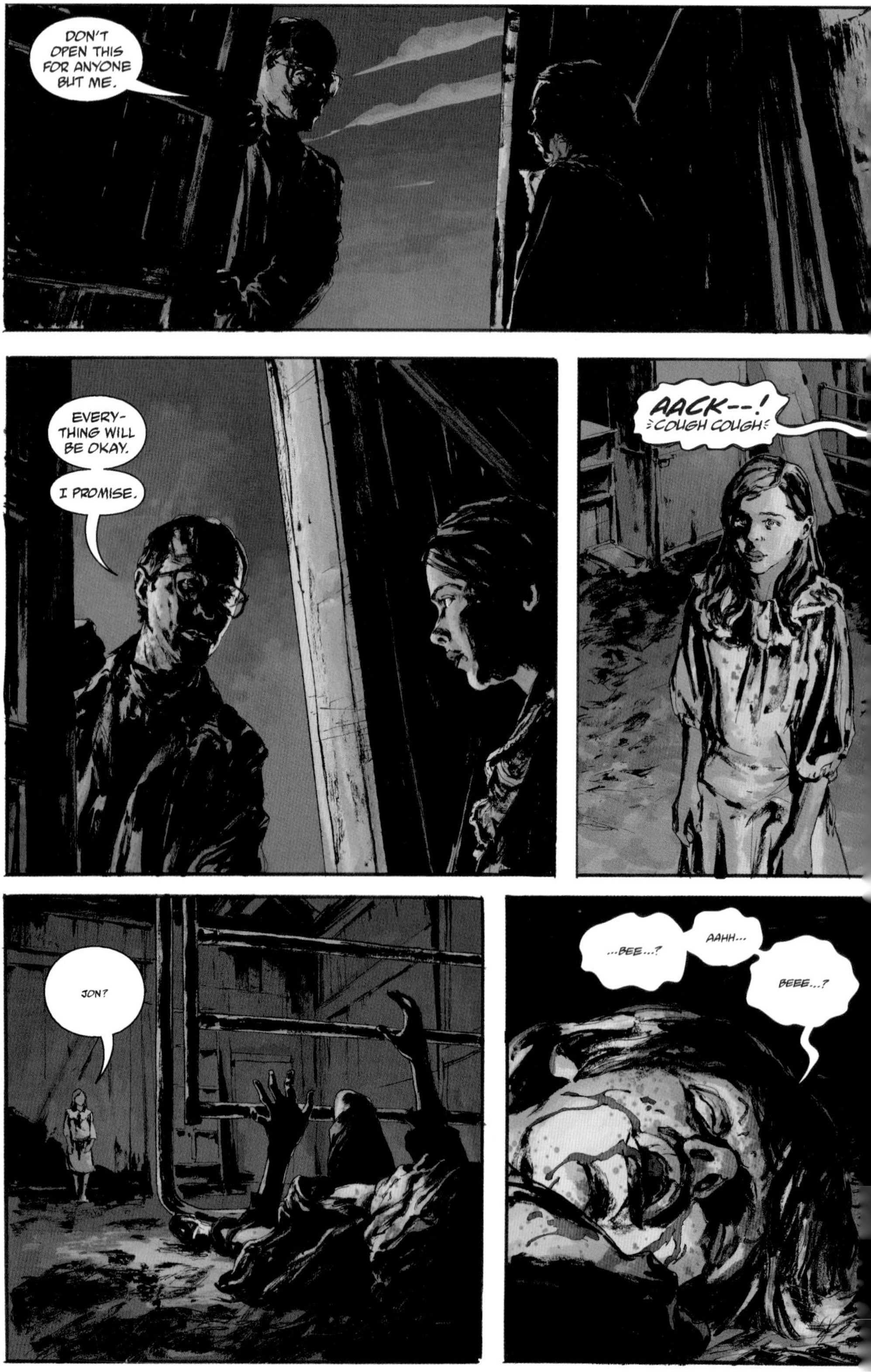
DON'T OPEN THIS FOR ANYONE BUT ME.
EVERY-THING WILL BE OKAY.
I PROMISE.
AACK--!
COUGH COUGH
JON?
...BEE...?
AAHH...
BEEE...?

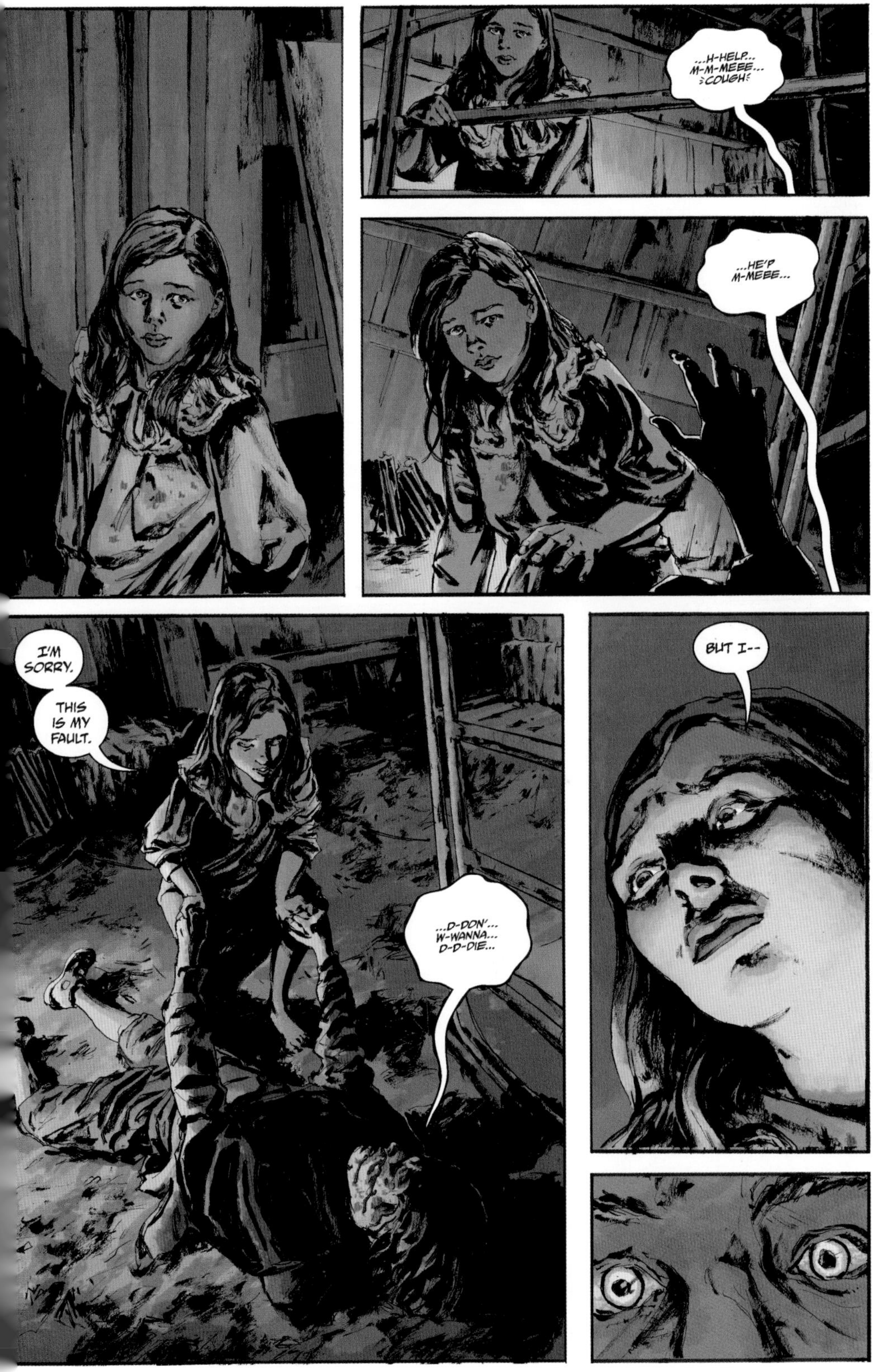
...H-HELP...
M-M-MEEE...
≶COUGH≷
...HE'P
M-MEEE...
I'M SORRY.
THIS IS MY FAULT.
...D-DON'...
W-WANNA...
D-D-DIE...
BUT I--

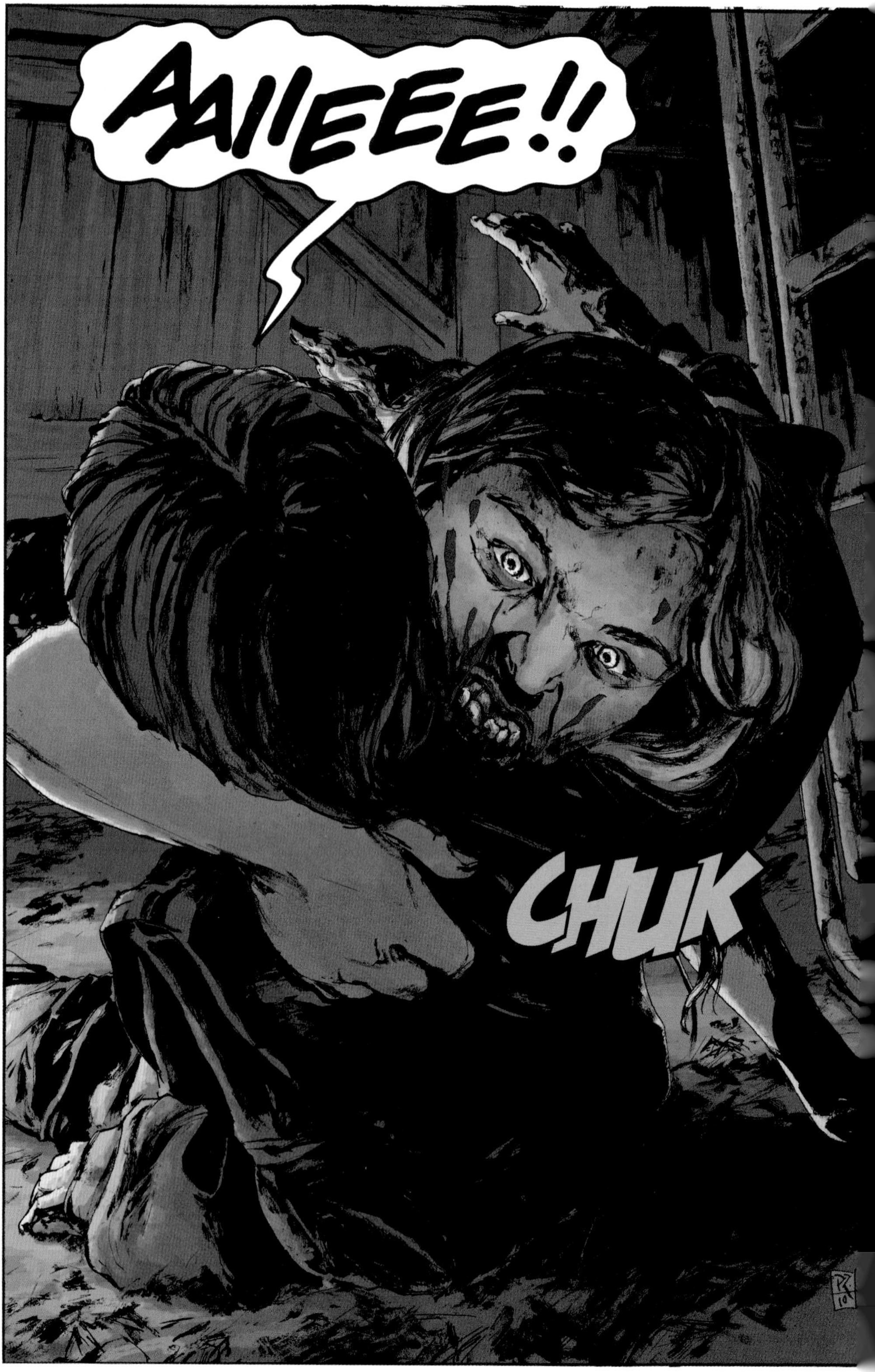
AAIIEEE!!
CHUK

CHAPTER FOUR

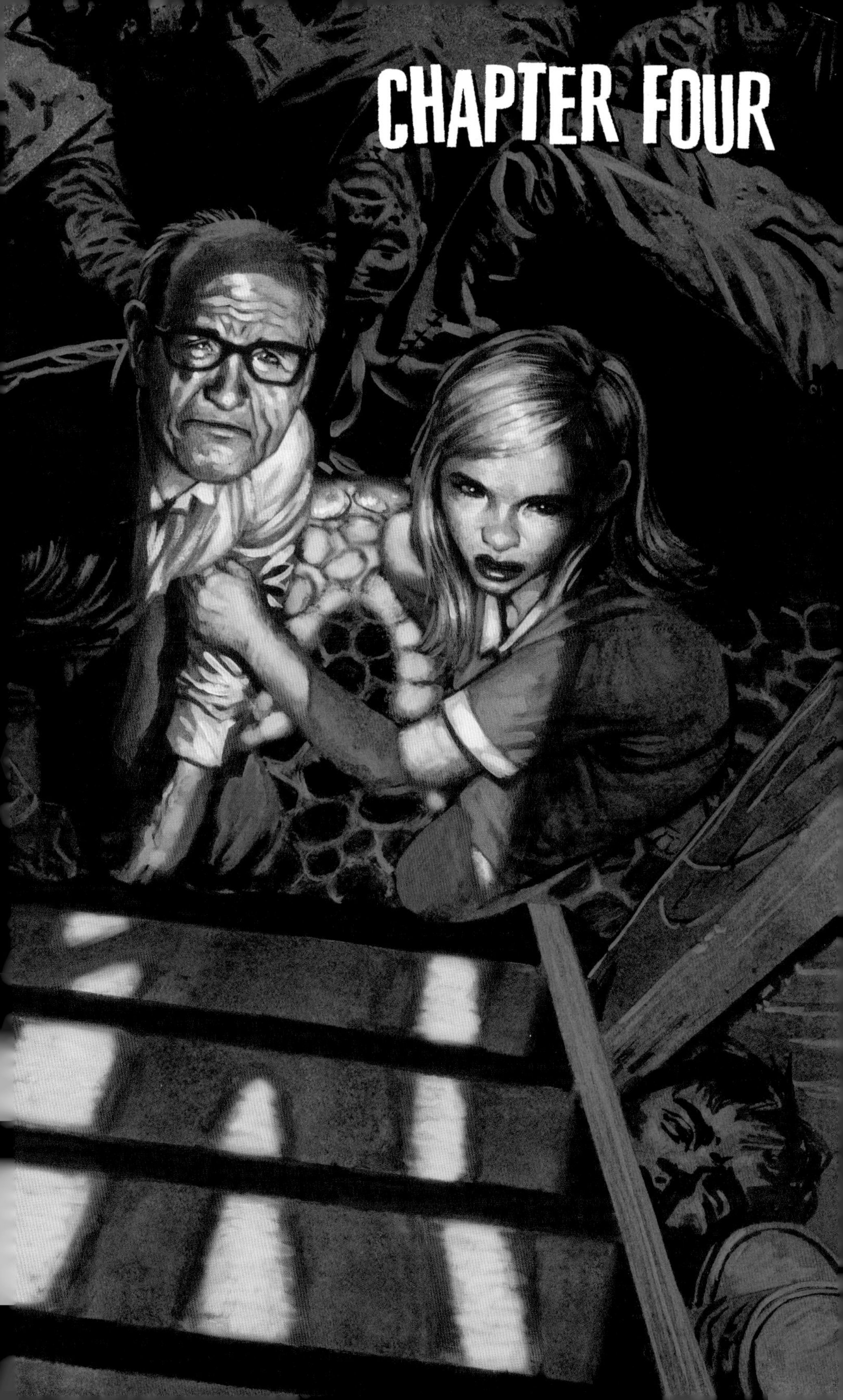

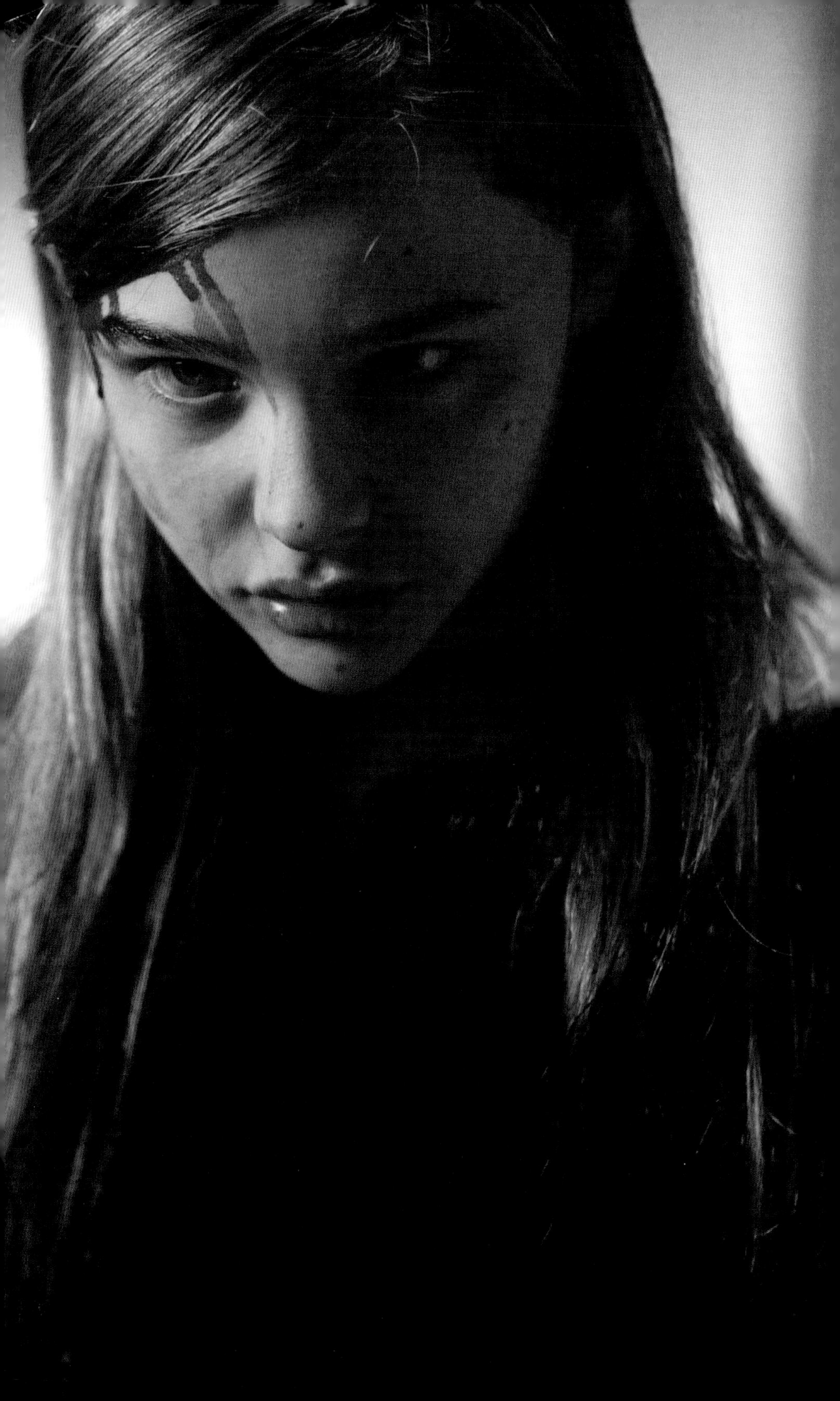

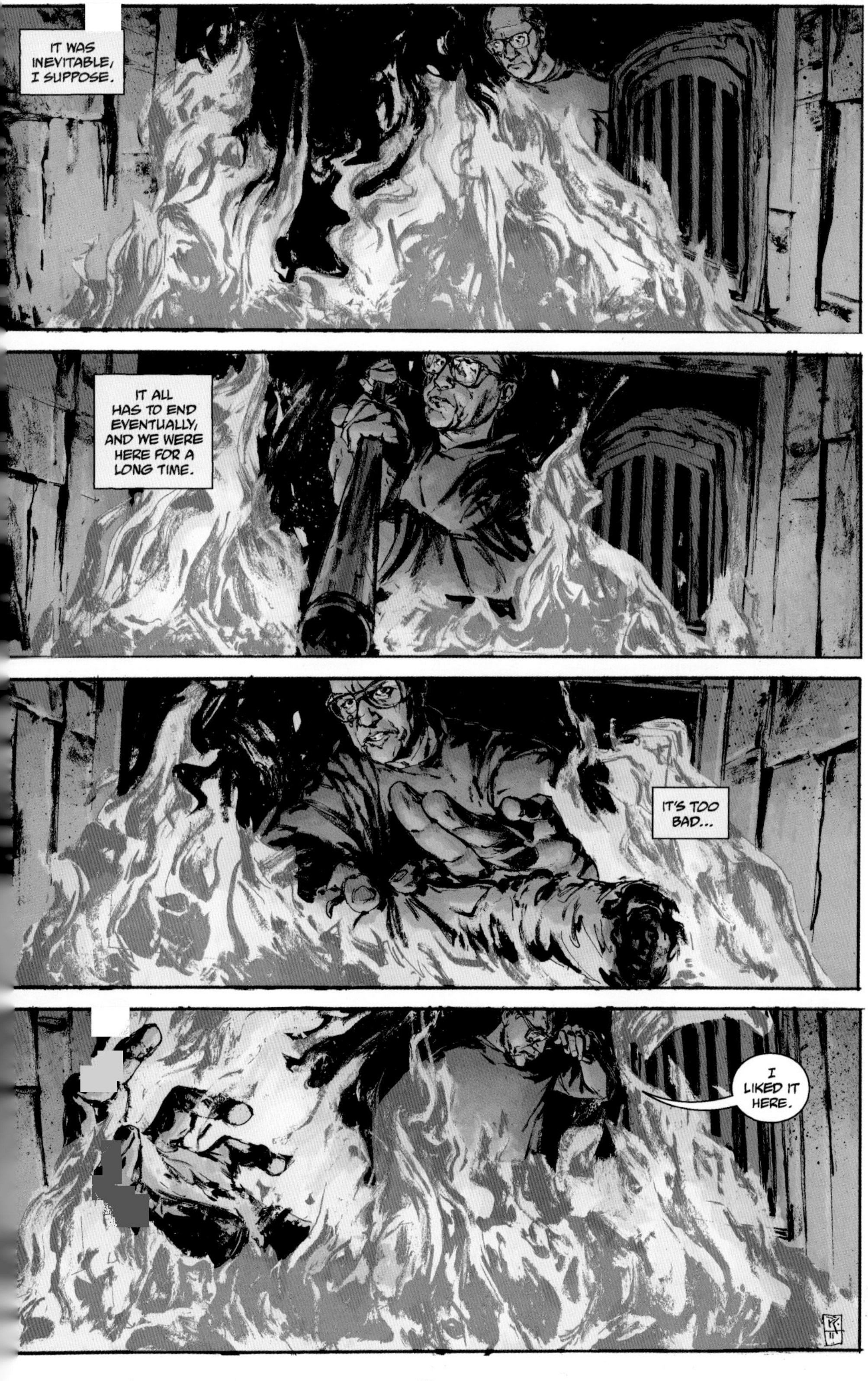

IT WAS INEVITABLE, I SUPPOSE.
IT ALL HAS TO END EVENTUALLY, AND WE WERE HERE FOR A LONG TIME.
IT'S TOO BAD...
I LIKED IT HERE.

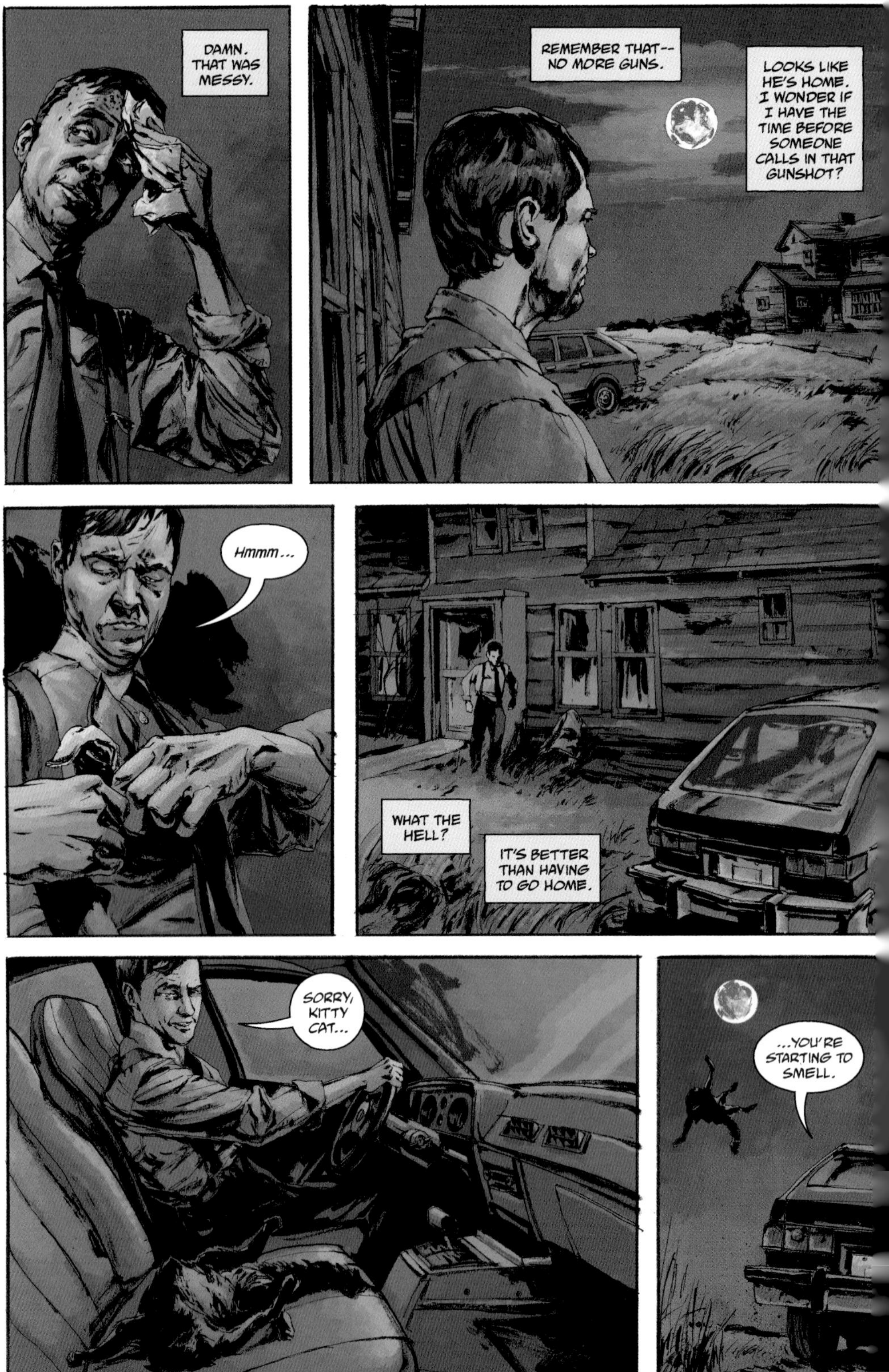
DAMN. THAT WAS MESSY.
REMEMBER THAT-- NO MORE GUNS.
LOOKS LIKE HE'S HOME. I WONDER IF I HAVE THE TIME BEFORE SOMEONE CALLS IN THAT GUNSHOT?
Hmmm...
WHAT THE HELL?
IT'S BETTER THAN HAVING TO GO HOME.
SORRY, KITTY CAT...
...YOU'RE STARTING TO SMELL.

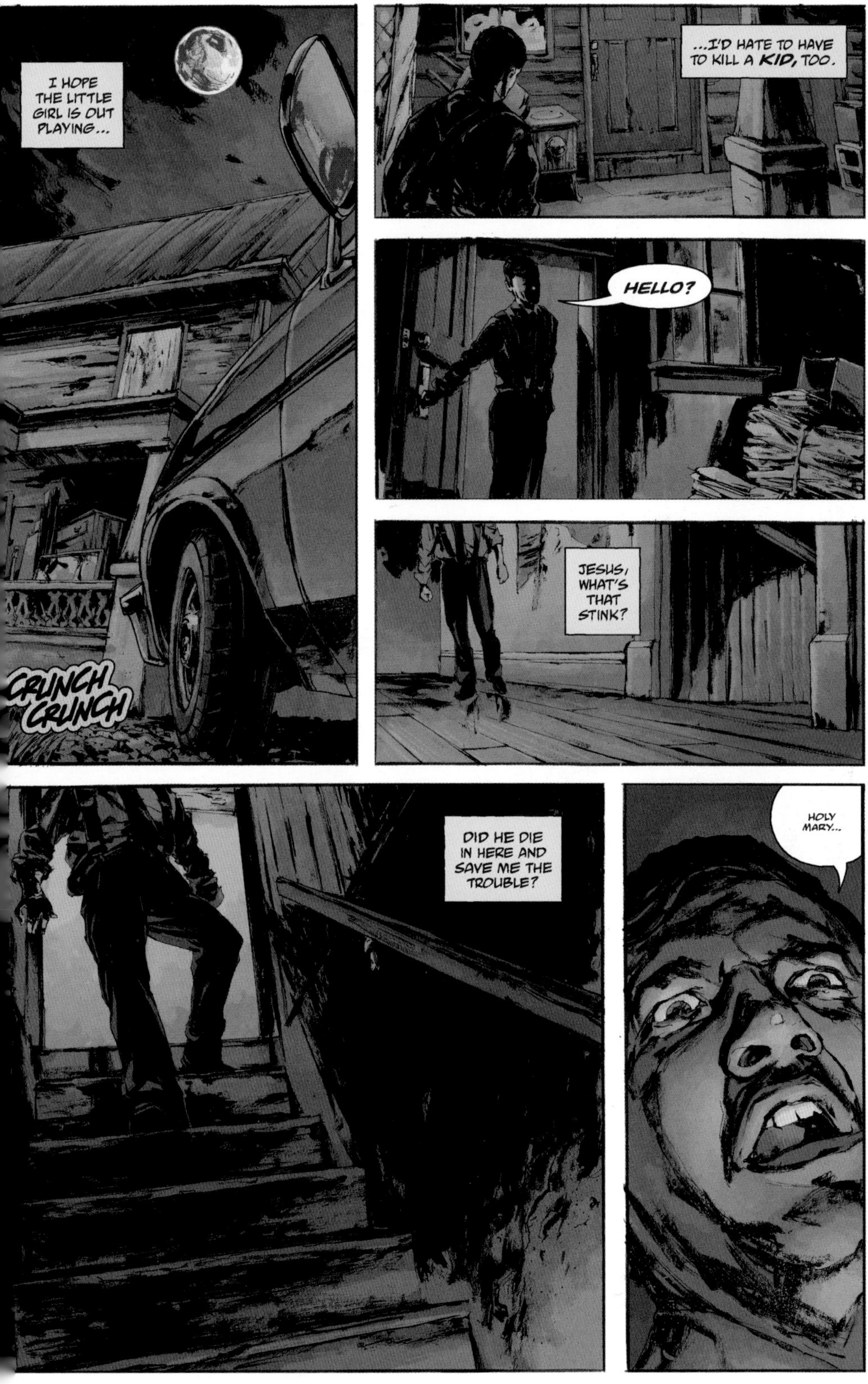
I HOPE THE LITTLE GIRL IS OUT PLAYING...
CRUNCH CRUNCH
...I'D HATE TO HAVE TO KILL A KID, TOO.
HELLO?
JESUS, WHAT'S THAT STINK?
DID HE DIE IN HERE AND SAVE ME THE TROUBLE?
HOLY MARY...

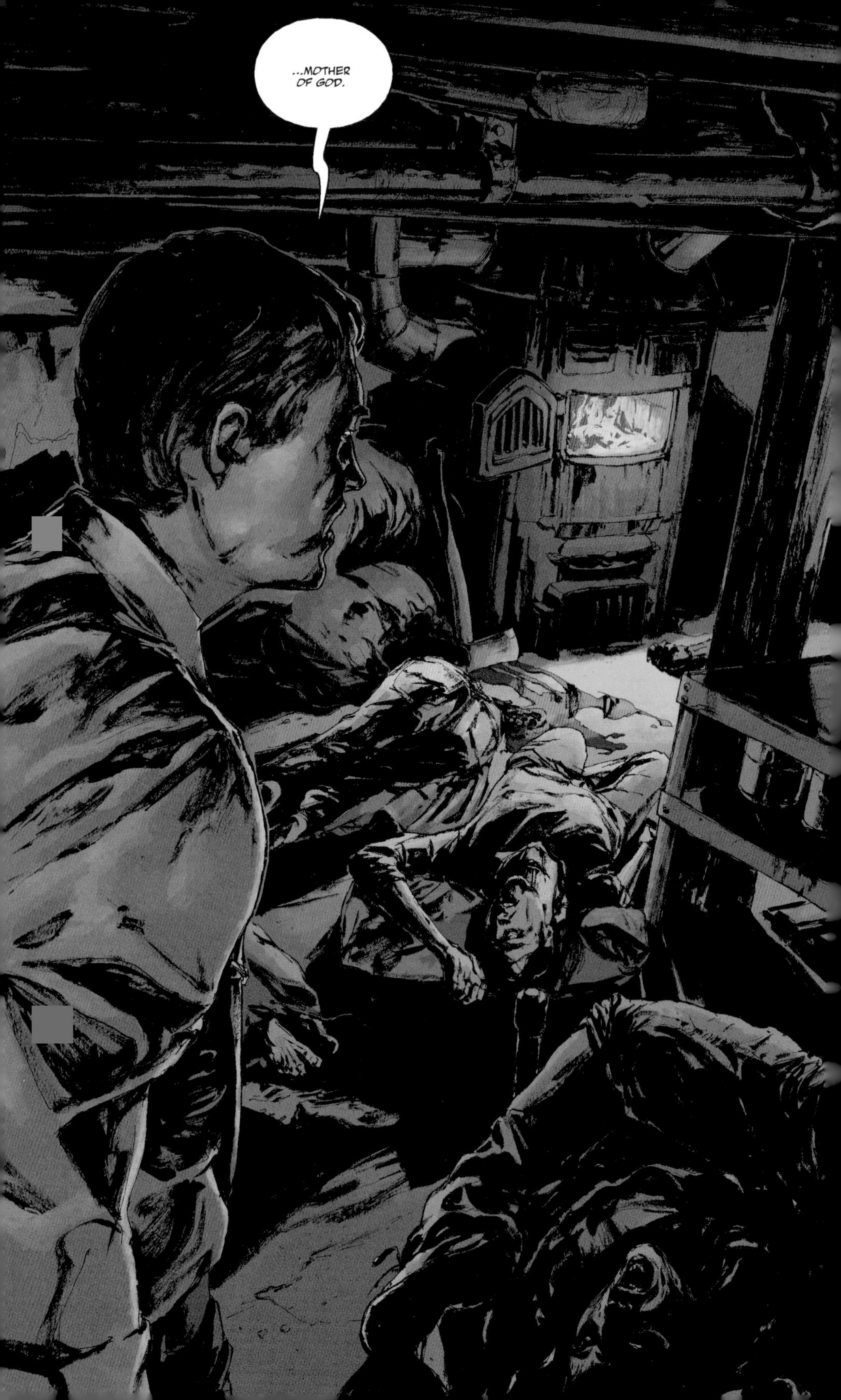
...MOTHER OF GOD.

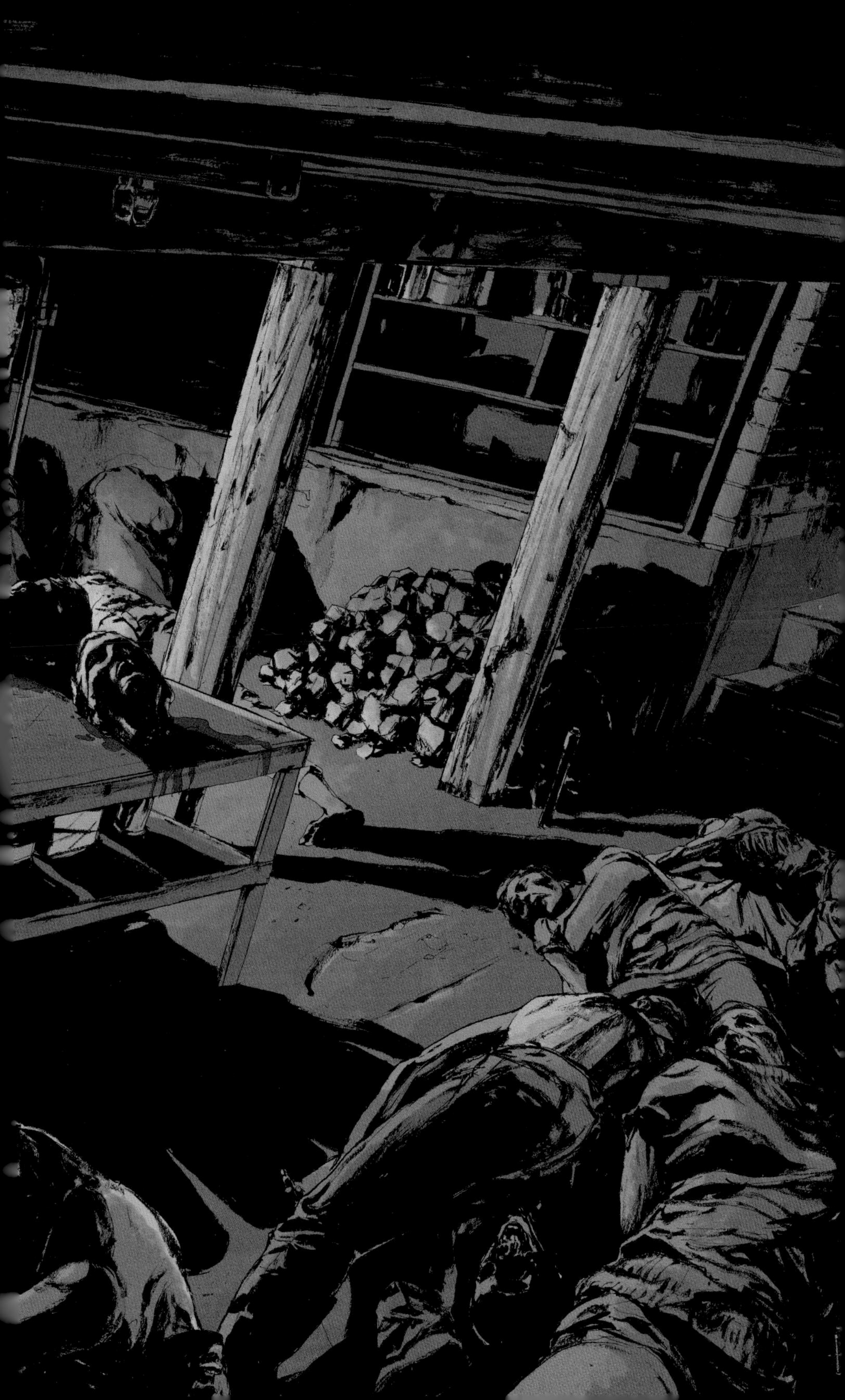

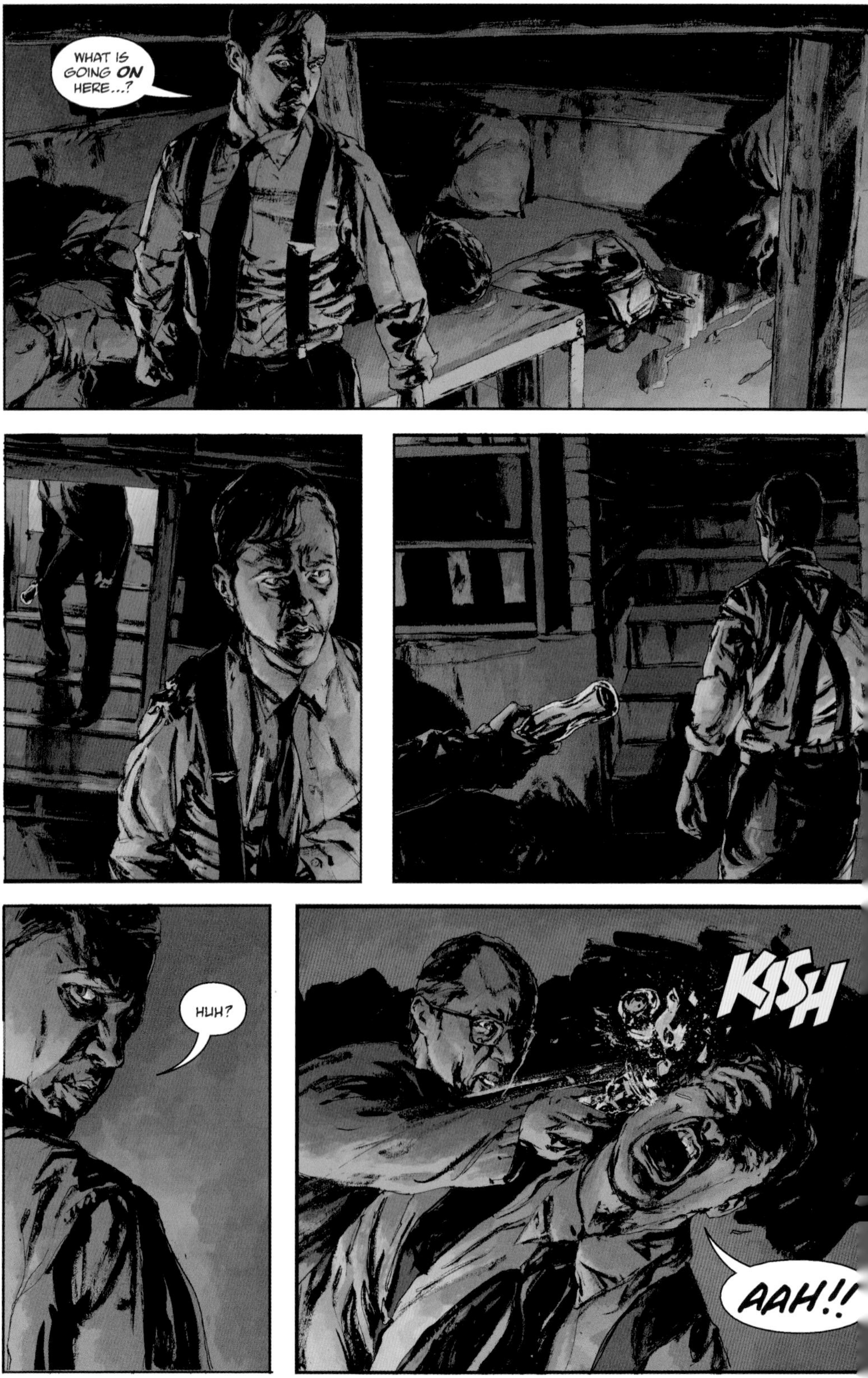
WHAT IS GOING ON HERE...?
HUH?
KISH
AAH!!

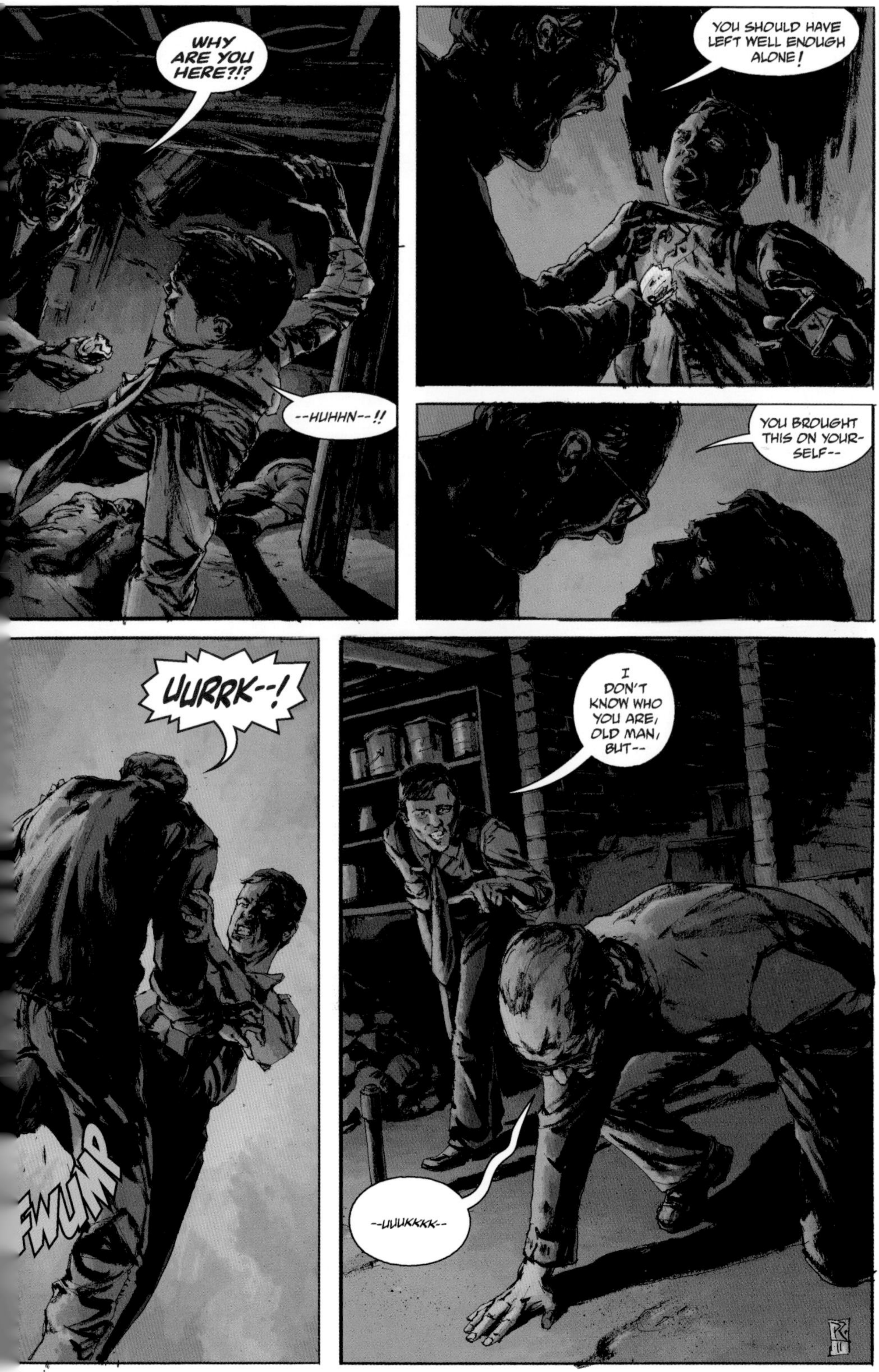
WHY ARE YOU HERE?!?
--HUHHN--!!
YOU SHOULD HAVE LEFT WELL ENOUGH ALONE!
YOU BROUGHT THIS ON YOURSELF--
UURRK--!
FWUMP
I DON'T KNOW WHO YOU ARE, OLD MAN, BUT--
--UUUKKKK--

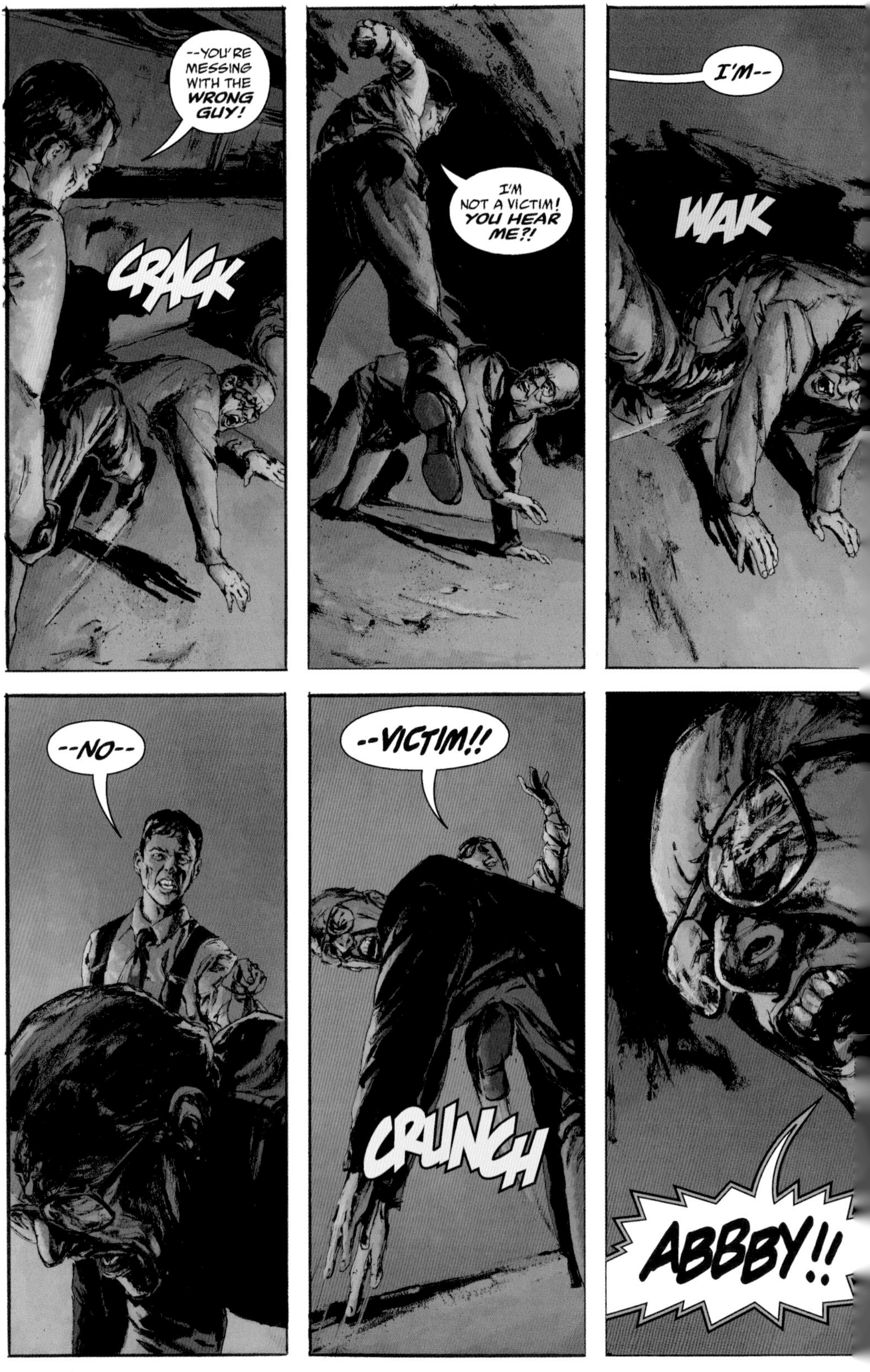
--YOU'RE MESSING WITH THE WRONG GUY!
CRACK
I'M NOT A VICTIM! YOU HEAR ME?!
I'M--
WAK
--NO--
--VICTIM!!
CRUNCH
ABBBY!!

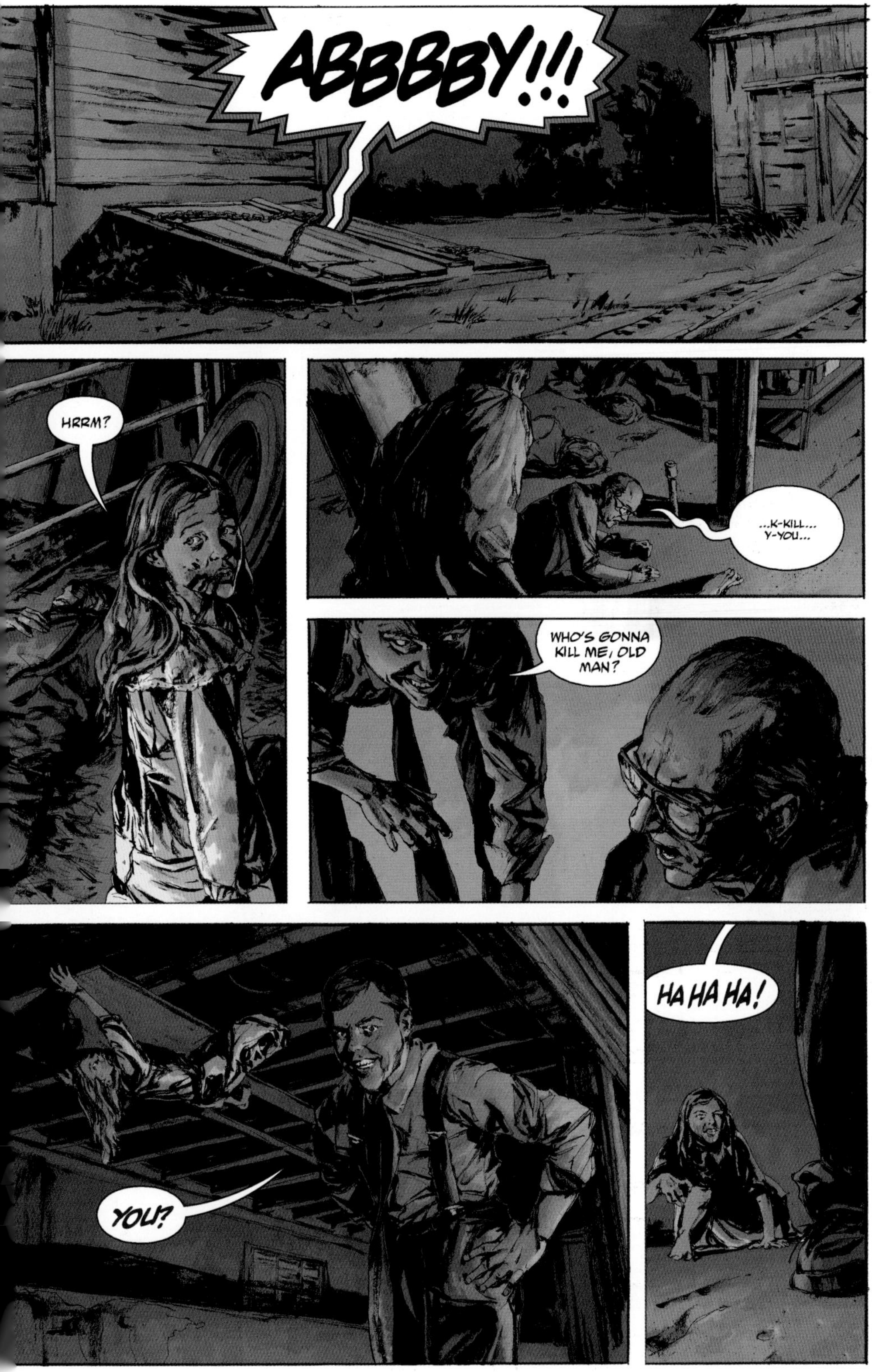
ABBBBY!!!
HRRM?
...K-KILL... Y-YOU...
WHO'S GONNA KILL ME, OLD MAN?
YOU?
HA HA HA!

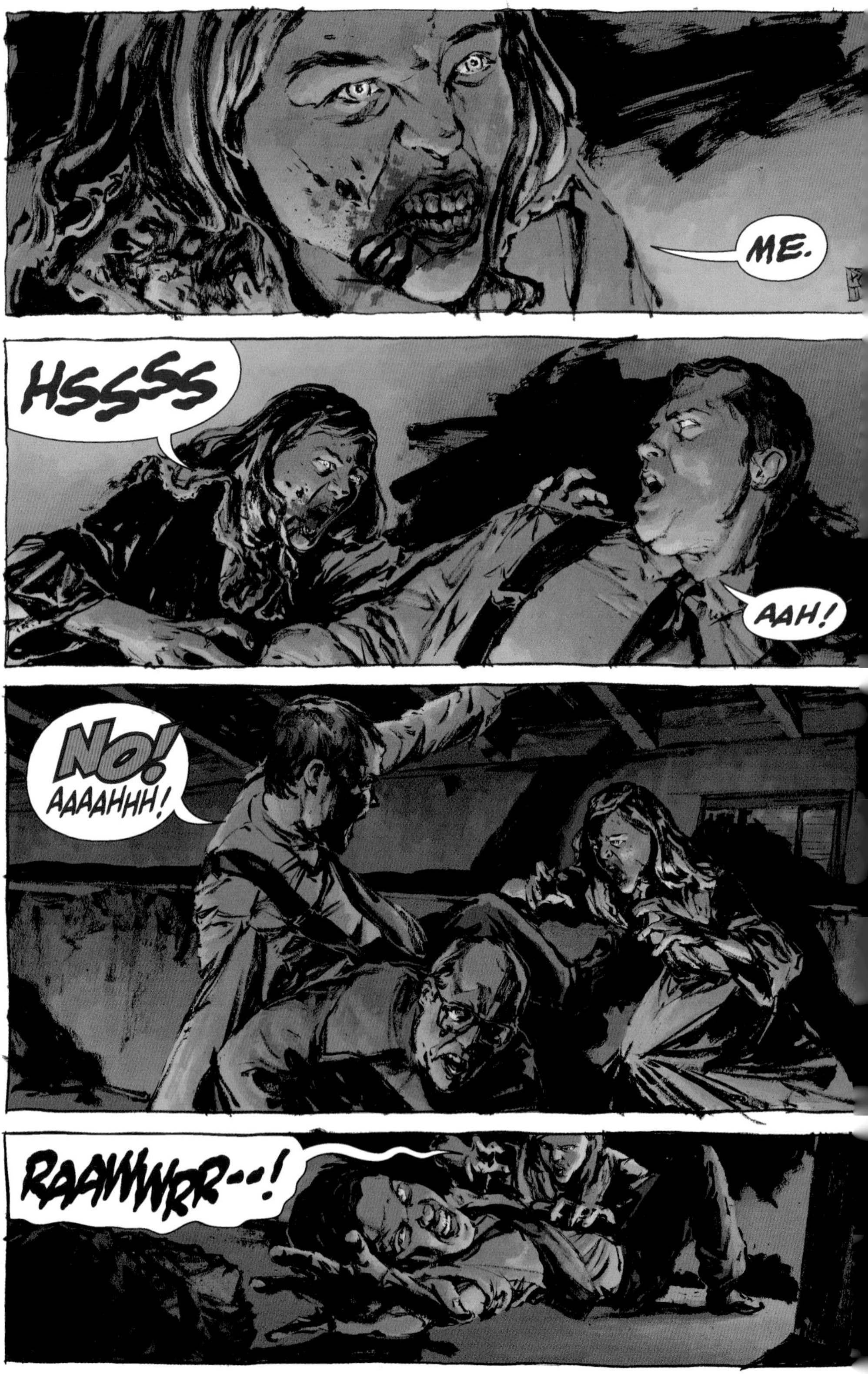
ME.
HSSSS
AAH!
NO!
AAAAHHH!
RAAWWRR--!

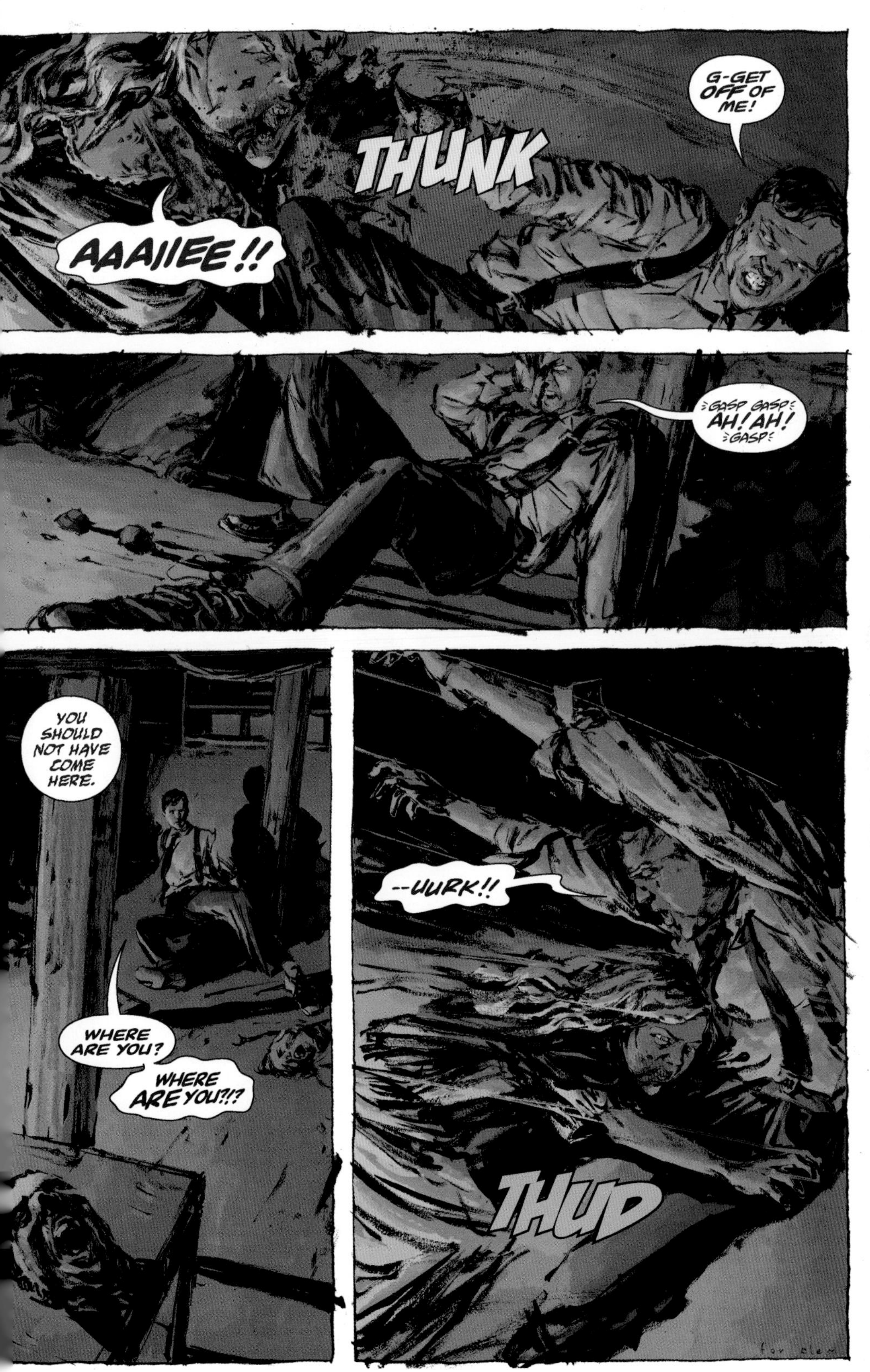
G-GET OFF OF ME!
THUNK
AAAIIEE!!
GASP GASP AH! AH! GASP
YOU SHOULD NOT HAVE COME HERE.
WHERE ARE YOU?
WHERE ARE YOU?!?
--UURK!!
THUD

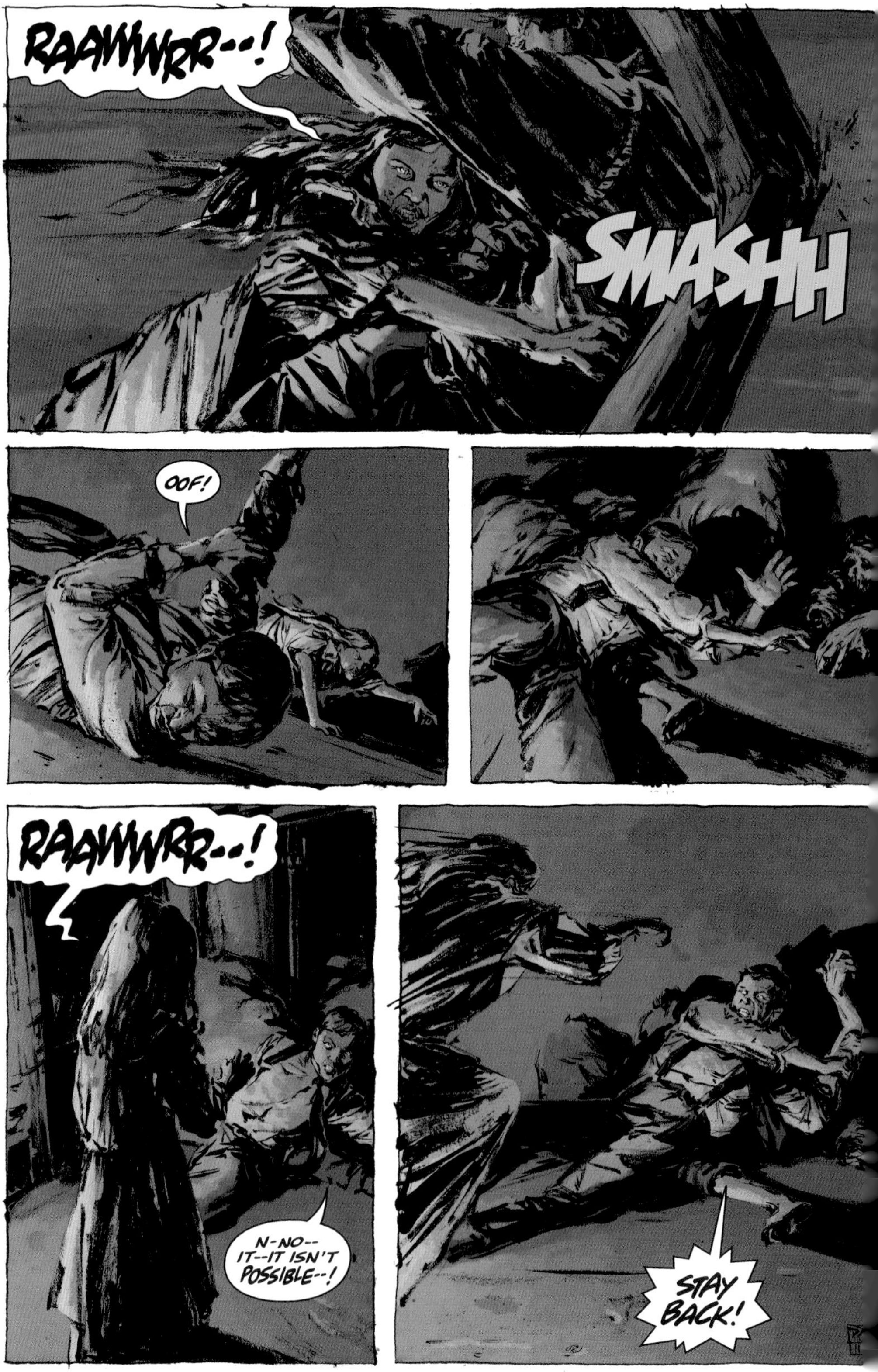
RAAWWRR--!
SMASHH
OOF!
RAAWWRR--!
N-NO--
IT--IT ISN'T
POSSIBLE--!
STAY
BACK!

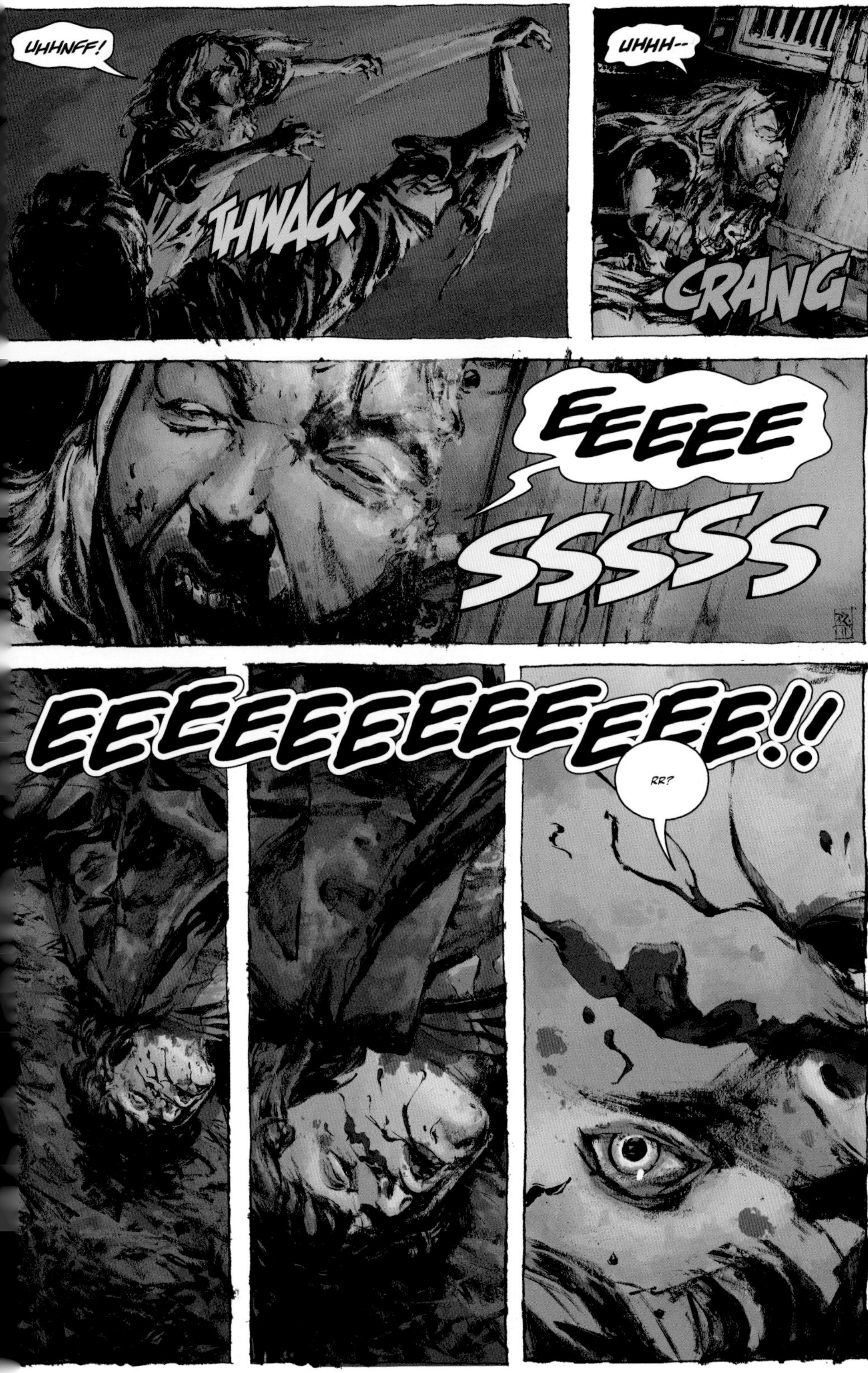
UHHNFF!
THWACK
UHHH--
CRANG
EEEEE
SSSSS
EEEEEEEEEEEEEEE!!
RR?

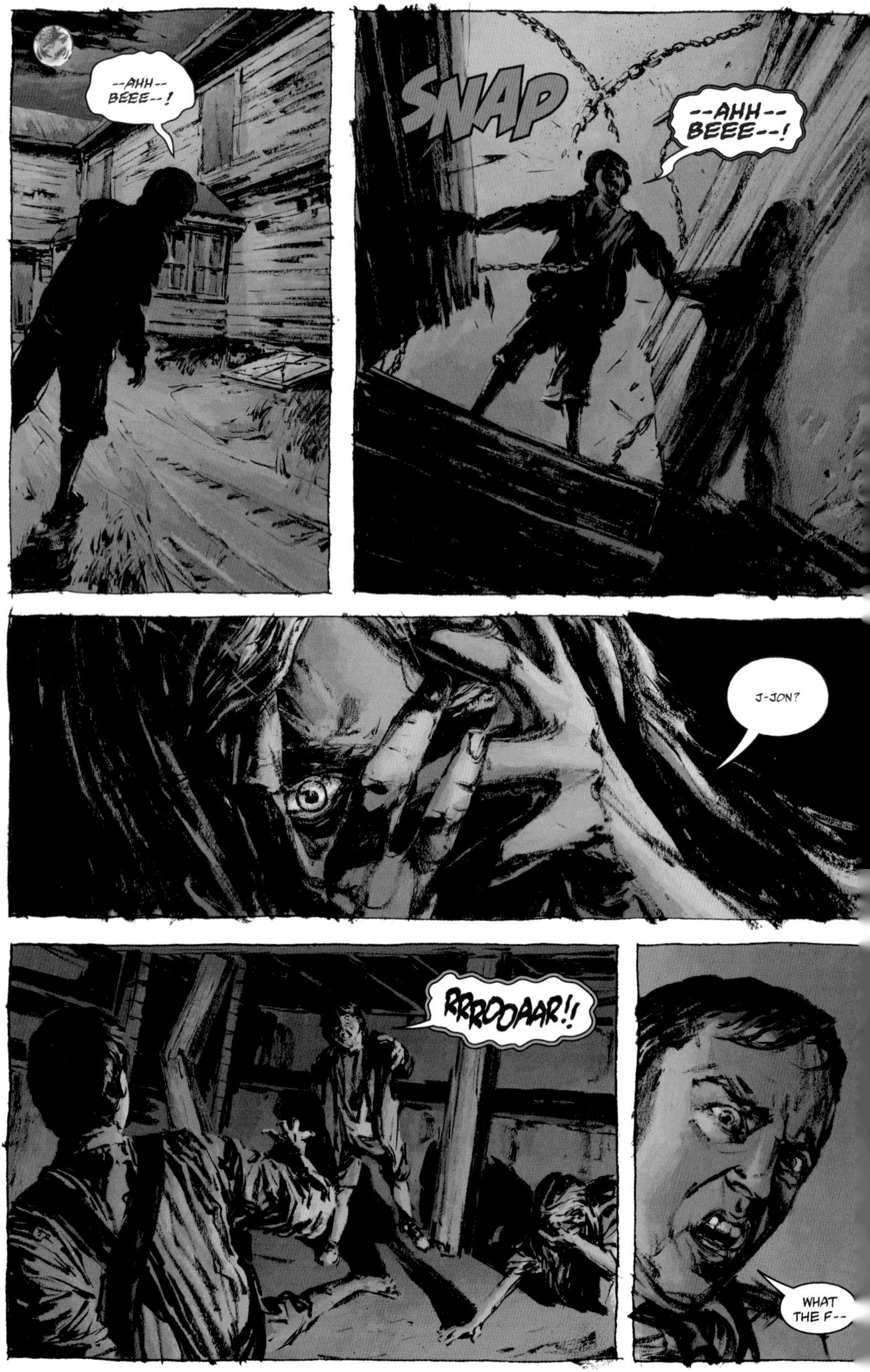

--AHH--
BEEE--!
SNAP
--AHH--
BEEE--!
J-JON?
RRROOAAR!!
WHAT
THE F--

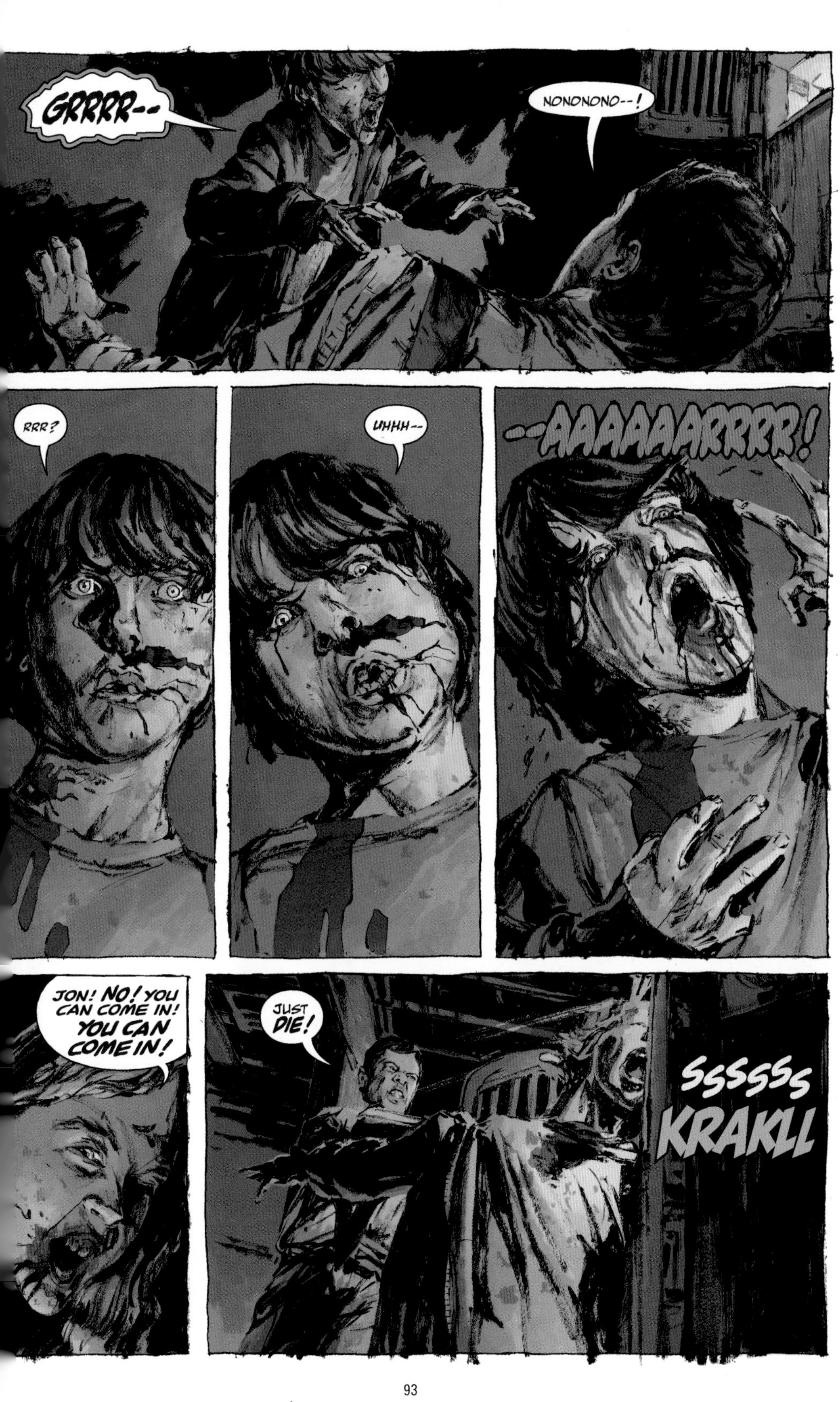
GRRRR--
NONONONO--!
RRR?
UHHH--
--AAAAAARRRR!
JON! NO! YOU CAN COME IN! YOU CAN COME IN!
JUST DIE!
SSSSSS
KRAKLL

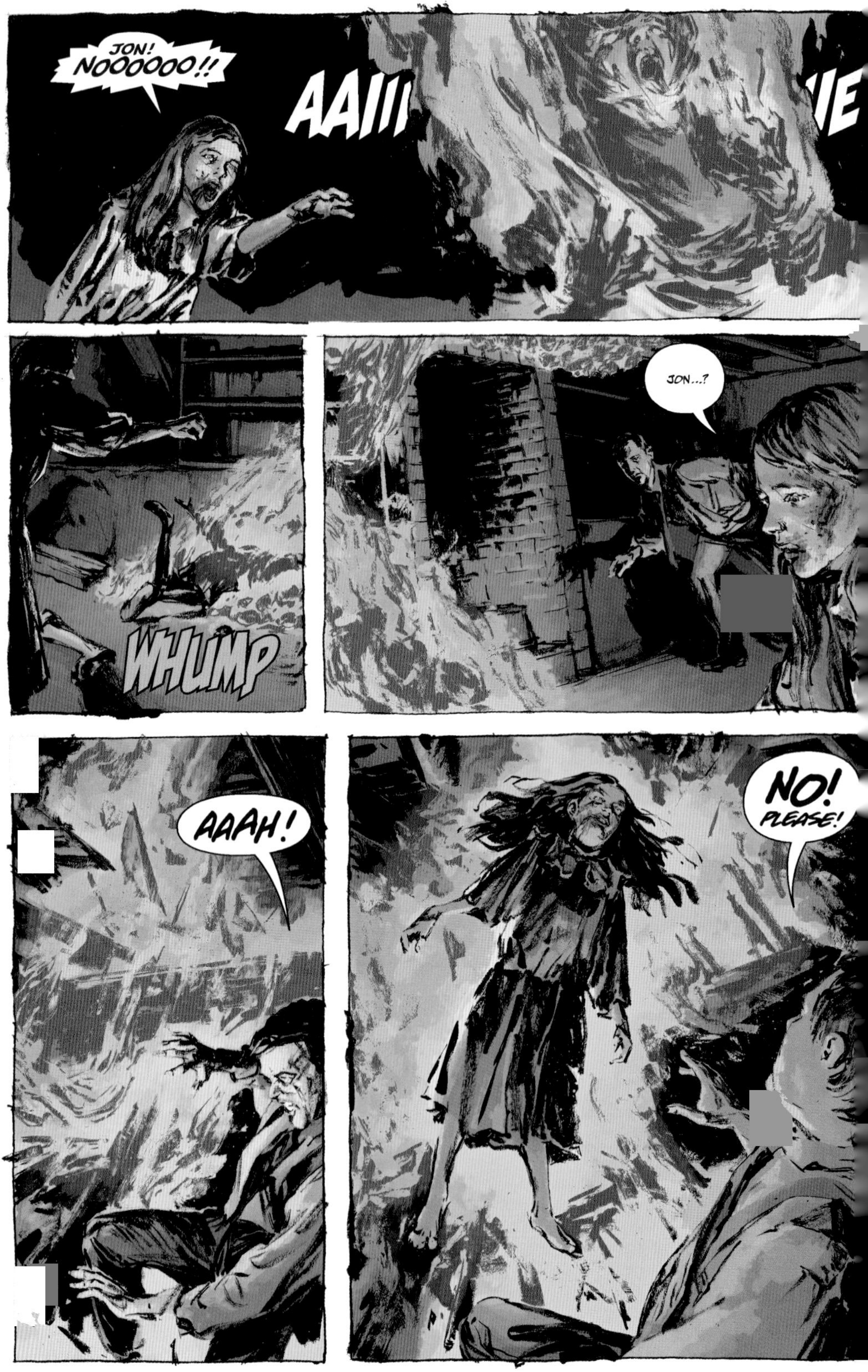
JON! NOOOOOO!!
AAIIIIEEE
WHUMP
JON...?
AAAH!
NO! PLEASE!

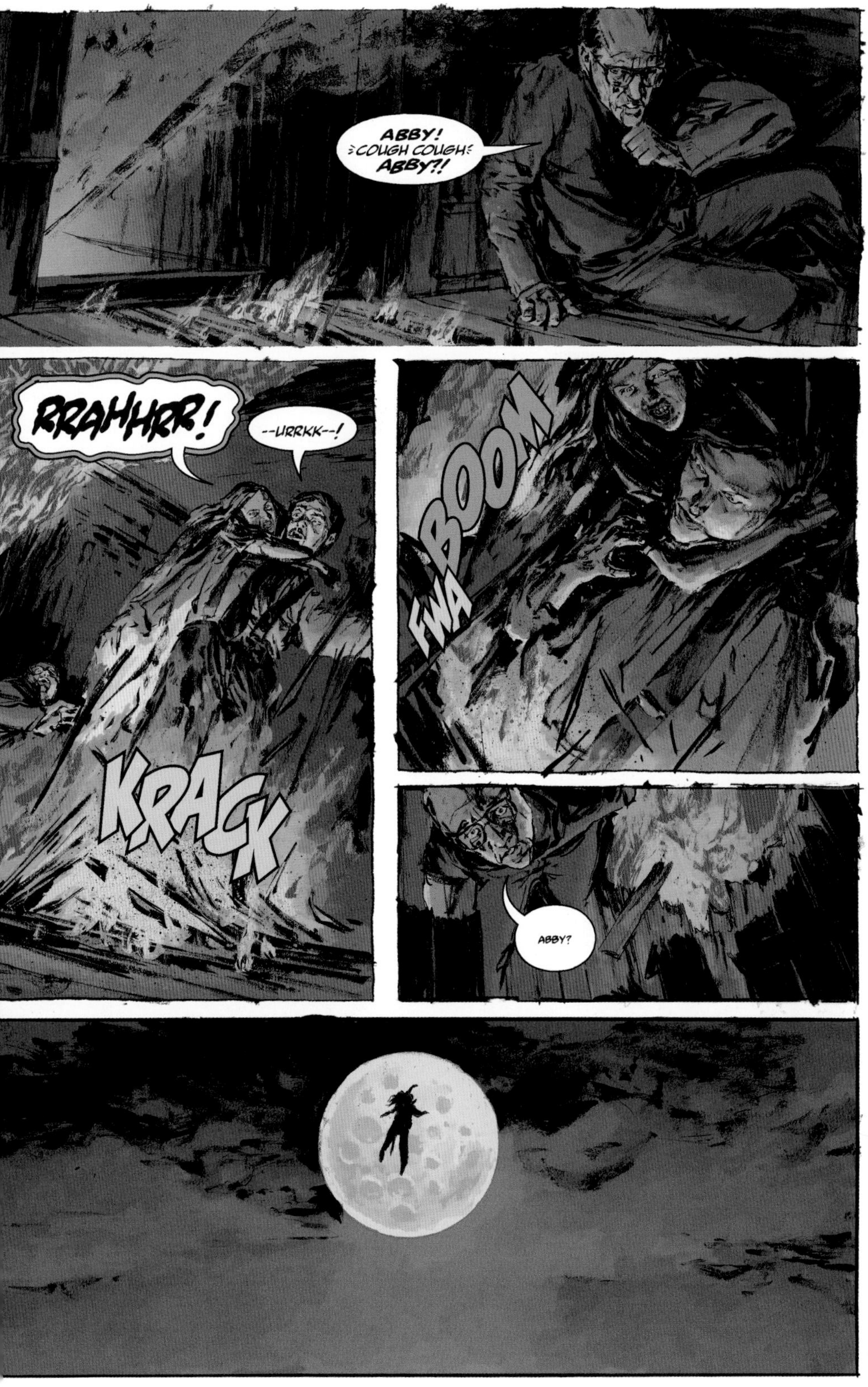

ABBY!
COUGH COUGH
ABBY?!
RRAHHRR!
--URRKK--!
KRACK
FWA BOOM
ABBY?

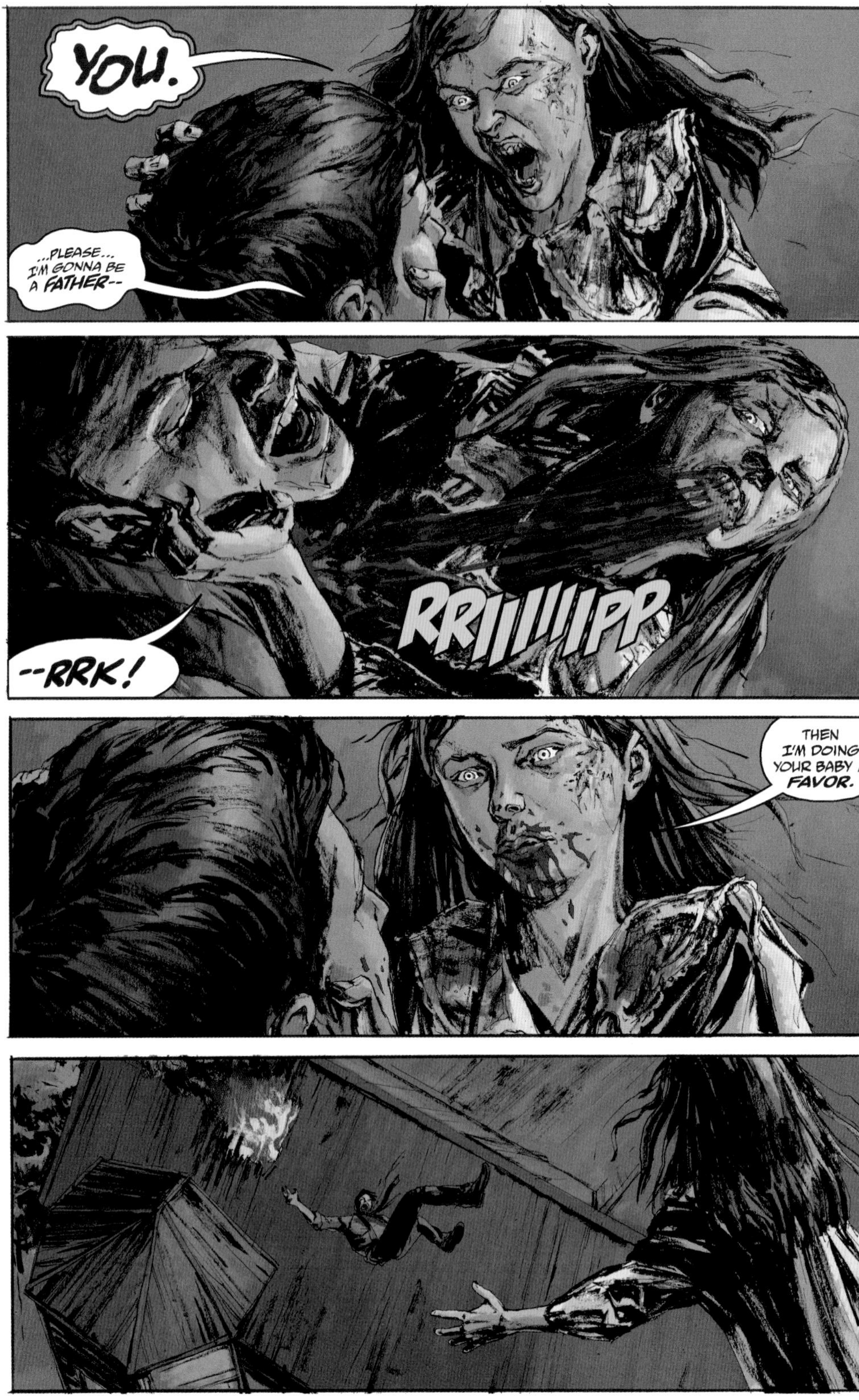
YOU.
...PLEASE... I'M GONNA BE A FATHER--
--RRK!
RRIIIIIIPP
THEN I'M DOING YOUR BABY A FAVOR.

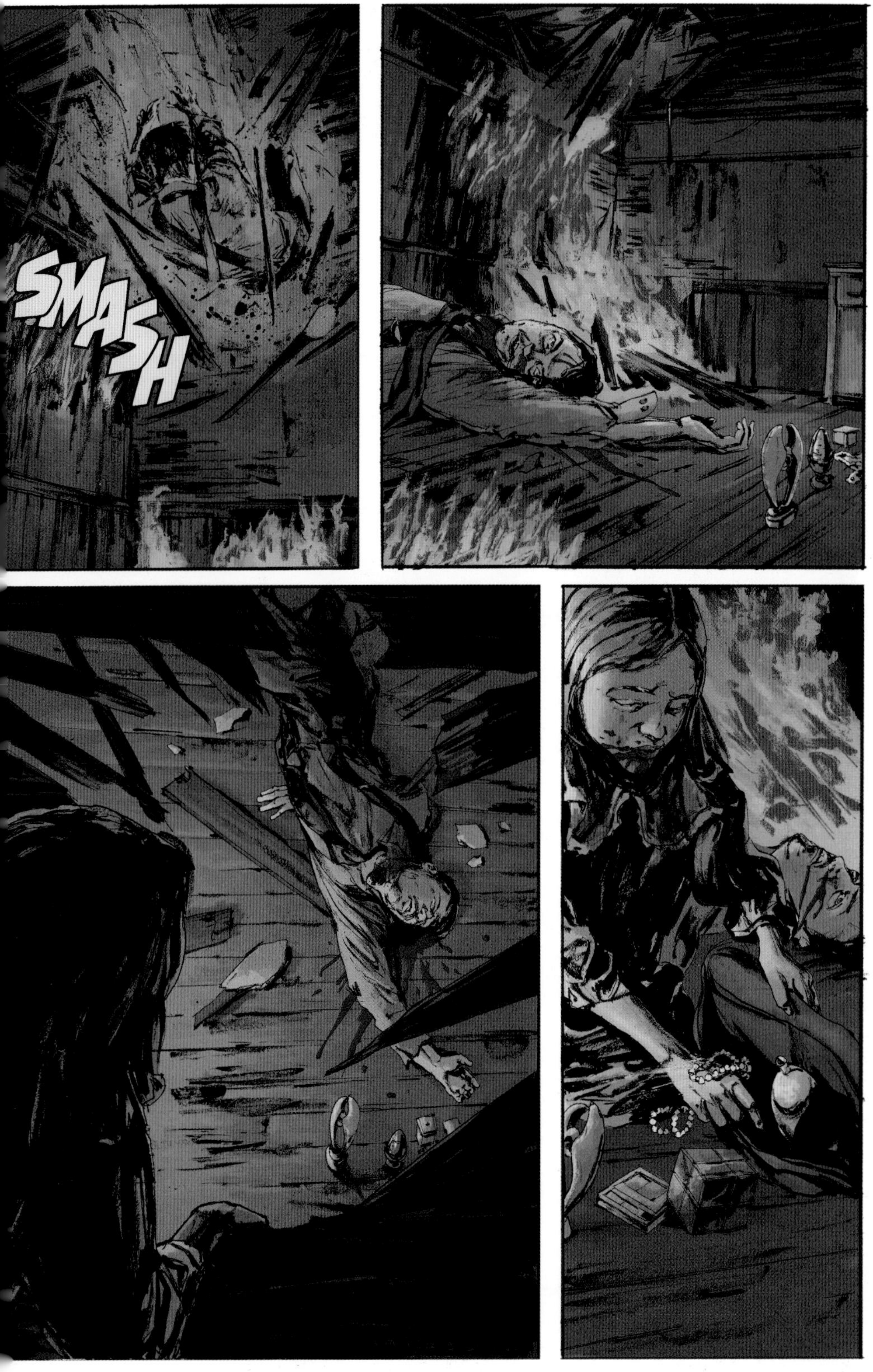
SMASH

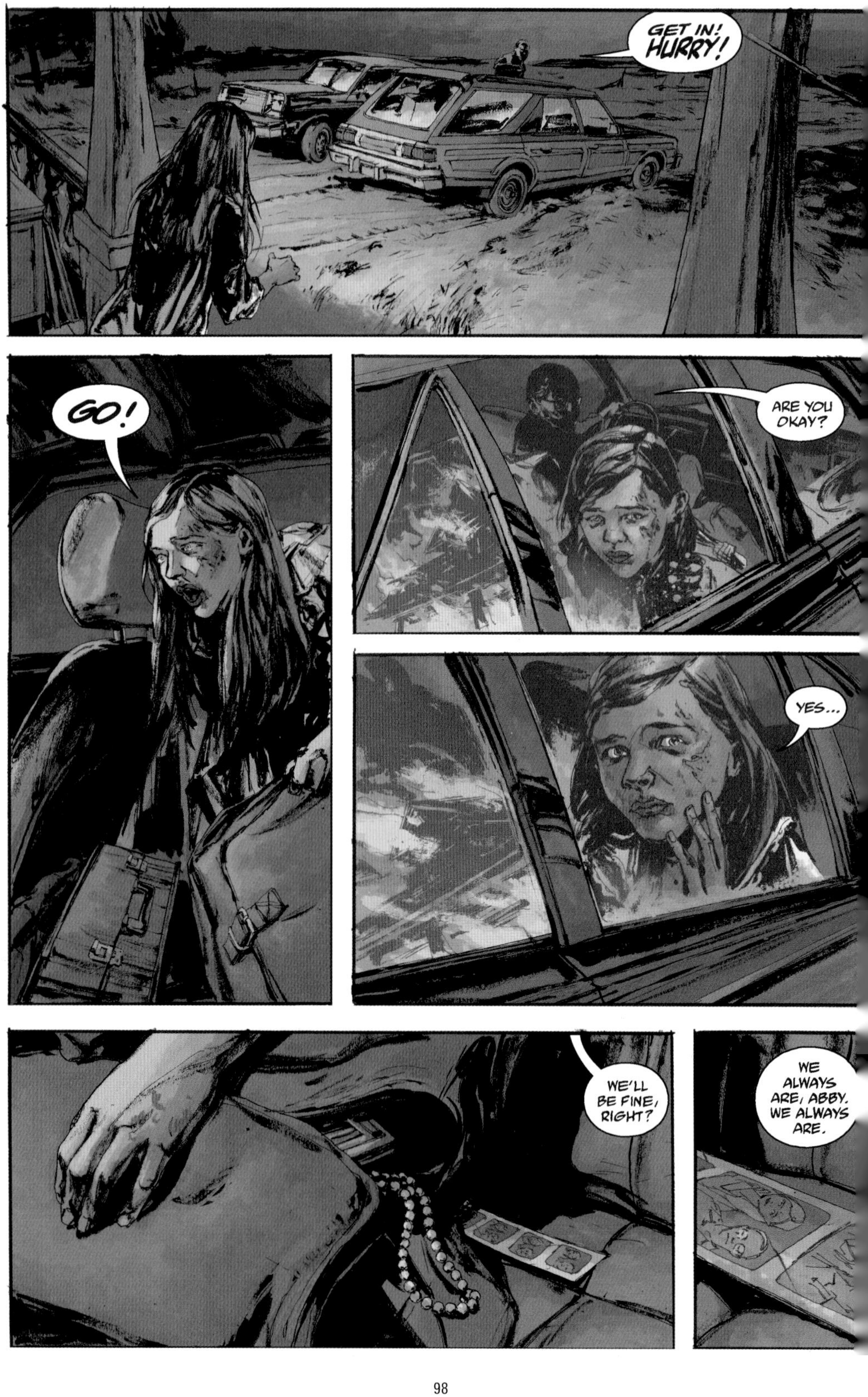
GET IN! HURRY!
GO!
ARE YOU OKAY?
YES...
WE'LL BE FINE, RIGHT?
WE ALWAYS ARE, ABBY. WE ALWAYS ARE.

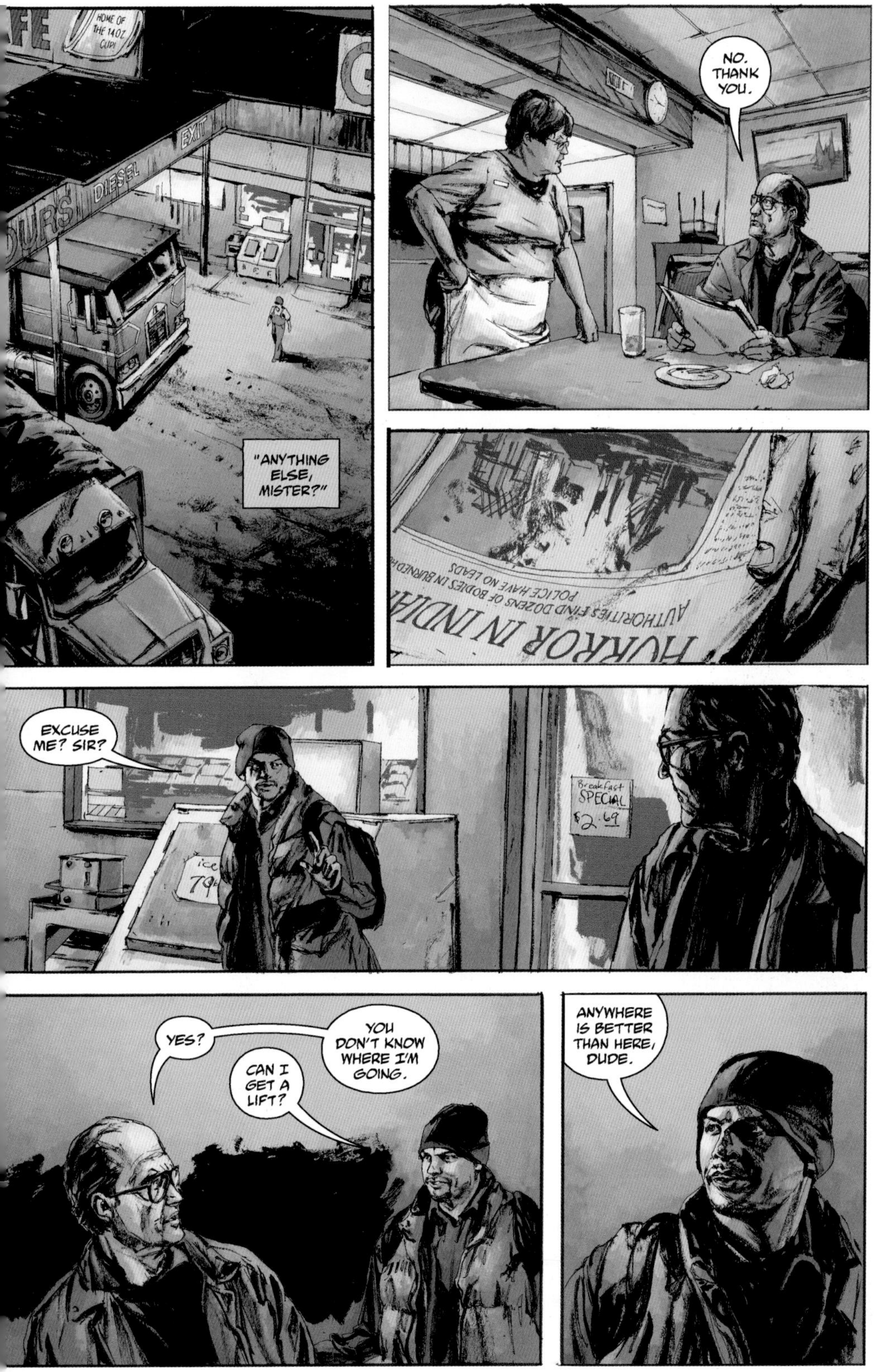
HOME OF THE 14 OZ CUP!
DIESEL
EXIT
"ANYTHING ELSE, MISTER?"
NO. THANK YOU.
HORROR IN INDIA
AUTHORITIES FIND DOZENS OF BODIES IN BURNED
POLICE HAVE NO LEADS
EXCUSE ME? SIR?
Breakfast SPECIAL $2.69
ice 79¢
YES?
CAN I GET A LIFT?
YOU DON'T KNOW WHERE I'M GOING.
ANYWHERE IS BETTER THAN HERE, DUDE.

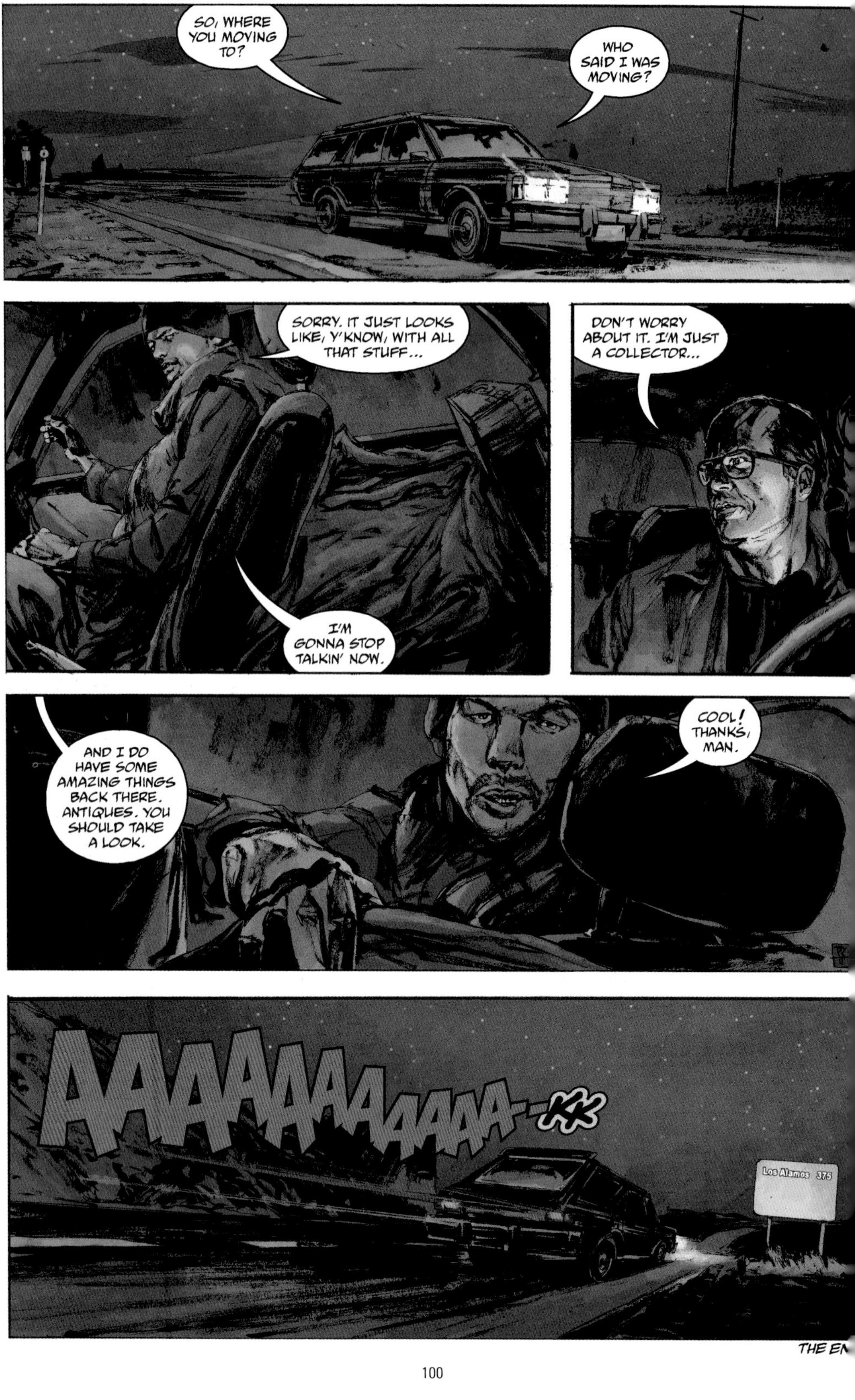
SO, WHERE YOU MOVING TO?
WHO SAID I WAS MOVING?
SORRY. IT JUST LOOKS LIKE, Y'KNOW, WITH ALL THAT STUFF...
I'M GONNA STOP TALKIN' NOW.
DON'T WORRY ABOUT IT. I'M JUST A COLLECTOR...
AND I DO HAVE SOME AMAZING THINGS BACK THERE. ANTIQUES. YOU SHOULD TAKE A LOOK.
COOL! THANKS, MAN.
AAAAAAAAAAAA-KK
Los Alamos 375

THE EN

LET ME IN

SKETCHBOOK

PATRIC REYNOLDS

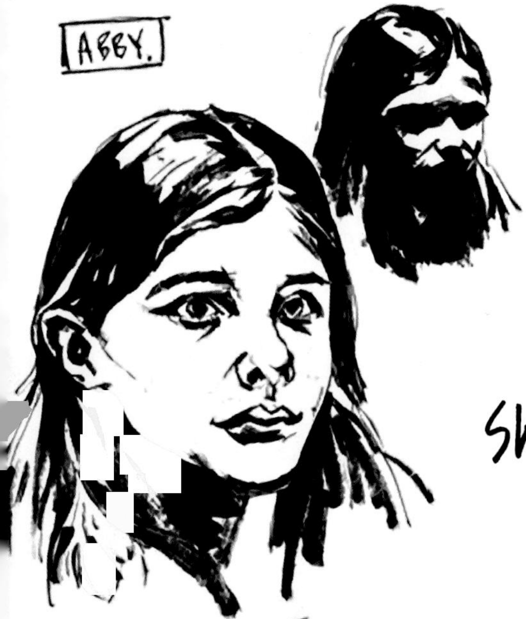
ABBY.

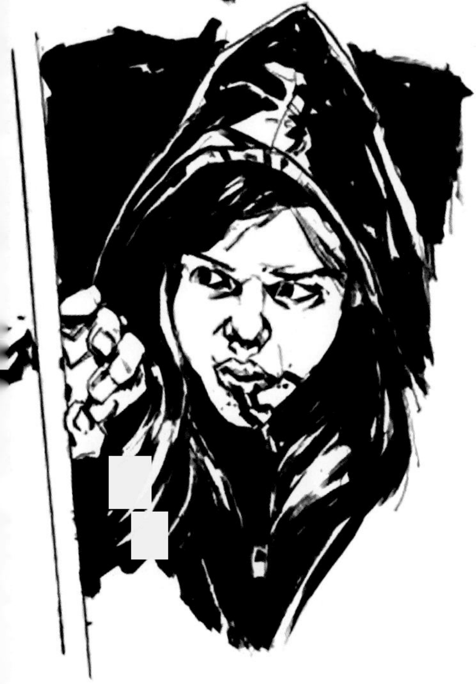

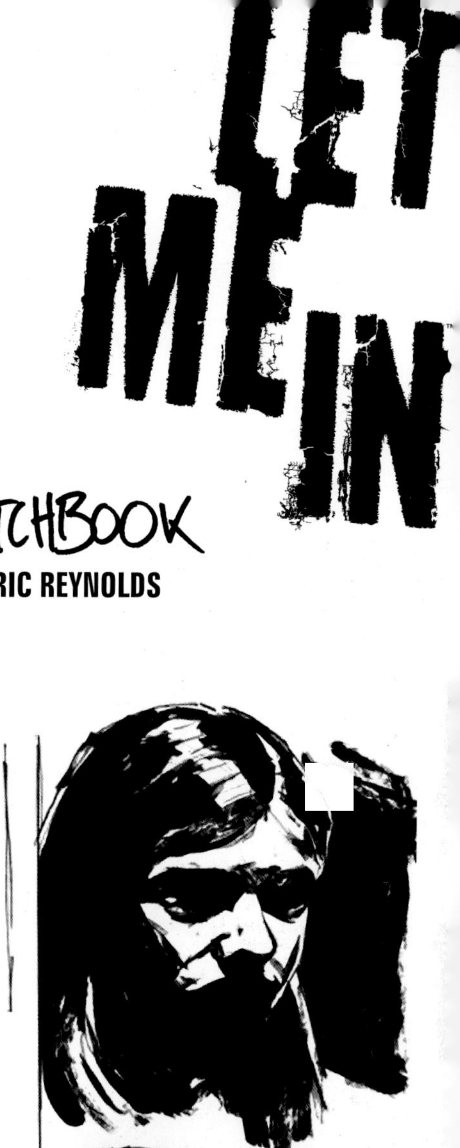

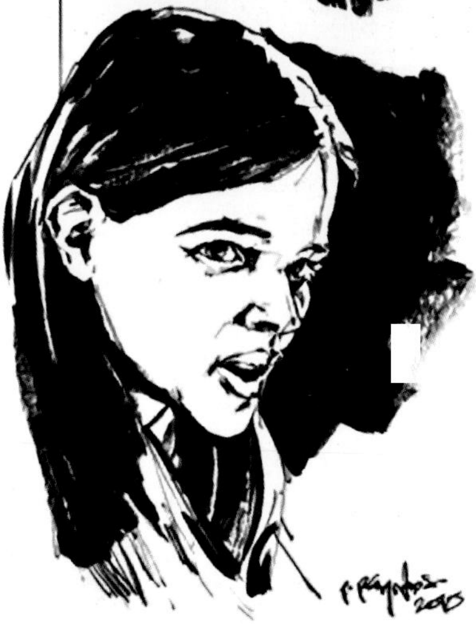

The star of the show is Abby, so one of my first priorities was getting Chloe Grace Moretz's likeness right. It's a tough spot to be in, since I can't make things look *too* referenced, or the drawing will lose that liveliness. So I figured if I focus on a few key features, I leave room for expressiveness. Chloe's eyes carry a lot of weight, and her lips and chin form a very specific shape. I knew if I could get those features right, everything else would fall into place.

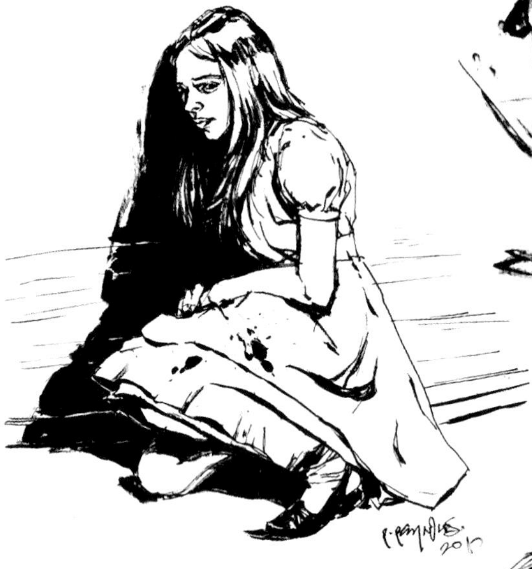
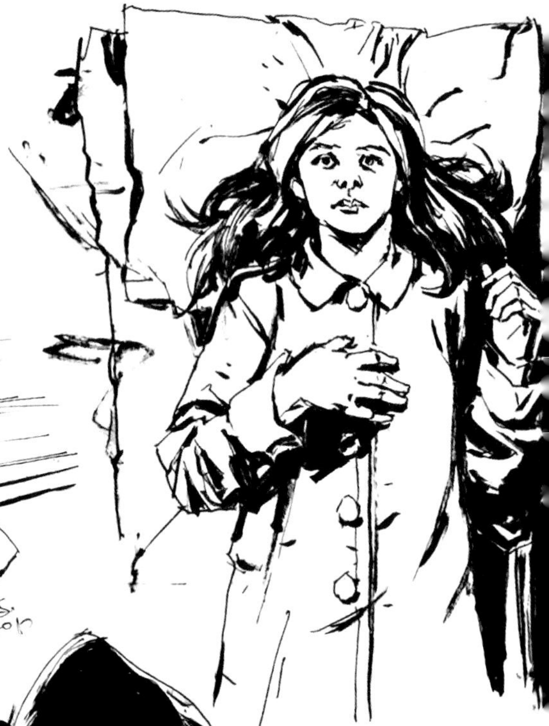
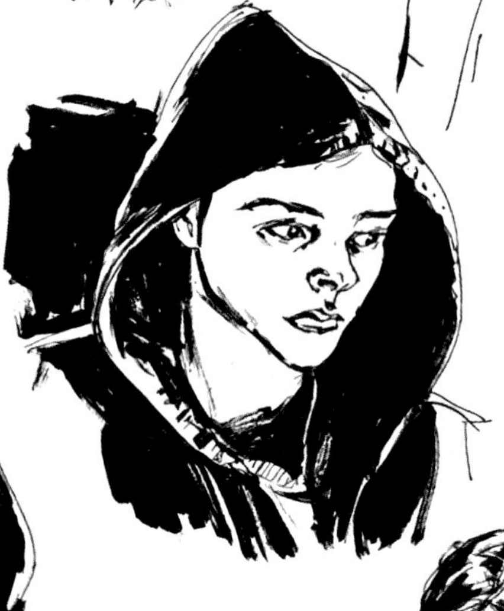
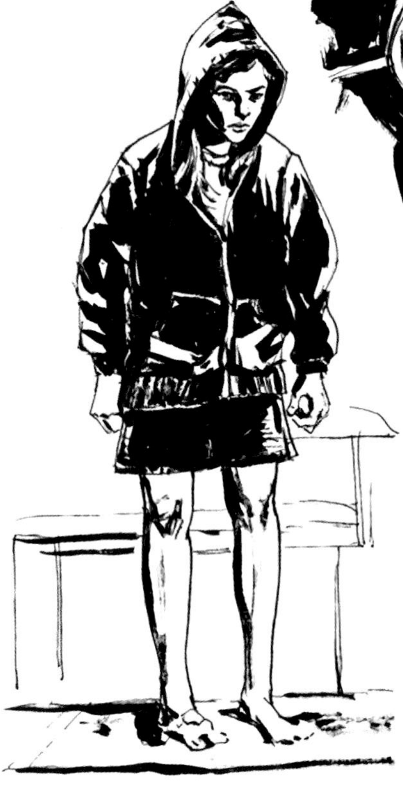
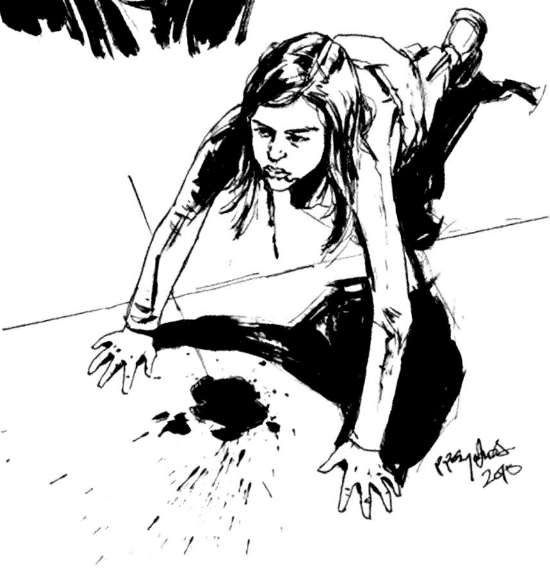

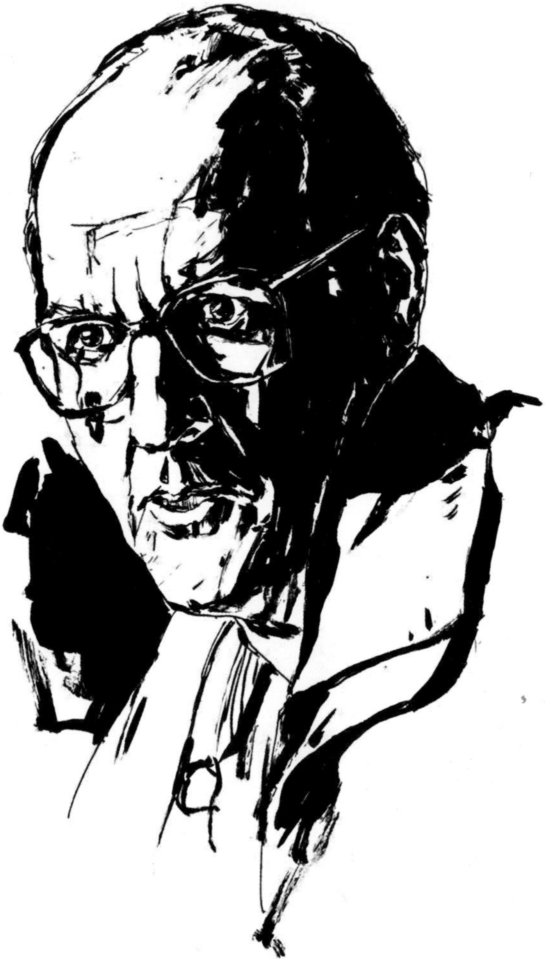

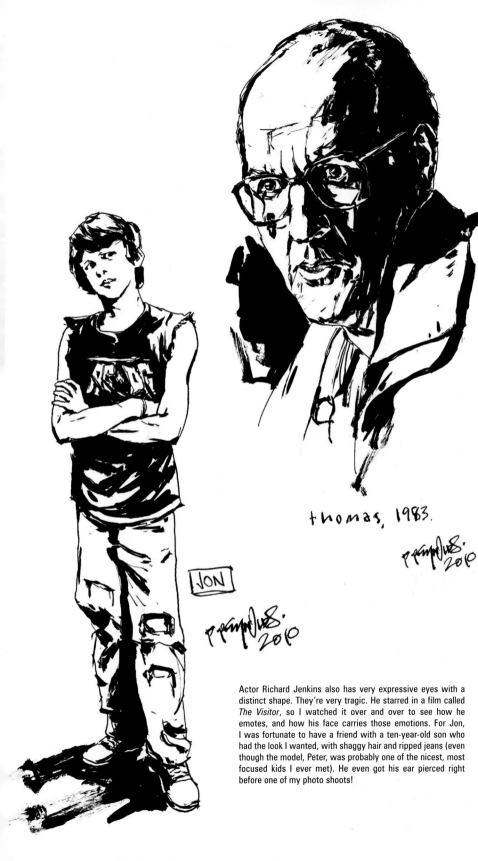

thomas, 1983.

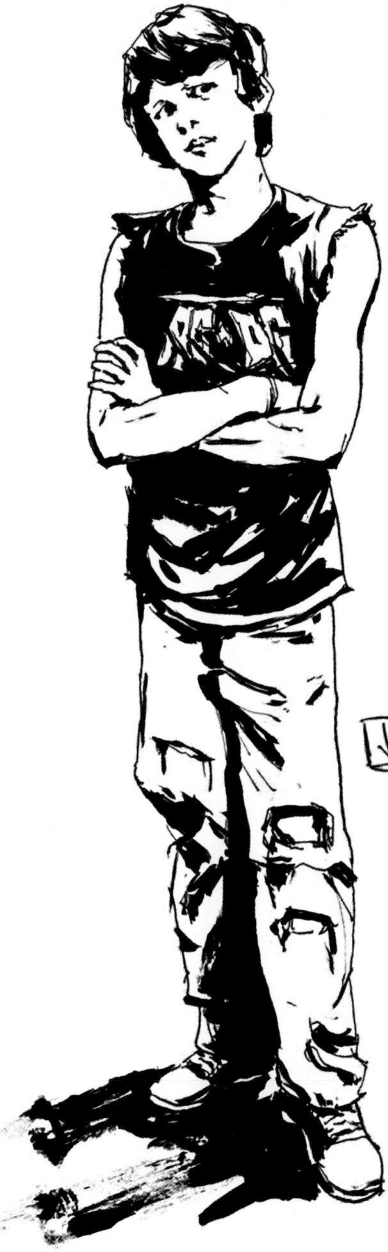

JON

Actor Richard Jenkins also has very expressive eyes with a distinct shape. They're very tragic. He starred in a film called *The Visitor*, so I watched it over and over to see how he emotes, and how his face carries those emotions. For Jon, I was fortunate to have a friend with a ten-year-old son who had the look I wanted, with shaggy hair and ripped jeans (even though the model, Peter, was probably one of the nicest, most focused kids I ever met). He even got his ear pierced right before one of my photo shoots!

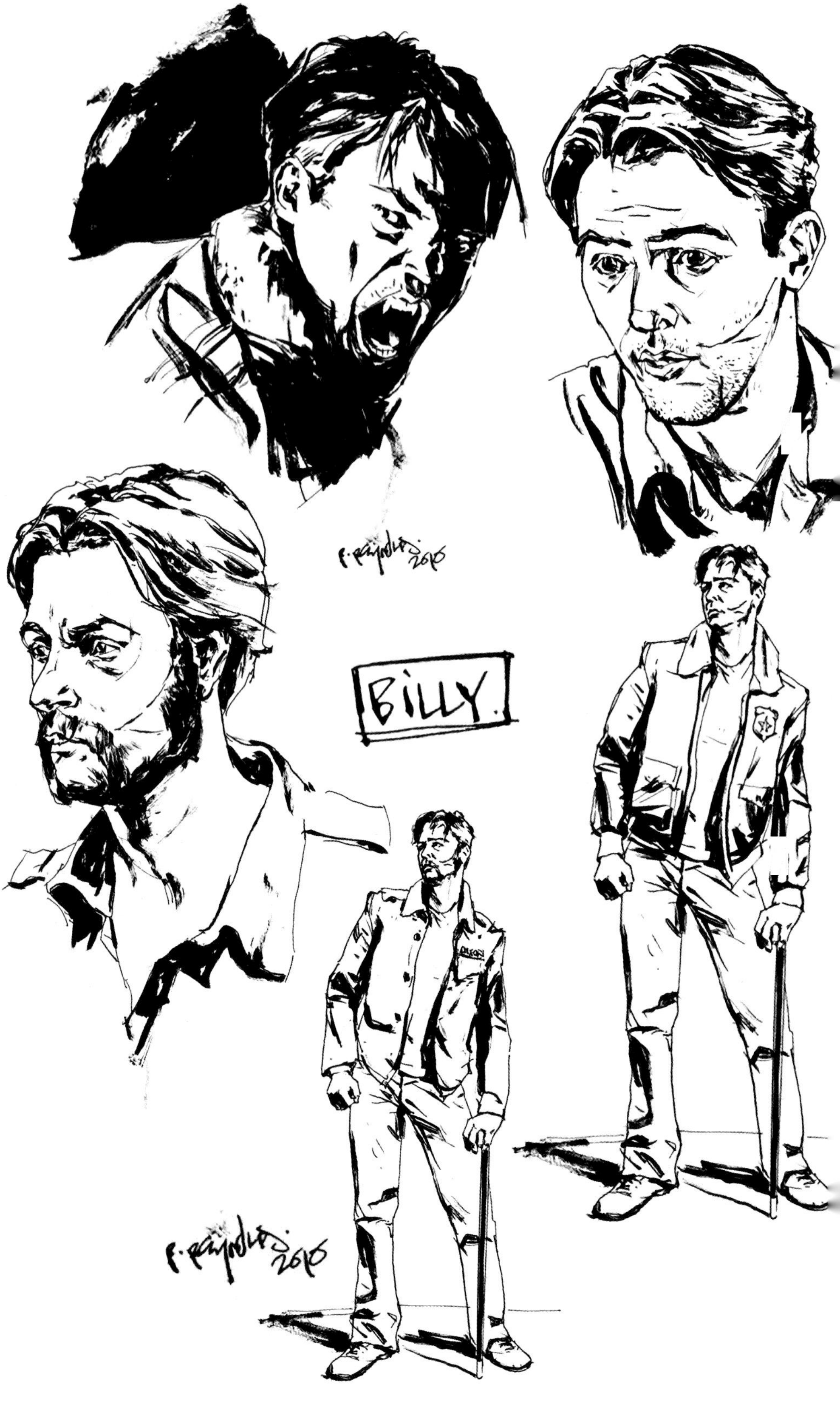
BILLY.

OPPOSITE PAGE: Once again, I was fortunate to find a model for Billy that had the look of the character I wanted. These drawings are essentially portraits of the model, Alex.

THIS PAGE: For Jamison, I tried to make up a character from scratch, but it just wasn't cutting it. Finally, one of my dad's best friends agreed to help me. He is probably one of the friendliest guys you'll ever meet, though.

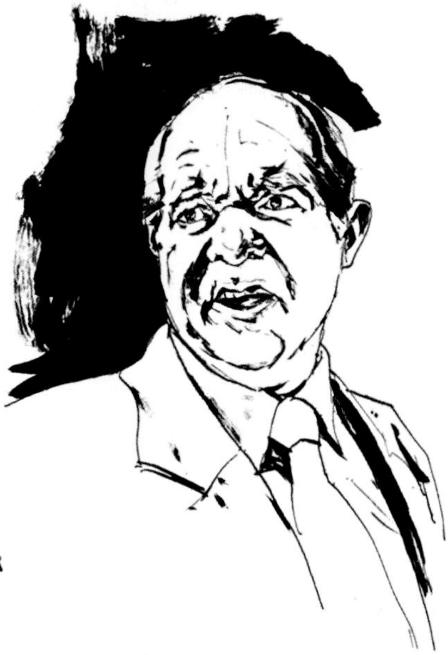

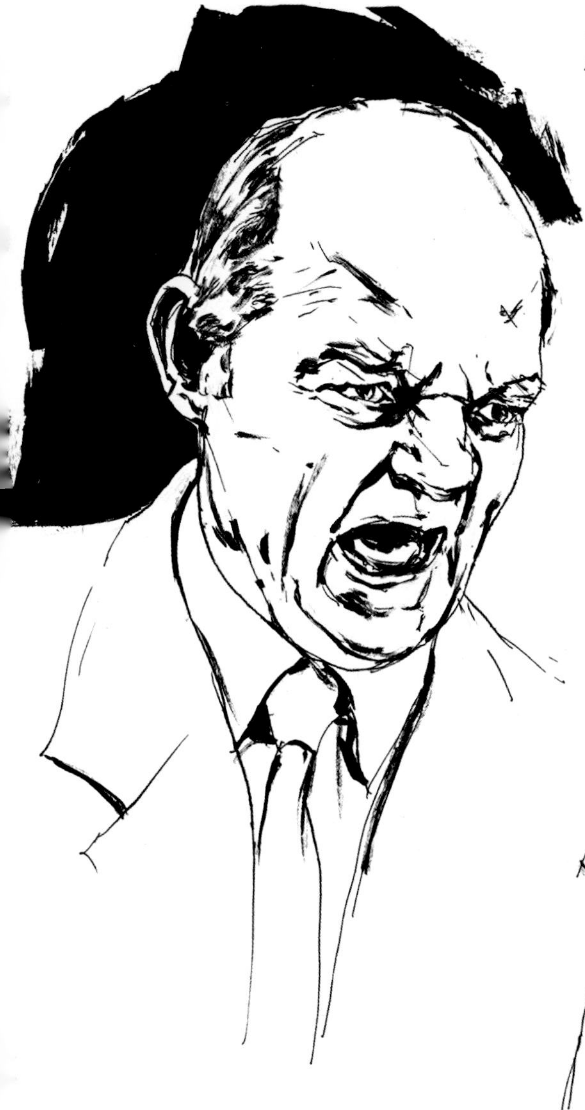

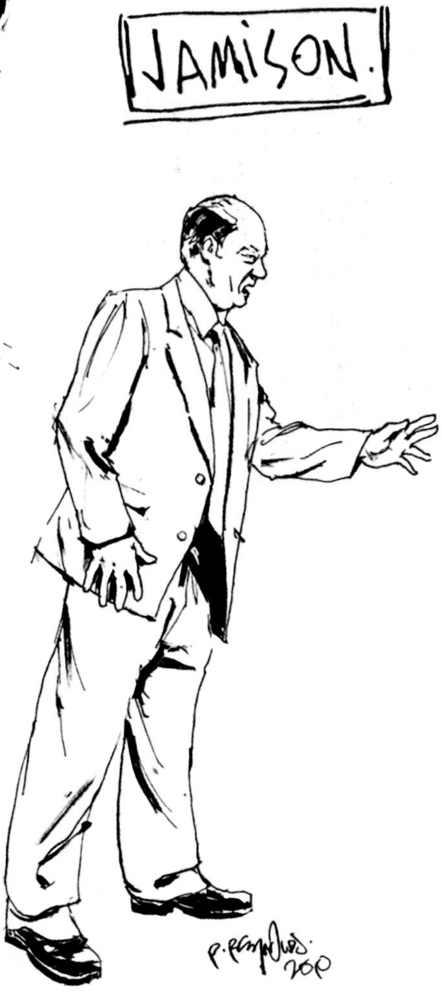
JAMISON.

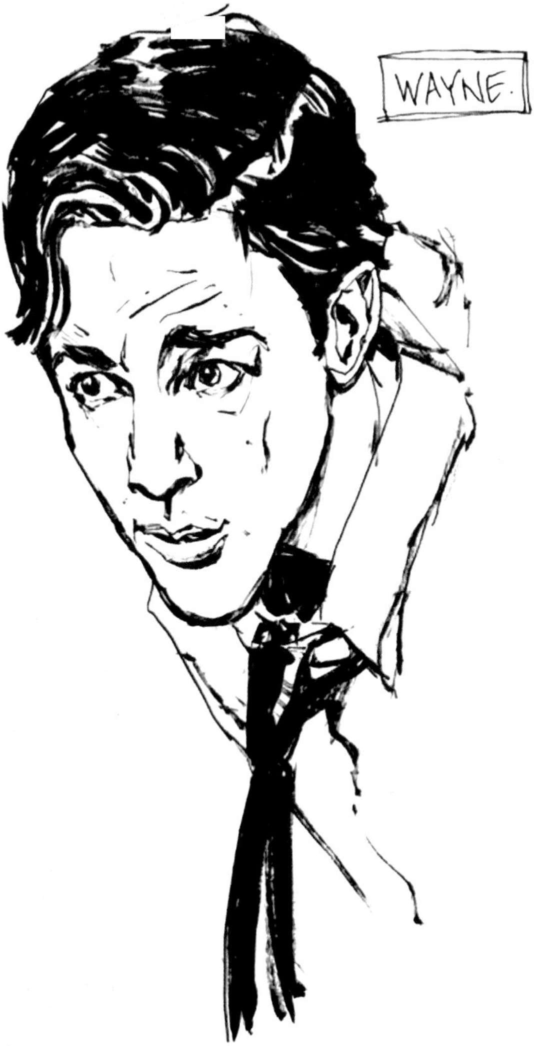
WAYNE.

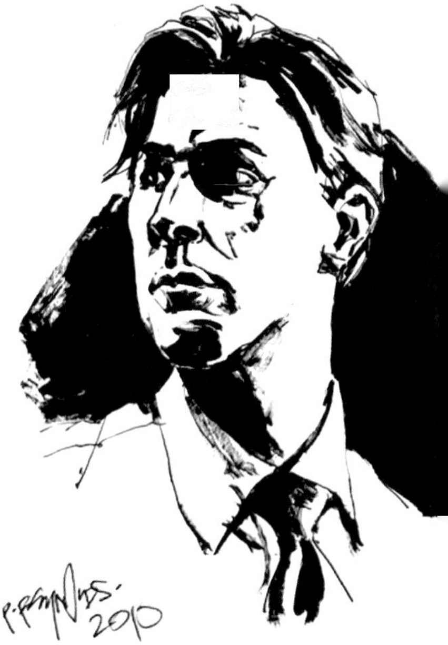

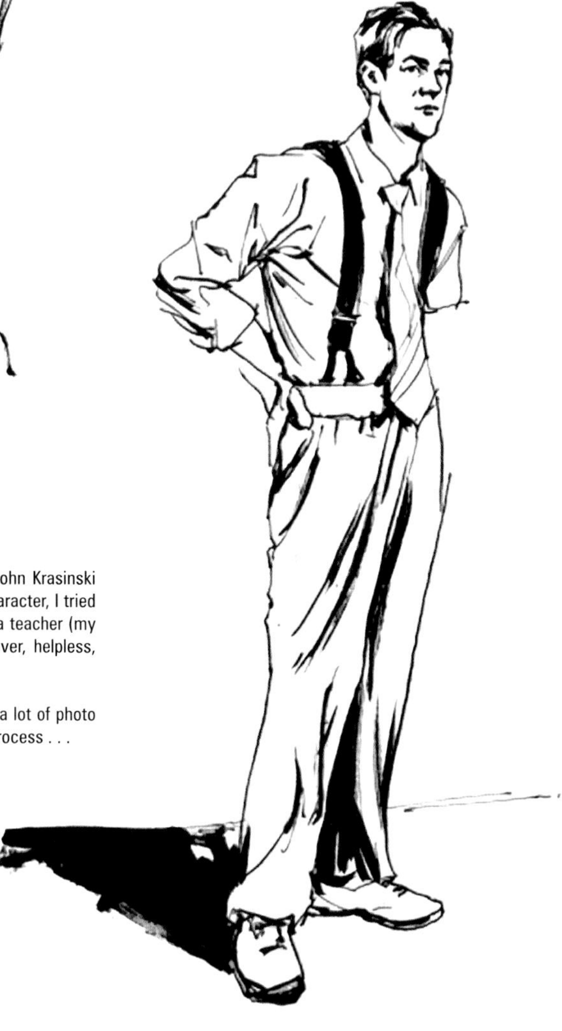

Marc Andreyko's note for Wayne says, "Think John Krasinski from *The Office*." Since I myself posed for this character, I tried to remember how I felt during my early days as a teacher (my former career). All dressed up, but tired, bent over, helpless, powerless . . . and seething.

To make these emotions believable, I had to use a lot of photo reference. The following pages let you in on my process . . .

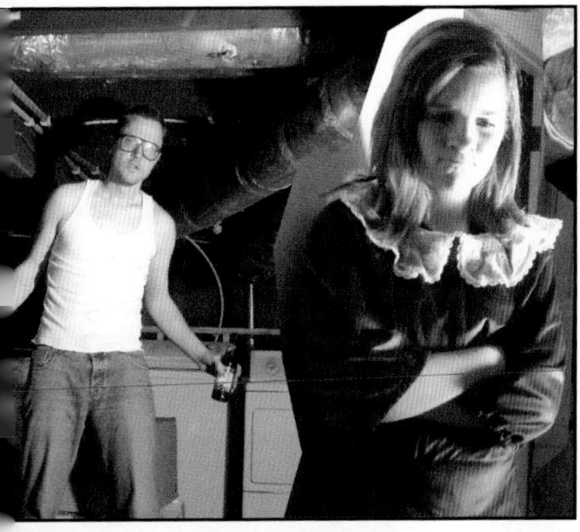

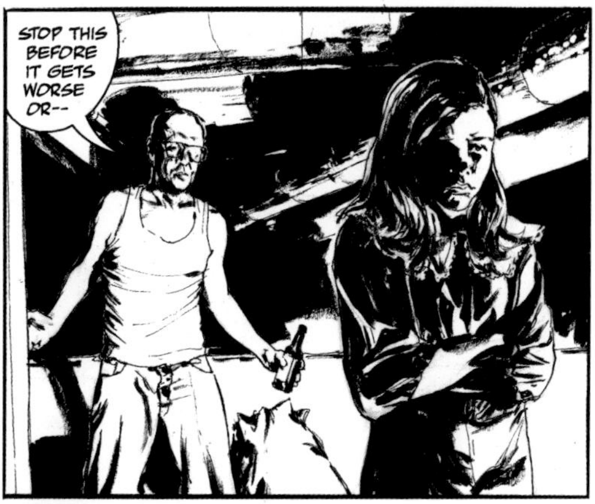
STOP THIS BEFORE IT GETS WORSE OR--

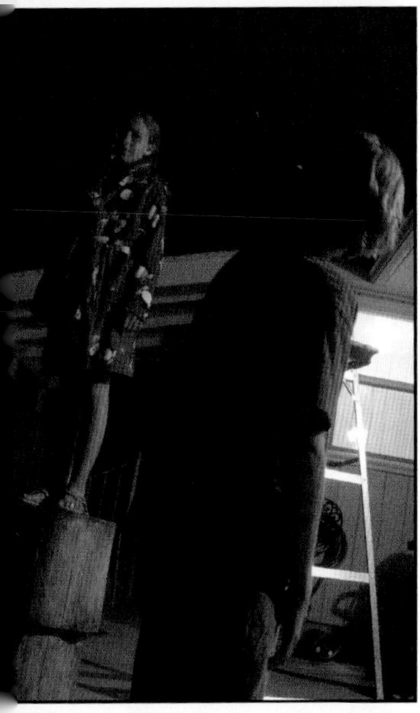

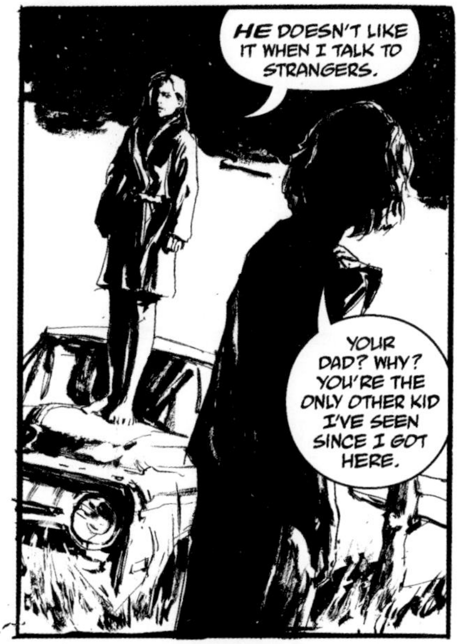
HE DOESN'T LIKE IT WHEN I TALK TO STRANGERS.
YOUR DAD? WHY? YOU'RE THE ONLY OTHER KID I'VE SEEN SINCE I GOT HERE.

ABOVE: Sometimes I had to splice two photos together. As long as I knew where the horizon line was in both photos (the red line), I could line them up proportionally pretty well.

LEFT: These two kids were terrific (they were actually brother and sister). I had them standing pretty close to the porch light to get the right amount of chiaroscuro.

BELOW: That's my poor friend Brandon hanging (actually holding onto the chain wearing a pair of gloves) from the rafters of my brother-in-law's barn. And that's my sister's car. I tilted the camera to make the image a bit more dynamic.

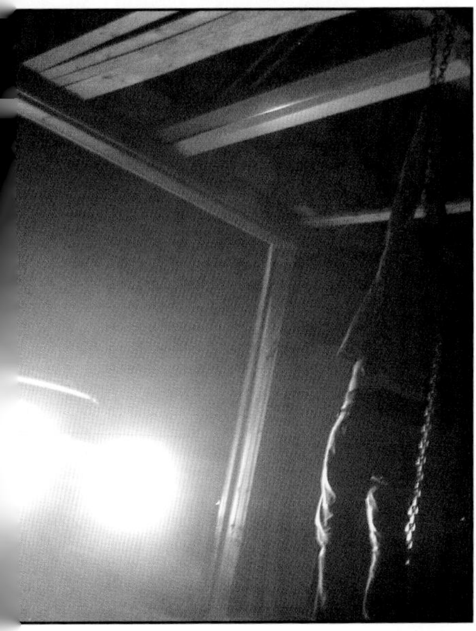

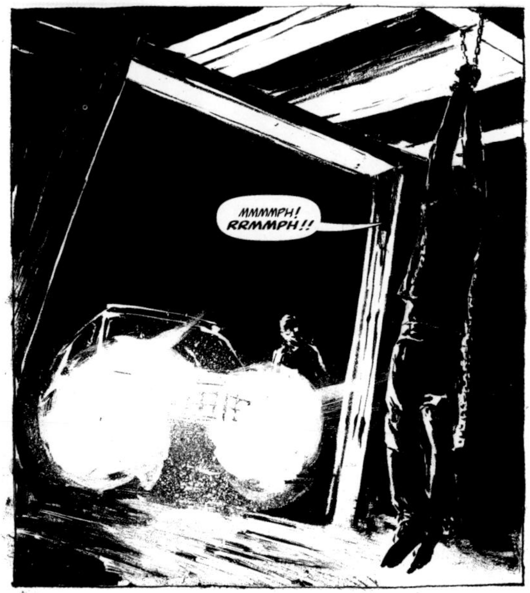
MMMMPH! RRMMPH!!

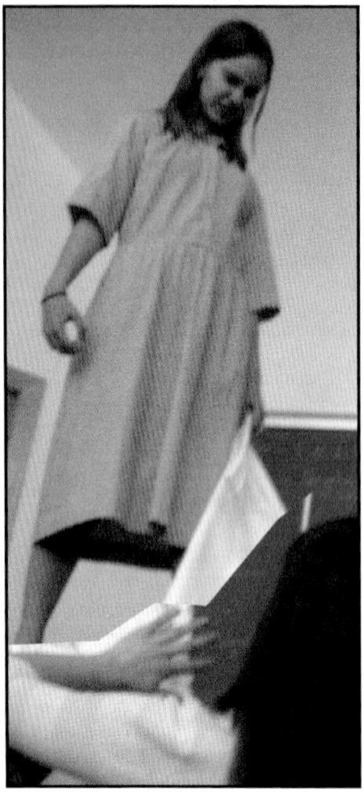

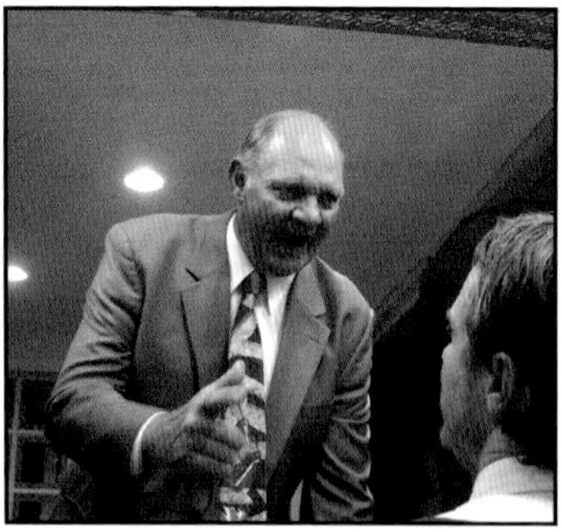

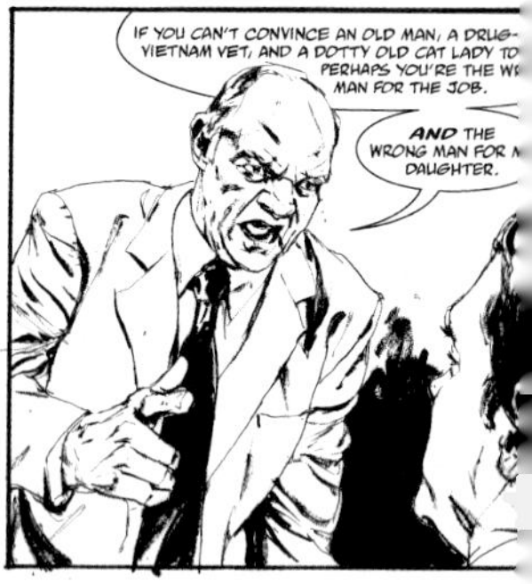
IF YOU CAN'T CONVINCE AN OLD MAN, A DRUG-
VIETNAM VET, AND A DOTTY OLD CAT LADY TO
PERHAPS YOU'RE THE W
MAN FOR THE JOB.
AND THE
WRONG MAN FOR
DAUGHTER.

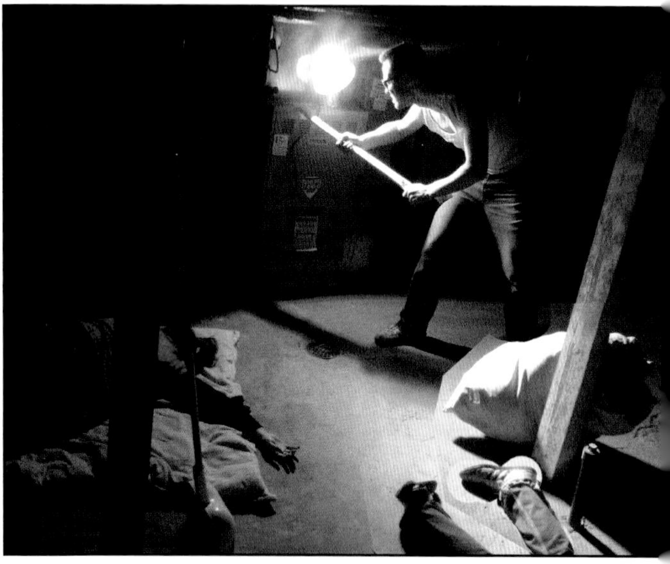

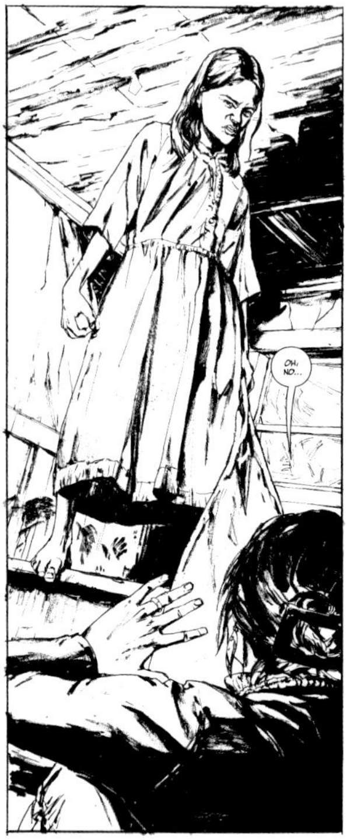
OH, NO...

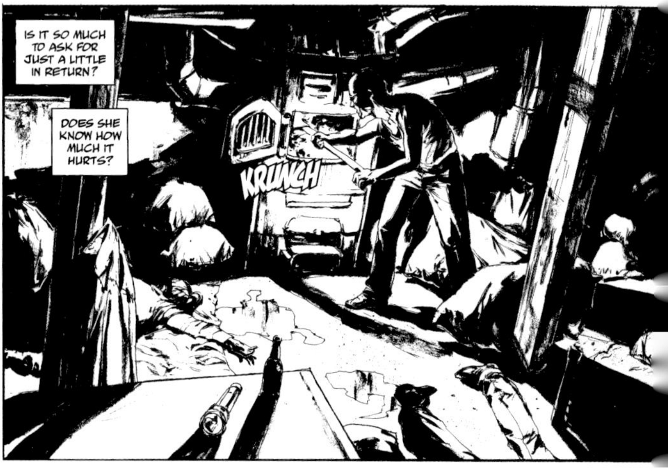
IS IT SO MUCH TO ASK FOR JUST A LITTLE IN RETURN?
DOES SHE KNOW HOW MUCH IT HURTS?
KRUNCH

THIS PAGE, LEFT: I used four different models for Abby. This girl was a high-school student, a bit older than Abby's character. So I had to from the photograph and adjust the figure by making her legs shorter and her head a bit bigger. We wanted her balancing on the edge tub to show her catlike nimbleness. As with the other photos, I tried to get close to what I wanted—just a basic sense of figure plac proportion, and lighting.

OPPOSITE PAGE, TOP: This panel uses a technique where there are no lines, just brush strokes. I thought that this would make the image more po less constrained, and more emotional. So I had to set up the shot so that there were massive amounts of contrast to make it work.

OPPOSITE PAGE, BOTTOM: That's my friend's brother, Alex, posing as Billy (he has terrific sideburns), and me holding a plastic dart gun to hi I like having normal, nonactor people model for me . . . The poses I get are more believable and natural.

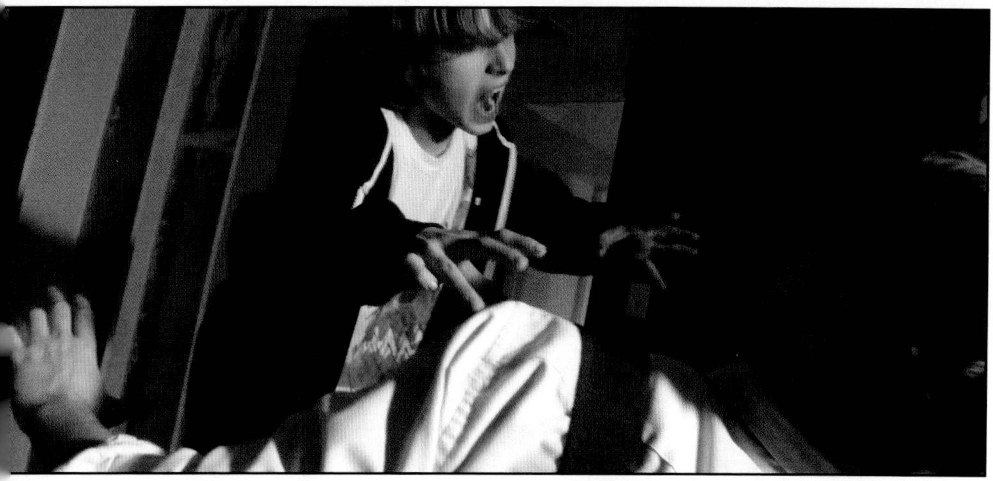

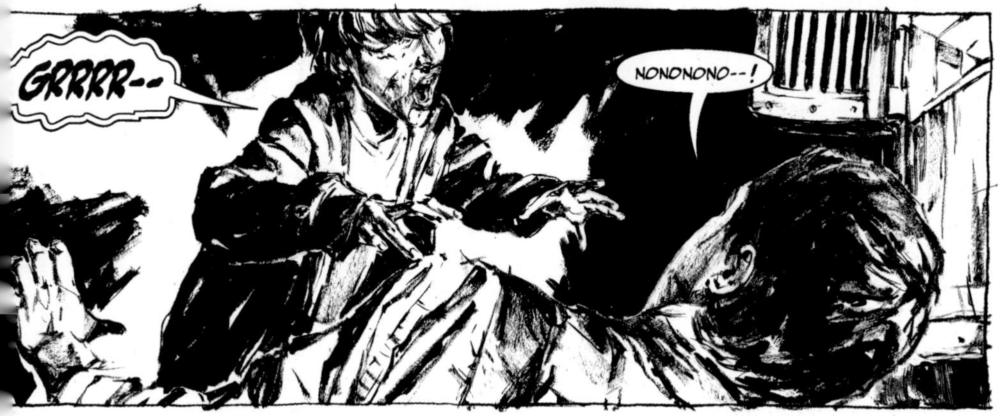
GRRRR--
NONONONO--!

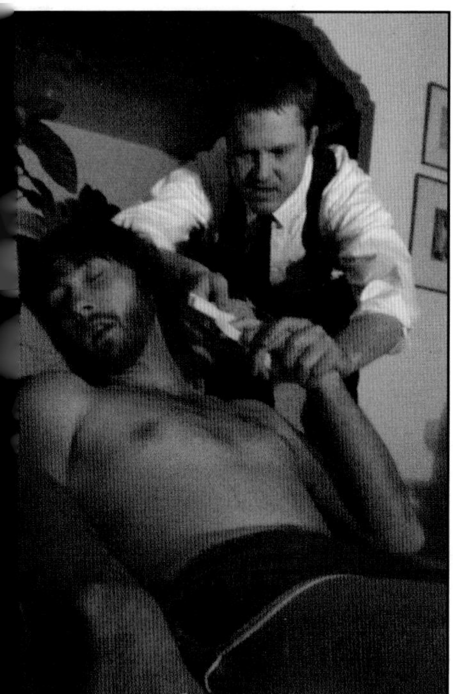

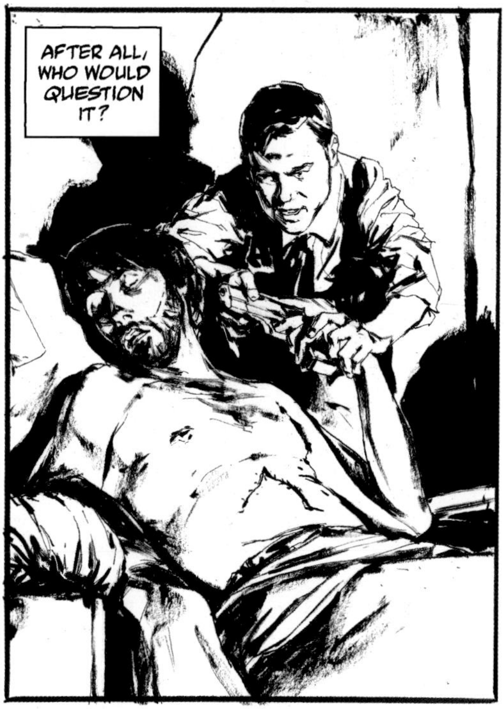
AFTER ALL, WHO WOULD QUESTION IT?

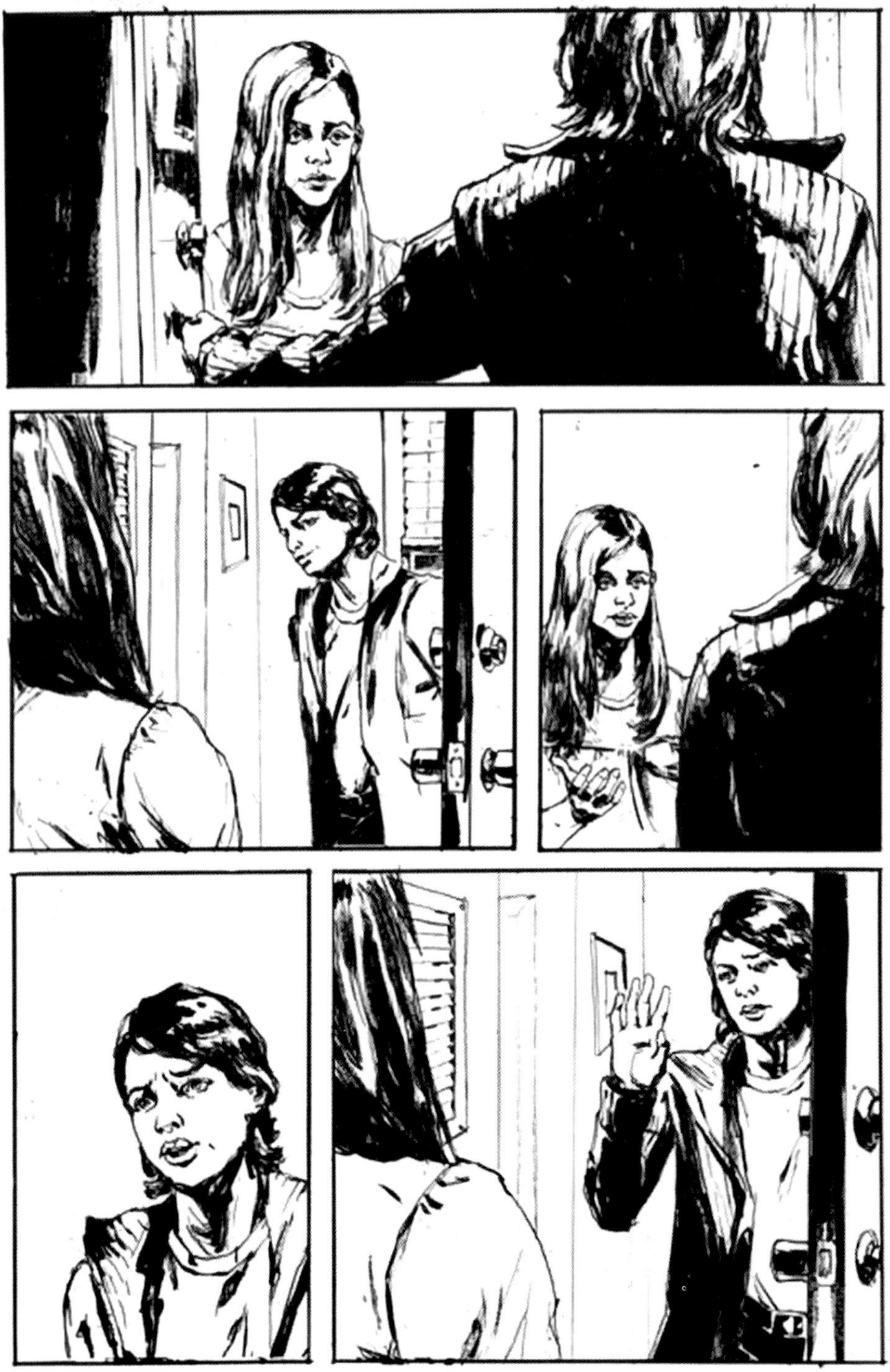

This was sort of an audition page I did for Scott Allie when he proposed the project to me, about a year before *Let Me In* came out. I hadn't heard *the Right One In*, so Scott sent me a clip of the swimming-pool scene. I remember it being one of the most elegantly crafted pieces of cinema I had even if people were getting their heads cut off. It was all about suggestion and what you didn't see. To me, that's how horror works best. It shoul you just enough to make your imagination scare the hell out of you.

Scott told me to do a few sample pages to show to Hammer, to see if I'd be a good fit for the project. Basically I took the scene from *Let the One In* where Oskar doesn't invite Eli in, and just replaced the Swedish actors with the American ones (even though Owen, played by Kodi Smit-Mc never appears in *Crossroads*, and I would never end up drawing him). Thankfully, they let me be a part of one of the best horror movies ever made

—Patric Re

RECOMMENDED DARK HORSE READING

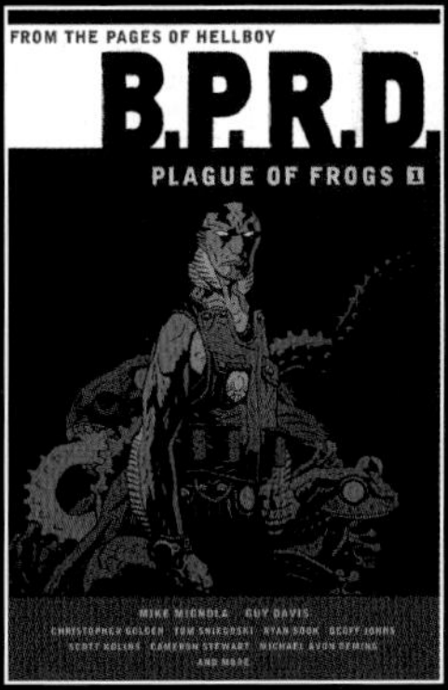
FROM THE PAGES OF HELLBOY
B.P.R.D.
PLAGUE OF FROGS 1
MIKE MIGNOLA · GUY DAVIS

B.P.R.D.: PLAGUE OF FROGS HARDCOVER COLLECTION VOLUME 1

Mike Mignola, Guy Davis, and more

n 2001, Hellboy quit the B.P.R.D., leaving Abe Sapien to lead Liz Sherman and a bizarre roster of special agents in defending the world from occult threats, including the growing menace of the frog army first spotted in *Hellboy: Seed of Destruction*. Mike Mignola and Dark Horse present the complete *Plague of Frogs* saga, from *Hollow Earth* to *King of Fear*. This first book explores the Bureau for Paranormal Research and Defense after Hellboy's departure, cracks open the secrets of Abe Sapien's origin, and sets the war on frogs in motion.

ISBN 978-1-59582-609-1 | $34.99

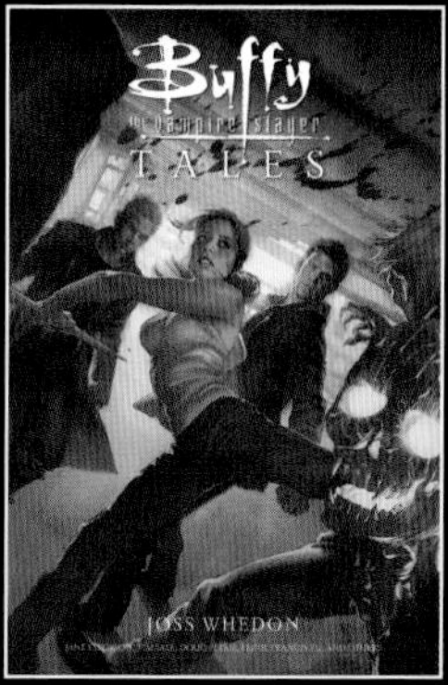
Buffy the Vampire Slayer
TALES
JOSS WHEDON

BUFFY THE VAMPIRE SLAYER: TALES

Joss Whedon, Cameron Stewart, and more

Before Season 8, Joss Whedon brought generations of Slayers and vampires to comics with the help of his acclaimed TV-writing team and some of the best artists to ever grace the comics page. Now all those stories, plus selected stories from Season 8, are collected in one deluxe hardcover, with a new cover by Jo Chen.

ISBN 978-1-59582-644-2 | $29.99

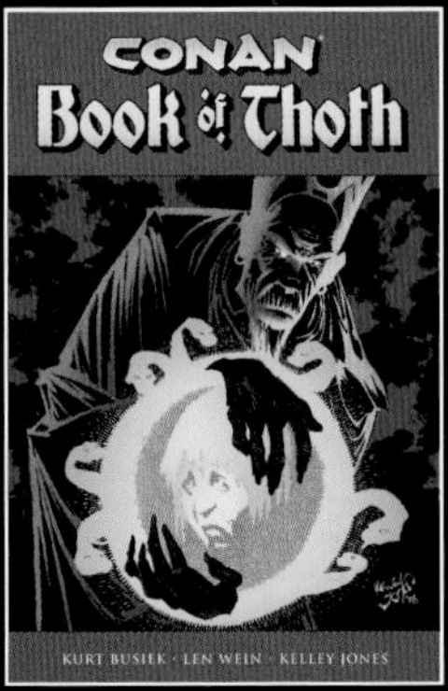
CONAN
Book of Thoth
KURT BUSIEK · LEN WEIN · KELLEY JONES

CONAN: BOOK OF THOTH

Kelley Jones, Kurt Busiek, and more

the dank alleys of a decaying city, a beggar child conjures visions of a ture where, instead of spitting on him in the streets, the rich and privi-ged cower in fear of his terrible authority. Through cunning, murderous eans, he ingratiates himself into a benevolent priesthood, only to turn e church and the nation itself over to the terrible snake god, Set!

ISBN 978-1-59307-648-1 | $17.99

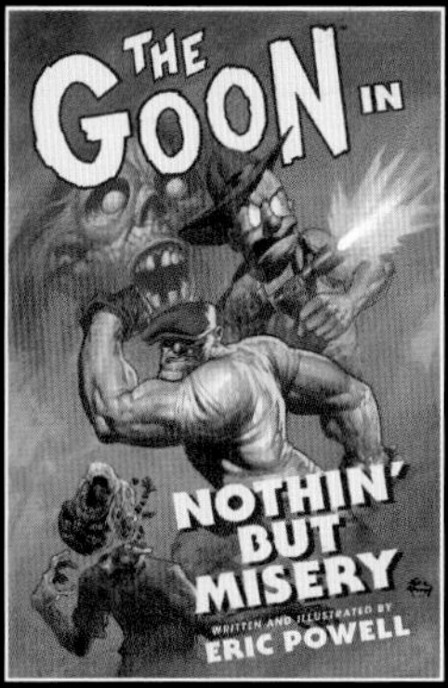
THE GOON IN
NOTHIN' BUT MISERY
WRITTEN AND ILLUSTRATED BY
ERIC POWELL

THE GOON VOLUME 1: NOTHIN' BUT MISERY

Eric Powell

The nameless man, the Zombie Priest, has come to town to build a gang from the undead. But even the undead fear the Goon, mob enforcer and protector of the downtrodden residents of Lonely Street. With Powell's stunning artwork, *The Goon*'s unique mash-up of horror, mob intrigue, and the sickest sense of humor in comics is an instant classic, and this new edition is the best time ever to find out what you've been missing!

ISBN 978-1-59582-624-4 | $16.99

AVAILABLE AT YOUR LOCAL COMICS SHOP OR BOOKSTORE! • To find a comics shop in your area, call 1-888-266-4226.
For more information or to order direct visit DarkHorse.com or call 1-800-862-0052 Mon.–Fri. 9 A.M. to 5 P.M. Pacific Time.
Prices and availability subject to change without notice.

ALSO FROM DARK HORSE BOOKS

PiXu
The Mark of Evil
Gabriel Bá Becky Cloonan
Vasilis Lolos Fábio Moon

PIXU: THE MARK OF EVIL

Gabriel Bá, Becky Cloonan, Vasilis Lolos, and Fábio Moon

This gripping tale of urban horror follows five lonely tenants—strangers—whose lives become intertwined when they discover a dark mark scrawled on the walls of their building. As the walls come alive, everyone is slowly driven mad—defenseless against the evil in the building, stripped of free will, leaving only confusion, chaos, and eventual death.

ISBN 978-1-59582-340-3 | $17.99

LIVING WITH THE DEAD
MIKE RICHARDSON
BEN STENBECK
Two boys, a girl, and
SEVEN BILLION
LIVING DEAD!

LIVING WITH THE DEAD

Mike Richardson and Ben Stenbeck

From the mind of Mike Richardson, creator of *The Mask* and *Th* *Secret*, comes this hilariously frightening tale of Straw and Whi two survivors of a global catastrophe who have lived through plague that's left the world with seven billion brain-hungry zombies

ISBN 978-1-59307-906-2 | $9.99

GUY DAVIS
THE MARQUIS
INFERNO

THE MARQUIS: INFERNO

Guy Davis

In eighteenth-century Venisalle, faith governs life and death, and the guilty hide their shame behind masks. It is to this stronghold of the Inquisition that the souls of hell have escaped to possess the living. Amid the carnage, one man is blessed with the clarity to recognize the demons—and the means to return them to Hell.

ISBN 978-1-59582-368-7 | $24.99

VAMPIRE BOY
CARLOS TRILLO
EDUAR

VAMPIRE BOY

Carlos Trillo and Eduardo Risso

Left nameless by his father and sentenced to eternal life by a tr of fate and fortune, the protagonist of *Vampire Boy* has spent fi centuries in a body that never ages, locked in an eternal strug with a rival as immortal as he. Acclaimed writer Carlos Trillo tea with legendary artist Eduardo Risso (*100 Bullets*) to produce a p gnantly engrossing twist on the classic vampire mythos!

ISBN 978-1-59582-562-9 | $24.99

AVAILABLE AT YOUR LOCAL COMICS SHOP OR BOOKSTORE! • To find a comics shop in your area, call 1-888-266-4226.

For more information or to order direct visit DarkHorse.com or call 1-800-862-0052 Mon.–Fri. 9 AM to 5 PM Pacific Time. Prices and availability subject to change without notice.

DARK HORSE BOOKS®

DarkHorse.com

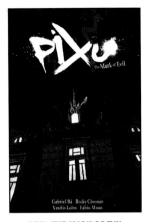

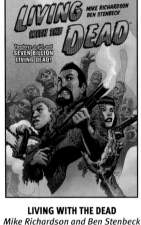

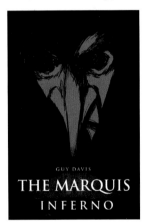

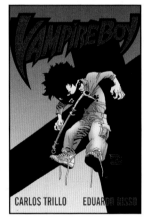